**W9-BEQ-336**

799

# KILL THE
# FÜHRER

## Dedication

*I dedicate this book to my supportive family and friends. I am particularly indebted to my wife Roe (Rosemary), who during much of the writing became 'widow Foxley'.*

# KILL THE FÜHRER

## SECTION X AND OPERATION FOXLEY

**DENIS RIGDEN**

First published in 1999
This edition published in 2009

The History Press
The Mill, Brimscombe Port
Stroud, Gloucestershire, GL5 2QG
www.thehistorypress.co.uk

© Denis Rigden 1999, 2002, 2009

The right of Denis Rigden to be identified as the Author
of this work has been asserted in accordance with the
Copyrights, Designs and Patents Act 1988.

British Library Cataloguing in Publication Data.
A catalogue record for this book is available from the British Library.

ISBN 978 0 7524 5473 3

Typesetting and origination by The History Press
Printed in Great Britain

# Contents

# Abbreviations and Designations

BSC      British Security Coordination
DAF      Deutsche Arbeitsfront (German Labour Front)
EH       The Foreign Office's anti-Nazi propaganda branch, taking its name from its location at Electra House
FANY     First-Aid Nursing Yeomanry
FBK      Führerbegleitkommando (Hitler's bodyguard)
FCO      Foreign and Commonwealth Office (formed in October 1968 by the amalgamation of the Foreign Office and the Commonwealth Office)
FHQ      Führerhauptquartier (Führer Headquarters)
ISK      Internationale Sozialistische Kampfbund
ITWF     International Transport Workers' Federation
MPGD     Mouvement des Prisonniers de Guerre et Deportés
OKW      Oberkommando der Wehrmacht (German High Command of the Armed Forces)
OSS      Office of Strategic Services
PIAT     Projector Infantry Anti-tank (a British hand-held weapon)
PID      Foreign Office's Political Intelligence Department
PWE      Political Warfare Executive
RSD      Reichssicherheitdienst
RSHA     Reichssicherheitshauptamt (Reich Security Main Office)
RUs      Research Units (the codename for PWE's 'German' broadcasting stations)
SD       Sicherheitsdienst (SS Security Service)
SHAEF    Supreme Headquarters Allied Expeditionary Force
SIS      Secret Intelligence Service
SOE      Special Operations Executive
STS      Special Training School

The staff officers of the Special Operations Executive (SOE) used Secret Intelligence Service-style designations, instead of their own names, when writing minutes and other documents circulated within the organisation's headquarters in Baker Street, London. For example, the designation of the Chief (executive head) of SOE was CD and that of the head of the German Directorate was AD/X.

# Introduction

Historians of the Second World War could hardly believe what they saw when they picked up their daily newspapers at breakfast time on 23 July 1998. Dominating the front pages were reports revealing something they had never even suspected: that British secret service officers of the Special Operations Executive had plotted to assassinate Hitler during most of the war years.

The media stories on this ultra sensitive Top Secret project, codenamed Operation Foxley, were based on official documents released that morning by the Public Record Office (PRO) at Kew. However, these few hundred papers – many of them written in dull military officialese – were but the contents of only three of the 971 files relating to SOE activities in Western Europe that the PRO was putting on public display for the first time. The media's sole interest was in Foxley and in a few other headline-grabbing operations, mostly those which, like Foxley, were organised by SOE's mysterious Section X, responsible for operations in Germany and Austria.

My own research into Foxley began much earlier – in mid-1996 when I was briefed on the operation by Gervase Cowell, the then SOE Adviser to the Foreign and Commonwealth Office (FCO), who was also Chairman of the Historical Sub-Committee of the Special Forces Club until his death in May 2000. Later, I had similar invaluable help from his successor in the FCO Adviser's post, Duncan Stuart. As well as providing much biographical information from SOE staff records, Stuart drew upon then unreleased 'headquarters files' to give me an overall picture of the many different sorts of sabotage and subversion engaged in by Section X and by the German Directorate, that section's name during the last six months of the European war.

Although the Adviser to the FCO (a post abolished early in 2002) has efficiently provided historians with all the help he could, the task of researching into what the Special Operations Executive achieved – or failed to achieve – has some distinctive problems. Most of these derive from the SOE's wartime archives being woefully incomplete. An estimated 85 to 87 per cent of the Executive's papers now no longer exist. Many were consumed by a fire at SOE's headquarters – 64 Baker Street, London – shortly after the war (arson was not suspected),[1] and some of the records held at SOE's Middle Eastern regional office in Cairo were deliberately destroyed when the German army came dangerously near. Yet other SOE documents were lost as a direct or indirect result of enemy action in the various theatres of war, or because wartime record-keeping was sometimes haphazard. Undoubtedly, office work was not always well organised at SOE headquarters, where there was no central registry and where each 'country section', including Section X, kept it own records in whatever way it thought fit. To top all this, some documents were 'weeded' after the war because they were judged to be unimportant and there was a shortage of shelf space. Historians also have problems with some of the SOE papers that have survived. Some are damaged and difficult to read. The 'economy' paper of the Second World War was thin and frail. Typing was often single spaced and on both sides of a page.

Even when the extant records are considered there are shortcomings. The documents on Foxley that have survived say nothing about how much planning of this never-to-be operation was undertaken between mid-1941, when Section X was given permission to investigate whether Hitler could be assassinated, and mid-1944, when the matter became a topic of regular discussion in SOE's governing Council, not just in Section X. Almost all the section's information about the dictator's movements and lifestyle must have been gathered during that three-year period. But that was when the section had a small staff who were almost certainly overstretched with work relating to current operations, most of them successful, some spectacularly so. Clearly, in such circumstances, it would have been impossible to allot many resources to the preliminary planning of Operation Foxley and its companion project, Operation Foxley II, which envisaged the assassination of selected members of Hitler's inner circle, such as Goebbels and Himmler.

A big batch of Foxley and Foxley II documents might, of course, have perished in the postwar fire. It is also possible that these assassination schemes were merely discussed, rather than formally written about, during the 'hidden' three years. My guess (I refrain from dignifying it as a theory) is that the research into Foxley and Foxley II during that straitened period was done largely or wholly by Major H.B. Court. The many thousands of surviving SOE personal files do not include his. It seems therefore that his was one of the many such files consumed in the fire. It is, however, known that he was an intelligence officer who, under the SOE symbol L/BX, wrote potted biographies of leading Nazis whom he chose as candidates for assassination. He was always a keen advocate of both Foxley and

Foxley II, having none of the misgivings about these schemes that were expressed in 1944 and 1945 by several of his SOE colleagues.

The surviving documents on these projects (or 'Foxley papers', as I call them) show that by the autumn of 1944, SOE was in possession of a great variety of information essential to the planning of the proposed assassinations. But there were always gaps in the intelligence picture. For example, the exact locations of Hitler and his principal henchmen at any given time in the last few months of the Third Reich were never discovered. If, by some catastrophic circumstance, the war in Europe had gone on much longer, say into 1946, these gaps might have been filled, and potential assassins might have been selected, trained and sent to Germany.

I wrote this book mainly to tell two stories: that of a highly controversial pipedream, Operation Foxley, and that of Section X. All the many previous books about SOE have either said nothing about the section or have represented it as having achieved little. In reality, however, it made a valuable contribution to the Allied war effort. I think the record needs to be put right.

The Special Operations Executive was created in the deepest secrecy on 22 July 1940. This was only two months after Winston Churchill had succeeded Neville Chamberlain as Britain's Prime Minister. Ironically, it was the previously ultra-dovish Chamberlain, who in his new post as Lord President of the Council, wrote a War Cabinet memorandum on 19 July describing SOE as a 'new organisation . . . to coordinate all action, by way of subversion and sabotage, against the enemy overseas'.

Although new, SOE was the product of pre-war secret planning by intelligence and military officers and by experts in propaganda.

In March 1938, shortly after the Anschluss, Hitler's annexation of his native Austria, the Secret Intelligence Service[2] created a small department, Section D, to formulate plans for sabotage and subversive operations in Europe in the event of war. Such schemes would include the selective destruction of key components in trains, factories, power stations and other assets of strategic importance. It was also envisaged that the enemy's war economy could be seriously damaged through fomenting labour unrest and other discontent. Section D was led by a seconded army officer, Major Laurence Grand, a future major-general. Often wearing a carnation in his button-hole, he was a flamboyant character.

At about the same time the Foreign Office persuaded Sir Campbell Stuart, a Canadian and a former managing director of the London *Times*, to set up and run a small branch to investigate ways of conducting anti-Nazi propaganda. The branch was called CS, after Stuart's initials, or more usually EH. (These initials stood for Electra House, the Thames Embankment building in which EH had its offices.) Stuart was an experienced publicist. Towards the end of the First World War he had assisted Lord Northcliffe, the newspaper proprietor, in organising schemes to undermine German army morale.

In October 1938, another future major-general, Lieutenant-Colonel J.C.F. Holland, was appointed to the staff of GS(R), later renamed MI(R), a small research section of the War Office. His assignment, overlapping that of Section D, was to study how to conduct irregular warfare in the conflict against Hitler that he and many other informed observers felt sure would begin soon. A Royal Engineers officer, nicknamed Jo (without an 'e'), he had won the Distinguished Flying Cross when attached to the Royal Flying Corps in the First World War.

In July 1940, Section D, MI(R) and EH were merged to form SOE. However, responsibility for producing propaganda material, as distinct from its dissemination, was given to the Political Warfare Executive (PWE) in the summer of 1941. Its staff were based at Woburn Abbey, Bedfordshire, and at Bush House, Aldwych, in London.

Churchill tasked the Special Operations Executive to 'set Europe ablaze' by helping resistance movements and carrying out subversive operations in enemy-occupied countries. SOE did not do all that the Prime Minister wished it to do. But it did make a big and unreported contribution to the Allied war effort, against both Nazi Germany and Imperial Japan's expansionist regime. General Dwight D. Eisenhower, the Supreme Commander, Allied Expeditionary Force, regarded European resistance movements, aided by SOE and American Special Operations, as a strategic weapon. In his view the activities of the disparate organisations comprising the French Resistance shortened the war in Europe by nine months.[3]

SOE had influence in all the theatres of war except the Soviet Union. Its liaison mission in Moscow received no information from Stalin and was always closely watched by his secret police, the NKVD (forerunner of the KGB). At its maximum size in mid-1944 SOE had a total strength of about 13,000 staff, about 3,000 of whom were women. Nearly half the men, together with a few of the women, worked clandestinely in enemy-occupied or neutral countries, controlling an even larger number of sub-agents. As one of the means of helping SOE staff to conceal the Top Secret nature of their work, they were told to tell friends and other enquirers that they were 'attached to the Inter-Services Research Bureau.'[4]

SOE was controlled by the Minister of Economic Warfare – Dr Hugh Dalton until February 1942 and the 3rd Earl of Selborne for the rest of the war. A Labour Party intellectual, Dalton reached the peak of his career when Chancellor of the Exchequer in the postwar Attlee government. He was made a life peer in 1960. Lord Selborne was a former Conservative MP who had held junior government appointments in the 1920s. He had also had important jobs in the cement industry. A grandson of Lord Salisbury, the nineteenth-century Prime Minister, he was nicknamed 'Top'.

In an undated memorandum, probably written in November 1943, Lord Selborne explained the command structure in which SOE operated. According to a summary of this memo,[5] the Minister of Economic Warfare reported direct to the War Cabinet on matters relating to SOE; SOE received directives from the British Chiefs of Staff regarding strategic objectives on which it should concentrate and on the countries to which priority should be given; and from the Foreign Office SOE received guidance on objectives for underground political activity.

SOE's ultimate controllers were, of course, the British and American political and military leaders. The implementation of grand strategy was the responsibility of the Washington-based Combined Chiefs of Staff Committee, comprising the US Joint Chiefs of Staff and the British Chiefs of Staff. Towards the end of the war the supreme commanders in the various theatres of conflict, in Europe and Asia, exercised more than a little direct control of SOE and other organisations engaged in irregular warfare. For example, SOE received directives from SHAEF, the Supreme Headquarters, Allied Expeditionary Force. General Eisenhower was advised on special operations by an SOE officer, Brigadier Robin Brook.[6]

Members of SOE were recruited from the armed forces, SIS, the business world, academia – indeed, from almost anywhere. They were an odd mixture of professionals and amateurs. There were a few duds among them but most had rare talents and lively minds that they put to good use, often with deadly consequences for the enemy.

Denis Rigden

# Chapter One

# *Operation Foxley – and much more*

The Special Operations Executive, Britain's secret organisation aiding Resistance movements during the Second World War, plotted to assassinate Adolf Hitler. A small department of SOE, Section X, formed in November 1940, had the tantalisingly complex task of investigating how, when and where the deed might be done. Only the staff of that section – renamed the German Directorate in October 1944 – and a tiny minority of others working at SOE's headquarters in Baker Street, London, knew about this Top Secret project. Even some members of the organisation's governing Council were unaware of it. However, one of SOE's principal staff officers and its Chief (executive head) from September 1943, Major-General Colin Gubbins, took a close interest in the scheme.

In mid-1941 the British War Cabinet, Chiefs of Staff and Foreign Office gave SOE permission to study the possibility of assassinating Hitler, and later that year a group of SOE-assisted Polish saboteurs nearly succeeded in killing him when they derailed a train in West Prussia.

By then Winston Churchill's coalition government had good reason for wanting to remove the heavily guarded dictator from the scene, as the Nazi war machine seemed unstoppable. Its huge forces had inflicted defeat after defeat since September 1939. First, the all but defenceless Poland had been invaded and territorially divided between Nazi Germany and its communist ally, the Soviet Union. In 1940 Hitler had overrun Denmark, Norway, Holland, Belgium and Luxembourg, and the German advance through France had resulted in more than 337,000 British, French and Belgian troops being evacuated from the Dunkirk beaches. The Führer had capped all this by forcing Marshal Pétain's French collaborationist administration to sign humiliating armistice terms. In April 1941 Hitler's forces had invaded Greece and Yugoslavia. By 1 June they had occupied Crete, with disastrous consequences for the defending British warships as well as for the British, Commonwealth and Greek troops on the island. The Nazi dictator had by then become so convinced of his own infallible judgment as a strategist that he went ahead with his long-planned invasion of Russia on 22 June.[1]

After the United States entered the war in December 1941, the American and British political and military leaders continued to hope that Hitler could be got rid of – somehow. However, they were worried that if he were seen to have been assassinated by anybody other than one or more of his closest henchmen, the Gestapo would make the death an excuse to murder vast numbers of actual or suspected members of resistance movements. All and sundry – men, women and children – would perish in such a bloodbath.

By 1943 the tide of the conflict had turned against the Nazis and Allied assessments of Hitler's impact had changed. Allied leaders were beginning to weigh the relative merits of having either a dead Hitler or a living one: they hoped that he would continue making strategic blunders so catastrophic that he would fast convert himself into one of the Allies' greatest assets. Indeed, some Allied politicians and generals already regarded him as an unwitting 'ally', worth many army divisions. In the last year of the war in Europe, another worry in London and Washington was that Dr Josef Goebbels, the Nazis' grandly styled Minister of National Enlightenment and Propaganda, would exploit any 'martyrdom' of his 'beloved Führer' in a desperate final attempt to galvanise the war-weary German nation into fighting harder for an unachievable victory, regardless both of strategic realities and the human and material cost to everybody involved, the Allies and Germany alike.

Despite all these factors inhibiting quick decision-making at the highest political and military levels, SOE was encouraged in June 1944 – perhaps by interest shown by Churchill – to intensify the planning of Operation Foxley, the codename for the proposed assassination of Hitler. General Gubbins arranged that the SIS be involved in the plotting by providing SOE with all available information on the Führer's travel arrangements and lifestyle; no details about his daily routine were to be regarded as too unimportant to be reported.

Plans for Hitler's liquidation, either on his private estate in the Bavarian Alps, or when he was travelling by rail or road, continued to be made until he himself settled the Allies' debate on his future by committing suicide on 30 April 1945, a week before the end of the war in Europe. These unrealised schemes – often the subject of differing assessments by SOE staff officers as well as by their political and military masters – included plans to kill Hitler using SOE agents or bombing by the RAF.

Section X and its successor, the German Directorate, also plotted to assassinate selected members of the Führer's inner circle. These schemes were codenamed Operation Foxley II and informally called 'Little Foxleys'. Various Foxley II projects were considered. These included a suggestion, quickly dismissed, that chemical or biological weapons might be used in an 'attack on a single person'. Another soon abandoned idea was that Rudolf Hess might be persuaded, perhaps under hypnosis, to participate in a Little Foxley.

Those on the Foxley II hit-list at various times towards the end of the war in Europe included: Goebbels, who as well as being Propaganda Minister since 1933 had sweeping powers from August 1944 as Special Plenipotentiary for Total War; SS Obersturmbannführer Otto Skorzeny,[2] leader of a ninety-member special detachment that freed Mussolini from custody in September 1943; Heinrich Himmler, head (Reichsführer) of the SS from 1929 and commander-in-chief of the Reserve Army from July 1944; and Ernst Kaltenbrunner, head of the Reich Security Main Office (RSHA) from January 1943.

In the course of planning Operation Foxley and the Little Foxleys, SOE's London headquarters received a vast quantity of highly classified information about the day-to-day routines of Hitler and his closest associates. This intelligence included detailed reports on where these Nazis lived and worked; on their travel arrangements; and on many other personal matters relating to their usually luxurious lifestyles, almost always heavily guarded and isolated from the German public on all but rare occasions, particularly towards the end of the Third Reich. All this information, assembled by Allied intelligence organisations, had been obtained over the war years either from prisoners-of-war, some of them former Nazis, or from many conspicuously brave men and women, Allied or German, associated with the resistance movements. If Hitler or any of his principal henchmen had been assassinated, the operatives chosen for that special Top Secret assignment would have needed an extraordinary blend of boundless courage, ingenuity and patience.

The planning of Operations Foxley and Foxley II was only a tiny part of the work done by the SOE staff officers controlling operations inside Germany and Austria. Their main task was to organise sabotage and the secret dissemination of a great variety of black propaganda literature which appeared to be German in origin and was in reality forged in Britain by the Political Warfare Executive (PWE).[3]

Although there were a number of major operations, such as train derailments and factory wreckings, most of the industrial sabotage comprised small but frequent acts not easily detectable as having been done deliberately. These included the wastage of scarce raw materials and the misuse of machinery, eventually causing its damage or destruction. Detailed information on how workers should engage in such unspectacular routine sabotage was given in literature clandestinely distributed by SOE agents. Section X and the German Directorate also organised what was called 'administrative sabotage' – operations to cause bureaucratic chaos, such as the mass circulation in Germany of forged ration cards and coupons for food and clothing (see Chapter Eleven).

In the propaganda sphere, the main aim of PWE and SOE was to undermine the morale of the German armed forces. SOE organised the spreading of literature telling soldiers and U-boat crews how to simulate illnesses, claim sick or compassionate leave, or even desert (see Chapter Thirteen). Similar black propaganda strove to intensifying the existing uneasy relationship between the Wehrmacht and the SS. The aim of yet other forgeries was to reveal the true nature of the Nazi regime to the majority of the German civilian population that still retained varying degrees of confidence in Hitlerism as late as 1944 and 1945 (see Chapter Fourteen).

Unlike the protracted discussions of the assassination schemes, there were no unduly long debates in Section X, and later in the German Directorate, over whether this or that operation involving sabotage or black propaganda could or should be undertaken. This was because SOE and the Allied leaders were agreed that these were acceptable methods of defeating Hitler which were guaranteed to be largely successful – unlike Operations Foxley and Foxley II.

Section X was set up on 18 November 1940 with extremely limited objectives: to establish channels of communication into Germany and Austria as a first step towards creating a network of agents within those countries, and to organise sabotage, initially on a small scale. This tentative planning was based on the assumption, made by the War Cabinet and the Foreign Office, that Hitler's 'Greater Germany' (Germany and Austria) possessed no effective indigenous opposition to his ruthless dictatorship. With a staff of only five, Section X could hardly have had a more modest beginning, though, if circumstances had been different, it should have been SOE's most important 'country section' with a lion's share of resources.

Section X did, however, have strong backing from SOE's first Chief, Sir Frank Nelson (1883–1966). As British Consul in the Swiss frontier town of Basle in 1939 and early 1940, he became exceptionally well informed about the Third Reich, particularly about its clandestine activities abroad. After completing his education in Heidelberg, Nelson had a highly successful business career in India, and during the First World War he served in the Bombay Light Horse. President of the Associated Indian Chambers of Commerce in 1923, he was knighted in the following year and sat from then until 1931 as the Conservative MP for Stroud, Gloucestershire.

The section was supervised for nearly a year by another informed advocate of clandestine operations: Sir Charles Jocelyn Hambro (1897–1963), a merchant banker and (only nominally during the war) Chairman of the Great Western Railway. Awarded the MC in the First World War, he joined the Ministry of Economic Warfare (or the 'Ministry of Ungentlemanly Warfare' as it was sometimes called) in September 1939. Transferred to SOE in August 1940 he was initially in charge of operations in Scandinavia. He arranged a small amount of sabotage in Swedish harbours serving Third Reich interests, and established contacts with the Resistance in Denmark, a task facilitated by his own family being of Danish origin. From December 1940 to November 1941, he had oversight of Section X and SOE's French, Belgian and Dutch sections. After a few months as the organisation's Vice-Chief, he was its Chief from May 1942 until succeeded by General Gubbins in September 1943. Hambro's greatest contribution to the war effort – and to mankind – was to initiate Operation Gunnerside: the destruction of the heavy water (deuterium oxide) plant in the Norsk Hydro complex at Vemork, near Rjukan, on the night of 27/28 February 1943. If there had been no Gunnerside, the Nazis would have obtained from occupied Norway all the heavy water needed for the manufacture of atomic weapons. Gunnerside, together with related guerrilla actions and aerial bombing, resulted in Hitler losing confidence in his scientists' research into splitting the atom.

Lieutenant-Colonel Brien Clarke, who later in the war supervised SOE activities in Iberia and much of Africa, was Section X's first head. But he was succeeded after only a few weeks by Lieutenant-Colonel Ronald Thornley, the section's guiding force from then until 30 October 1944 when, much enlarged, it became the German Directorate, with Thornley as its deputy head.

Internal SOE documentation from 1940 reflects the British authorities' prevailing lack of confidence in the fragmented German Resistance (Der Widerstand). For example, Section X minuting referred to the 'so-called anti-Nazi elements in Germany' which, it claimed, were 'in the vast majority of cases neither willing nor able to undertake any subversive activities against the German regime'. Most of the German people were judged to be 'solidly behind the Nazi leadership'. This situation contrasted sharply with that in the occupied countries. All of these had resistance movements which their respective SOE country sections assisted throughout the war in Europe, providing arms and other supplies, as well as training. Also, many nationals of the occupied countries became SOE agents.

It is clear from all this that Section X faced problems that no other SOE country section had. Trying to establish any militarily worthwhile opposition movement in Germany or Austria was considered to be impossible. It was therefore decided that the section should engage only in 'subversive activities in the real sense of the word', 'sporadic sabotage wherever possible, to alarm the enemy security services and to encourage genuine subversive elements', and 'administrative sabotage, which is always a most valuable weapon against methodically-minded Germans'.

In this early period of the war Section X also judged – probably wrongly – that it had no source of recruits for clandestine work in Germany. The estimated 70,000 Germans and Austrians living in Britain in 1939, most of them Jews, were considered unsuitable for active service because of their age or because they had no personal experience of conditions in the wartime Third Reich. Many of these refugees had fled from persecution in the early or mid-1930s.

However, Section X was given invaluable advice – mainly on sabotage and clandestine communications – by three groups of refugees, nearly all of them Germans, who were exceptionally well informed about many of the industries in Germany and the occupied countries. One of these groups, the Demuth Committee (or Central European Joint Committee) received a monthly subsidy from British secret funds – initially £150, but soon raised to £200. The committee was run by Dr F. Demuth, President of the Emergency Society for German Scholars in Exile, from 6 Gordon Square, London. He was in contact with about forty refugees, mostly German Jews, who in pre-war days had held senior positions in industry, commerce or banking.[4] His discretion in performing this go-between role deservedly earned praise from the War Office and Britain's counter-espionage service, MI5. However, his contacts were not always handled well. For example, one of them, Dr J. Seligsohn Netter, a former chairman and managing director of the Wolf Netter and Jacobi Werke, was told to visit his 'nearest labour exchange' when he offered his services to the Ministry of Economic Warfare in December 1940.

Section X's other exiled special advisers belonged either to the International Transport Workers' Federation (ITWF) or the

Internationale Sozialistische Kampfbund (ISK), a small and unusual socialist party, most of whose members were German, the others being Swiss, French, Belgian, Dutch or Scandinavian. The ITWF (called the International Transport Federation in some SOE documents) moved its head office from Amsterdam to London shortly before Hitler invaded Holland. By 1940 those German ISK members still in Germany were either in concentration camps or, if at liberty, were actively anti-Nazi whenever possible. The ISK, whose members were teetotal, vegetarian and in other ways ascetic in their personal lives, was the only mainly German political party that gave Section X any significant amount of help. Section X particularly valued the advice of two ISK leaders, René Bertholet in Switzerland and Willi Eichler in London, who had contacts with the Swiss secret service.[5]

One of the Section X's first decisions was to appoint its own representatives in SOE missions in important neutral countries, such as Switzerland and Sweden, and to ask other country sections of SOE to assist it in penetrating Germany – clearly, something it could not do on its own. However, these country sections were preoccupied with their own efforts to establish links with resistance groups and refused to give Section X enough of the help that it needed. The section was therefore almost always forced to rely on its own limited resources – its own representatives in the neutral countries and its own agents, for a long time few in number.

In December 1940 Section X arranged with the British censorship authorities to receive copies of all correspondence relating to certain individuals in whom it was interested. Postal censors worked in a central bureau in Liverpool and in many other offices in Britain and overseas. In Bermuda a mass of postal, telegraphic and radio traffic between the western hemisphere and Nazi-occupied Europe was intercepted by an outstation of British Security Coordination (BSC). Established in New York in August 1940, BSC represented SOE and SIS interests in the western hemisphere, and shortly after the US entered the war in December 1941 it became their chief liaison office with the Office of Strategic Services (OSS)[6] and later also with the Federal Bureau of Investigation. British Security Coordination was headed by a personal representative of Winston Churchill, William Stephenson. Knighted in 1945, he was a Canadian-born millionaire businessman, electronics pioneer, and in the First World War, an ace fighter pilot.[7]

In January 1941 Section X began a regular and fruitful dialogue with MI9, the branch of the War Office's Military Intelligence Directorate that organised escapes from prisoner-of-war camps in

Germany and the occupied countries. Section X arranged to be shown MI9 documents that would be helpful when planning operations. The section also compiled a questionnaire for use by MI9 when debriefing former prisoners of war after their repatriation. Many of these men provided intelligence valuable to Section X.

However, the section initially received little useful information from SIS. This was partly because almost everything related to the gathering, assessment and distribution of political, military and economic intelligence was badly organised in the immediate pre-war years. As a result, the Foreign Office, the armed services' ministries and the intelligence community often failed to coordinate their efforts during the war. Another problem was the under-funding of services related to defence. In 1935, at the height of the Abyssinian crisis, the head of SIS, Admiral Sir Hugh 'Quex' Sinclair, complained that financial stringency had forced his organisation to abandon activities in several countries that had been bases for obtaining information about Fascist Italy. He added that SIS's budget had been so reduced in recent years that it now equalled only the normal cost of operating one destroyer in home waters.[8]

In July 1938, Sinclair defended criticism of SIS from within Whitehall. He admitted that except on naval construction, where it was 'excellent', SIS's intelligence on military and industrial matters was at best 'fair'.[9] Already handicapped by having only a thin spread of agents in Europe, SIS suffered severe setbacks shortly before the war. As a result of the Anschluss, its head of station in Vienna was arrested, and its network in Czechoslovakia was broken up after the Nazi seizure of Prague in the spring of 1939. In the first two months of the war, SIS lost its Berlin, Vienna and Warsaw stations, and, during the Soviet–Finnish 'Winter War' of 1939–40, the stations in Helsinki and the Baltic States had to take refuge in Stockholm. The Nazi conquests in 1940 caused SIS to lose its stations in Oslo, Copenhagen, Paris, Rome, Brussels and The Hague. By early 1941 all the Balkan stations had been compelled to move to Istanbul, and within Europe SIS had become heavily reliant on its presence in four neutral countries, Switzerland, Sweden, Portugal and Spain.[10] It was against this background of few resources and severely limited initial objectives that Section X began its work. However, before examining the section's activities in detail, it is worth mentioning an operation which the SOE officers in London did not plan but which was in line with Allied policy on sabotage. More importantly, this operation gave Section X food for thought when, in 1941, it began studying whether Hitler could be killed during one of his journeys by rail.

# Chapter Two

## *Hitler's train a target*

The SOE documents on Operation Foxley record that a group of Polish Resistance fighters nearly succeeded in killing Hitler in the autumn of 1941 when he was travelling in his personal train, the Führerzug, in West Prussia – an area mainly comprising the pre-war Polish Corridor.

This party of highly trained saboteurs, whose orders were to destroy any fast train, not necessarily Hitler's, had laid several kilograms of explosives on the railway line between Freidorf and Schwarzwasser about 20 to 30 minutes before the Führerzug was due to race by. However, for reasons unknown, Hitler's train made an unexpected stop at a nearby station. But the operation was far from being wholly unsuccessful as another train was let through and it detonated the charges, killing 430 of the Germans on board. They were probably SS personnel and others closely associated with the Nazi regime, although the Foxley papers do not say so. Much material damage was also done, as it took two days to unblock the line. The Poles had been able to place the explosives because the railway police (Bahnpolizei) who guarded the track were less vigilant in 1941 than they were later in the war. Armed with rifles and hand grenades, they patrolled the line periodically but spent most of the time near the points and the already heavily guarded signal boxes.

In 1941 the members of the Polish Resistance engaged in railway sabotage were organised in twelve-member detachments, each comprising a radio operator, six men who laid the explosives, and five who acted as lookouts. Each detachment – there was one for every district (kreis) – had a short-wave radio set used to communicate with the Polish Resistance headquarters and with other sabotage detachments, and to detonate the charges from a distance of 400 metres. The charges were attached to the rails by spring clips.

Polish saboteurs played a major role in disrupting Nazi railway traffic to the eastern front. They destroyed or seriously damaged an estimated 6,000 locomotives and an unknown number of other rolling-stock. These guerrilla actions, together with much else done by members of Poland's heroic resistance movement, benefited greatly from assistance by SOE in the form of training and the clandestine dropping of military supplies from the air.[1] During the war years 485 successful drops were made on Polish soil, the first on 15 February 1941. This was a pioneering venture undertaken at great risk to the RAF Whitley bombers involved, since never before had SOE arranged such an airlift on to any enemy-occupied territory.

All this was made possible by the close relations established between intelligence officers serving Poland's exiled government (in London after a short period in Paris) and Colin Gubbins, the future major-general and executive director of SOE (from September 1943). A specialist in irregular warfare, he had been Chief of Staff of a British military mission to Poland in the summer of 1939. From there he had brought back to Britain a Polish time pencil, a device that detonated a plastic explosive charge after a pre-set period ranging from ten minutes to thirty hours. Invented (ironically) by the Germans in the First World War, the time pencil had been improved by the Poles and was perfected by SOE's Station IX, a secret research establishment at The Frythe, a former hotel in Welwyn Garden City, Hertfordshire. Training in the use of the time pencils, as well as in many other sorts of industrial sabotage, was given to SOE agents at another Hertfordshire location, Brickendonbury Manor (Station XVII). The time pencils contributed significantly to the Allied war effort in enemy-occupied countries, not least in Poland. More than 12 million of them were manufactured during the Second World War.

Hitler's train, which was so nearly destroyed by Polish saboteurs, was a great source of interest to Section X. Between 1940 and 1944 SOE assembled a wealth of detailed information about the Führerzug and the other Sonderzüge, the Special Trains used by only a few members of the Nazi leadership and their entourages. These favoured men included Himmler, Göring, Joachim von Ribbentrop, the Foreign Minister, and Field Marshal Wilhelm Keitel, Hitler's sycophantic principal military adviser and nominally Chief of Staff of the High Command of the Armed Forces (OKW). The Führerzug, a streamlined express train, was given to Hitler by a group of industrialists. He used it as a mobile headquarters and when making his few visits to fellow dictators – Benito Mussolini, head of the Italian Fascist regime, and General Francisco Franco of Spain.

The train was made up of three sections which were linked together during only part of the journeys. The front section (Vorzug) was codenamed 'Kleinasien'; it carried some members of Hitler's staff. The second and main section (Hauptzug) was codenamed 'Amerika' and was where he nearly always travelled, accompanied by his immediate entourage, including twenty or so members of the SS-Führerbegleitkommando, Hitler's escort detachment. The rear section (Nachzug) was codenamed 'Asien' and carried other security personnel.

The Führerzug was long. For example, the Hauptzug section alone comprised two locomotives and fourteen coaches when travelling in 1940 between Freilassing, Salzburg and Hitler's various headquarters (FHQs). Anti-aircraft guns were mounted on the first and last coaches. The second and third coaches were the Führerbegleitkommando's quarters. The train staff had accommodation in coach four. Radio and telephone equipment were in the fifth coach. Hitler's secretariat was in the sixth, and Martin Bormann and his staff were in the seventh. A dining car and kitchen comprised the eighth. Adjutants occupied the ninth, and the tenth was Hitler's saloon coach, at the entrances to which two bodyguards were always on duty. 'Various high personages' (Section X's description) were in the eleventh, twelfth and thirteenth coaches.

At other times the Hauptzug section of the Führerzug was believed by Section X to have between six and twenty coaches. In 1943, during the Russian campaign, it had two locomotives and ten or eleven coaches defended by surface artillery as well as anti-aircraft guns.

Railway police, usually armed with revolvers but sometimes with rifles or machine-pistols, and detachments of train and local Gestapo, some in civilian clothes, were on duty on the platforms wherever the Führerzug stopped at stations. Whenever Hitler left the train, such as for stops lasting up to half an hour, he was surrounded by bodyguards. Early in the war, when Goebbels was still successfully brainwashing much of the German population into believing that his idol was worthy of hero-worship, admiring crowds were allowed to go right up to Hitler's personal coach at stops en route. But, Section X estimated, by 1944 members of the general public were being kept at a distance from the train, and even the railway workers servicing it were not permitted to loiter unnecessarily.

Information about the routes and travel times of the Führerzug and of the other Special Trains (Sonderzüge) was a State secret. The Nazi-controlled central management of the railways, in both Germany and the occupied countries, telegraphed unpublished timetables to its subordinate area offices and to the stations concerned. The arrival of a Special Train was announced by number only, with the seeming intention on some occasions of giving the misleading impression that it was a goods train.

However, Section X did not believe that the Nazis went one step further still and ran 'duplicate Führerzüge' – trains disguised to look like the real Führerzug. This belief was based on information from one of Hitler's former servants who often travelled on the Führerzug until mid-1940, and on subsequent evidence from other sources that such 'duplicates' were never seen on the eastern front. The nearest approach to any such deception was the running of an advance train, which, according to three well-informed Austrian railwaymen, always went some distance in front of every Sonderzüg, at least in Germany. This advance train had one or two coaches carrying railway police sent to reinforce their local contingents. Running a 'duplicate' would never have fooled the general public for long, as the Führerzug (and the other Sonderzüge) were distinguishable from ordinary trains by their luxurious coachwork, larger windows, and wider concertina gangways between coaches.

Section X also assembled detailed information about the servicing and provisioning of the Special Trains. For example, on Ribbentrop's train the exterior of the coaches, excluding the roofs, was washed outside Salzburg station by six French women and the interior of the coaches was cleaned by railway workers, presumably Austrians or Germans. The Führerzug was usually serviced at the Schloss Klessheim sidings in a western suburb of Salzburg by Führerbegleitbataillon personnel thought to be fanatically loyal to Hitler, but the train was also seen on sidings at Salzburg beside Göring's Sonderzüg, close to a place normally reserved for Ribbentrop's train. Section X knew about the cafés and other locations where the various train personnel spent their leisure time.

It also knew that water for drinking and cooking purposes was supplied to the Führerzug at stations where it stopped. Hydrants were connected either to the train's fresh-water tank on the dining car roof or to water cocks on either side of the train. At Anhalter railway station in Berlin, beer, mineral water, chocolate, malt and coffee were taken on board in sufficient quantities to last four to six weeks. Meat, vegetables and fruit were usually supplied at Salzburg. Arthur Kannenberg (1896–1963), a senior official of the Reich Chancellery in Berlin and a former cook, waiter and accountant, was responsible for ordering this food; Hitler's was specially brought from the Chancellery or from the Berghof, his villa on the Obersalzberg in the Bavarian Alps.

The level of defence on the trains was also thoroughly researched by Section X. This was information that would be essential if any attack were to be made on the Führerzug. The similar sounding Führerbegleitkommando and Führerbegleitbataillon had different but complementary functions. Members of the Führerbegleitkommando (or FBK, Begleitkommando des Führers) were bodyguards accompanying Hitler wherever he went. The Führerbegleitbataillon, a unit of the Division Grossdeutschland, usually provided guards at Hitler's headquarters but were otherwise not directly concerned with his personal safety. The FBK was formed in February 1932, eleven months before Hitler came to power. By 1944 it had 143 SS personnel. Responsibility for his safety was also entrusted to an even more important and more sinister organisation, the Reichssicherheitsdienst (RSD), which by 1944 had 250 personnel. The RSD had wide-ranging powers of investigation and prosecution as well as responsibility for the safety of not only Hitler but also the other leading Nazis. It was formed early in 1933 as the 'Command for Special Duties' but was renamed the RSD two years later. Its leader throughout was a former police lieutenant, Johann Rattenhuber (1897–1957), eventually as an SS-Gruppenführer (major-general).

With all this information on the Führerzug and the other Special Trains, and undeterred by the Polish saboteurs' failure to kill Hitler in 1941, Section X was in 1944 studying the possibility of assassinating him when he travelled to Berlin from Berchtesgaden or Schloss Klessheim, or from Munich to Mannheim.

On the first of these journeys the Führerzug stopped at Landshut, Regensburg, Hof and either Halle or, less often, Leipzig. Also the Führerzug and the other Sonderzüge sometimes stopped at Juterbog or Luckenwalde where Hitler, Himmler, Ribbentrop and other leading Nazis might disembark with their entourages and complete the journey to Berlin in cars. The Führerzug travelled between 90 and 120 kilometres per hour and went through two tunnels. On the Munich–Mannheim route the train was 'believed' (Section X's word) to pass through Augsburg, Ulm, Stuttgart, in which there were two tunnels, and Heidelberg.

Four dissimilar methods of assassination based on information about the Führerzug were proposed: shooting Hitler, poisoning him, blowing up the Führerzug in a tunnel or derailing the train when it was travelling on the surface.

The first plan envisaged shooting Hitler beside the Schloss Klessheim railway sidings when he was stepping out of his car to begin a rail journey. Unfortunately, Section X did not know whether his motorcade took a left-hand or a right-hand fork after leaving or passing the Schloss. This imposing eighteenth-century palace[2] on the western edge of Salzburg had been used since January 1944 as part of one of Hitler's personal headquarters (Führerhauptquartier – FHQ) because the advancing Soviet army was threatening the Rastenburg FHQ in East Prussia.[3]

Schloss Klessheim, outlying buildings and the railway sidings were protected by an estimated 1,250 troops equipped with anti-aircraft guns, searchlights and armoured cars. If the left-hand fork were taken, the road ran towards sidings beside a wood. Though thickly leaved in summer, this wood, made up largely of deciduous trees, might not provide much means of concealment in winter. Nevertheless, Section X officers thought, perhaps too optimistically, that there was 'adequate cover' for a sniper with a rifle, or a small party armed with a PIAT anti-tank gun,[4] to be hidden at the edge of the wood (and the road) opposite a building at the north-western end of the sidings. Thus precariously positioned, the sniper or PIAT handlers would shoot Hitler from a distance of less than 90 metres as he got out of his car.

In the event of his motorcade taking the right-hand fork after leaving or passing the Schloss, even greater difficulties would have been encountered. The Section X officers thought that in that situation Hitler would probably get out of his car near a building at the south-eastern end of the railway sidings. This would place him well over 270 metres from the point of fire. He would therefore be too far away for a sniper to be sure of killing him, but, the officers believed, he would 'probably' be within range of a PIAT. This seems another example of Section X's unjustified optimism, as according to *The Oxford Companion to the Second World War*, the PIAT, manufactured from mid-1942, was 'effective' to only 90 metres.

A second plan relating to the Führerzug considered the possibilities of poisoning. Section X thought that it would be impossible to poison the Führerzug's drinking and cooking water, or in other ways interfere with the train, when it was standing overnight in the Schloss Klessheim sidings. This caution was almost certainly justified, as Klessheim was (as described in the Foxley papers) 'a private station and not open to the public' and the train was guarded and washed by Führerbegleitbataillon troops. However, the idea of 'doctoring' the water when the Führerzug was parked in the sidings of Salzburg railway station was not rejected out of hand. Section X believed that the train was occasionally serviced there; in July 1944 it was reportedly seen standing alongside Ribbentrop's Sonderzüg.

In view of all that has already been said about the extreme precautions taken to ensure Hitler's personal safety, it may seem surprising to present-day readers that in Salzburg in 1944 the sides of the coaches of his Special Train were being cleaned by citizens of a Nazi-occupied country, that is by the six French women mentioned previously as doing the same job on Ribbentrop's train. Section X hoped, and it was only a cautiously expressed hope, that one or more of these women might be persuaded to drop a strong solution of poison into the Führerzug's fresh-water tank, located above the dining car's kitchen. However, even after nearly five years of the war, it was not known whether fresh water was taken into the train at Klessheim or Salzburg. And even if it were discovered that Salzburg was indeed where this was done, the water could be 'doctored' only during the night before the train began a journey in which it was certain that Hitler would be on board.

There were also unanswered questions about who guarded the stationary Führerzug: how many men were on duty and how alert and otherwise capable were they? In the second half of 1944 Section X still needed to find out this essential information. It did know that Ribbentrop's Special Train was watched over by only two armed railway policemen, but the Führerzug was almost certainly more heavily protected. Yet another problem was how to distract the guards' attention while the fresh-water tank on Hitler's train was being polluted. This would be no easy task, even in the extremely poorly lit Salzburg railway station. One operative would have to play the decoy role while another agent climbed on to the roof of the dining car and put the poison in the tank.

If this operation had been undertaken, about 768 grams of the lethal substance would have been used. Section X expected that the jolting of the train when travelling at speed would have evenly dispersed the high concentration of the poison throughout the tank, which had a capacity of 540 litres.

The Foxley papers do not identify the substance, describing it only by the code-letter 'I'. SOE chose it – in preference to the faster reacting 'R' and 'F' (also unnamed) – because it took an estimated six to seven days for the symptoms of 'I' to appear. By then there would be no antidote, or so it was hoped. 'I' had neither taste nor smell, and neither hard nor soft water was visibly affected by one lethal dose – two grams to 1.4 litres. If 'treated' in the same ratio, both black and white coffee remained unchanged in appearance, as did tea with milk. However, as described in the Foxley papers, milkless tea 'immediately becomes opalescent and in the course of an hour or so becomes quite turbid and deposits a brown sediment'. Similarly, wines and spirits adulterated with a lethal dose of 'I' became 'turbid or cloudy at once' and gradually deposited a dark brown sediment. By contrast, the same amount of 'I' did not alter the appearance of half a pint of beer, or of apples, prunes and cabbage that had been stewed or boiled in water given the fatal dose.

Clearly, SOE had learned much about poisoning. It had had to do so because, apart from envisaging 'I' as one of several means of killing Hitler, it sometimes included lethal 'L' tablets among the stores it gave its own operatives. If one of these exceptionally brave men and women were captured and then interrogated by the Gestapo, the SOE leadership in London recognised that the torture inflicted upon them would be so intense that there would be no shame in committing suicide. SOE also chose poisoning as one of several methods of assassinating traitors who had betrayed resistance fighters to the Nazis. For example, at the request of the Norwegian High Command exiled in Britain, SOE sent a team of four agents to Norway in October 1942, solely to kill selected individuals who had a notorious history of collaboration. The four operatives, codenamed Bittern, were equipped with fifteen bottles of poison, eight lethal tablets, morphia syringes and ether pads, as well as ordinary weapons.[5]

The Foxley papers say that there was 'reliable information' (intelligence reports from various sources) that Hitler was addicted to tea, always drinking it with milk. Section X officers thought, perhaps over-optimistically, that as the milk was poured first into the cup, it was 'unlikely' that the tea's opalescence would be noticed in the second or so that it took for the tea to pass from the teapot to the cup. Reports in the popular press that Hitler drank enormous quantities of black coffee were denied by a prisoner of war who had been a personal servant of the dictator from 1936 to 1940. However, a later witness, a former dining-car attendant on Ribbentrop's train, said that Hitler was indeed a heavy drinker of coffee and that he personally served him with milked coffee at the Berghof. Section X concluded from this conflicting evidence that Hitler might have greatly increased his coffee drinking during the course of the war.

The third assassination plan being considered by Section X would have involved destroying the Führerzug in a tunnel. By mid-1944 the Nazi dictatorship was becoming ever more desperately short of military manpower. In consequence, as the Foxley papers note, tunnels and bridges in Germany were less heavily guarded than were those in the occupied countries. Similarly, railway track in Germany was 'relatively free from Bahnpolizei or military patrols'. In Austria, the guarding of the railway was lax; each bridge and tunnel was thought to be protected by only two men, reportedly 'very slack in performing their duties'.

With the overwhelming majority of well-trained German soldiers serving at or near one of the front lines, Section X expected, reasonably enough, that the inefficient category of troops known as Landesschützen would in future be employed more often to guard the railways. If that were so, a tunnel sabotage party disguised as Landesschützen or as railway police, with one member pretending to be a Gestapo man in civilian clothes, would not arouse suspicion. Section X's plan involved the saboteurs bluffing their way into taking over the guarding of a tunnel. They would then lay explosive charges and detonate them as Hitler's train sped by. The section also briefly considered a method of laying explosives that might have been used in the longer tunnels, such as those in Stuttgart (700 and 340 metres in length). Saboteurs would have had to enter the chosen tunnel down its ventilation shaft but this might have involved the noisy task of cutting through the ventilation grating with a blowlamp. If either of these tunnel operations had been attempted, an agent with a radio set would have had to warn the saboteurs when the Führerzug was coming towards them.

The fourth assassination plan envisaged derailing Hitler's train when it was travelling at speed on the surface. This would have been done either by diverting the Führerzug on to a siding through changing the points or by performing the almost certainly suicidal act of throwing a suitcase full of explosives under the train's wheels.

Of course, all these and others of Section X's various schemes to assassinate Hitler would have required the approval of the Allied leaders, political and military, before operatives would have been sent into action. Also, more than halfway through 1944, the section still had big gaps in its knowledge relating to the 'possibilities of action in connection with the Führerzug'. However, Section X did have the addresses of houses and flats in the Salzburg area where agents could be hidden 'with no questions asked'. It also knew the Salzburg cafés and similar meeting places frequented by military and SS personnel, railway police, engine drivers, and sleeping-car and dining-car staff. In addition, Section X knew where to find the French women employed on train washing.

Even more important, the section thought it 'probable' that agents able to derail the Führerzug could be recruited from German or Austrian prisoners of war 'with sufficient hatred of Hitler'. Among these Germans, Bavarians were considered to have a particularly strong loathing of him, as well as of Nazis in general.

Section X also regarded Poles and Czechs living in wartime exile as having potential assassins of Hitler among their number. Whoever was eventually chosen to do the deed would have had to have been extraordinarily brave and resourceful. After being trained in Britain or abroad, such as Italy or Slovenia, they would have been infiltrated into Nazi-held territory, overland or by parachute. In or near Salzburg they would then have sought sanctuary and other essential help from anti-Nazi relations and friends, Austrian or Bavarian, or from selected members of the large communities of foreigners, mainly Poles and Czechs, who were being forced to work in the area.

Could a Section X agent have killed Hitler during one of his railway journeys? Not without a much fuller briefing than SOE's London headquarters was able to provide. As it was, in the last months of the war in Europe, some of the section's information on the running of the Führerzug dated from as far back as 1940. The four assassination schemes described in this chapter (it was also suggested that a time-bomb be smuggled on to the train) were only outlines of what might have been done. They were, nevertheless, imaginative projects. In more favourable circumstances, one of them might have had its desired result.

# Chapter Three

## *The Führer's mountain retreat*

Section X also studied the possibility of killing Hitler in or near the Berghof, his villa on the Obersalzberg, in the Bavarian Alps. It was in this isolated mountain retreat, high above the medieval town of Berchtesgaden, that the dictator spent much of his time and where he apparently felt less unsafe than anywhere else, particularly after the narrowly failed Bomb Plot of 20 July 1944.

Rather in the way that he admired beautiful but unintelligent women (dumb blondes), Hitler was fascinated by spectacular (and speechless) alpine scenery. There is certainly an abundance of that in the Berchtesgaden area, with its limestone peaks, glacier-scaped slopes and foothills covered by forests and grassland. This was what he saw from the villa and even more clearly from the Eagle's Nest, a small house on the Kehlstein mountain top at the highest altitude on the Berghof estate (1,834 metres). Hitler also looked deep into the verdant territory of his native Austria, then swallowed into his so-called 'Greater Germany' (since the Anschluss). The Berchtesgaden area also almost certainly appealed to him because of the weird superstitions associated with it. According to the oddest of these, the Emperor Charlemagne is still alive, held captive in a mountain cave.

However, most important of all for Hitler was the Berghof's rarefied position, seemingly on top of the world. This was a place where, isolated from everybody except bodyguards and members of his sycophantic entourage, he could indulge to the full his megalomaniac illusion of possessing infallible judgement. For him the Berghof was therefore the ideal setting for several pre-war and wartime conferences with members of his inner circle, political and military. In the same way it was the best available location for receiving – and if possible browbeating or bemusing – foreign dignitaries such as Kurt von Schuschnigg, the Austrian Chancellor ousted on the eve of the Anschluss, Neville Chamberlain, the British Prime Minister from May 1937 to May 1940, Admiral Horthy, the Hungarian Regent, Count Ciano, Mussolini's Foreign Minister and son-in-law, and Marshal Antonescu, the Romanian dictator.

On 18 April 1945, twelve days before his suicide, Hitler ordered the establishment of an 'inner fortress' (Kernfestung) in the Bavarian Alps, presumably in or near the Berghof. He hoped that a contingent of Nazi fanatics would continue fighting from there after the rest of his 'empire' had collapsed. This absurd order – the outcome of thoughts put in his mind by Himmler and others – could, of course, never by obeyed. On 25 April an RAF bombing raid made the Berghof villa and its outbuildings uninhabitable.[1] On 4 May American troops entered Berchtesgaden, ending the last dreams of a Nazi revival.

Judging from the Foxley papers, Section X had by the summer of 1944 become well informed about the Berghof and the Führergebiet, the collective name of more than fifty buildings, camps and amenities surrounding, protecting and otherwise serving the villa. Section X knew the location of each of these properties and the topography and climate of both the Obersalzberg and the nearby countryside on the road to Schloss Klessheim. The section had also gathered detailed information about the enormous resources put into guarding Hitler twenty-four hours a day. In addition, it knew which members of his inner circle lived on the estate or visited it often. Armed with all this essential intelligence, but acutely aware that much more was needed, Section X identified various places where an agent might have a chance of killing Hitler.

Originally called the Haus Wachenfeld, the Berghof villa was Hitler's most valuable personal possession, bought from the sales of *Mein Kampf*.[2] After he came to power he greatly enlarged it and furnished it luxuriously. The massive amount of building work, much of it done by slave labour, included digging deep into solid rock to provide the villa with a labyrinth of underground rooms. The most important of these was Hitler's vast air-raid shelter, which was 15 to 20 metres below the Berghof's surface rooms. A tunnel leading to the shelter zigzagged near the entrance, turning left, left again and then right, finally linking with a central passage. This led into the shelter itself, which, according to Section X's information, was 80 to 100 metres long, lavishly furnished, and centrally heated by a boiler under the richly carpeted parquet floor. The shelter had three exits and was ventilated but had no air shafts – important pieces of information for a would-be assassin. This shelter, in which Hitler would have been safe from even the heaviest Allied bombing, was part of a vast complex of air-raid and observation shelters built into the Obersalzberg mountain side in 1943 and 1944. The Führer's shelter and a similar one for his personal secretary, Martin

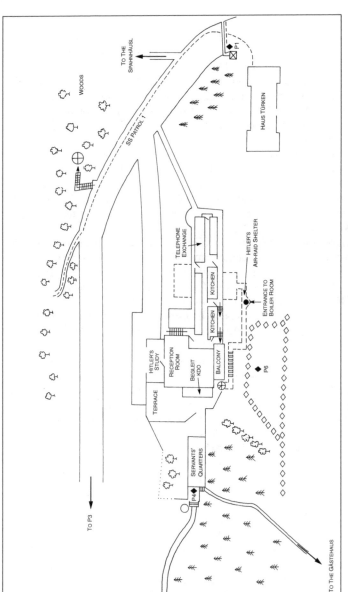

*Map of the Berghof based on Section X's intelligence reports.*

Bormann (1900–45), were completed in May 1944 and eleven shelters were being linked by tunnels at about that time.

The Foxley papers include a sketch-map of the Berghof's ground floor as it was in April–May 1944 – another indication that some of Section X's information was slightly out of date in the autumn of that year. As well as Hitler's personal quarters, the villa had several grand rooms for formal occasions. It also had accommodation for bodyguard troops and contained one of the three telephone exchanges on the Obersalzberg.

The other principal buildings and amenities on the Berghof estate included the Haus Türken, the Gästehaus Hoher Göll, the Platterhof, SS barracks, the Vordereck, the Haus Bormann, the Landhaus and Adjutantur Göring, the Haus and Atelier Speer, the Beckstein Haus, a theatre, manual workers' accommodation, a farm and the Mooslaner Kopf tea-house.

A former hotel, the Haus Türken contained sleeping quarters for pickets of the SS-Wachkompanie Obersalzberg, an SS guardroom and accommodation for the Obersalzberg detachment of the RSD. Also in the house was another of the Obersalzberg's telephone exchanges. The Gästehaus Hoher Göll was in woods behind the Berghof in the direction of the Eagle's Nest. Eva Braun, Hitler's mistress, and various RSD personnel lived there. It also had quarters for SS-Gruppenführer Dr Otto Dietrich (1897–1952), the Nazi Party's press chief from 1931 to 1945, on his visits to the Berghof. Other visitors sleeping there included Hitler's aides-de-camp and lesser functionaries. The guest-house, named after the nearby Hoher Göll mountain (2,522 metres), was managed by Fräulein Josepha Guggenbichler, who also supervised the women on the Berghof estate. Führerbegleitbataillon personnel operated teleprinters in the building.

A military hospital in 1944, the Platterhof was originally intended to be a hotel and was completed only in 1942. The manager of its barber's shop spoke Italian fluently and German with a Bavarian accent. He employed three Italian assistants. The Foxley papers contain much seemingly unimportant personal information like this – just one of many indications of how well Section X was informed about locations where it hoped to send agents and where potential assassins of Hitler might be found working alongside diehard Nazis. Nurses and other hospital staff lived in a house associated with the Platterhof, with porters, clerks and waitresses in back rooms. In the SS barracks there were the living quarters of the SS-Wachkompanie and the offices of the SS-Kommando Obersalzberg and of the Stollenbaukompanie, manufacturers of air-raid shelters. The building, whose layout Section X knew in some detail, also contained garages and a gymnasium.

The Vordereck comprised two houses. The first one contained the Verwaltung Obersalzberg, the local administrative headquarters, on the ground floor, with servants' quarters above it. Führerbegleitkommando members slept there when Hitler was in the Berghof. In the second house was the estate's air-raid control room, with SS-Untersturmführer (Second Lieutenant) Bredow in charge. The Haus Bormann was the home of Bormann, his wife and, according to the Foxley papers, his 'nine to eleven children'. Associated with it were the Modellbau and the Kindergarten. Built into rock, the Modellbau was thought to be safer than many other buildings on the estate, and for that reason Bormann used it for storing his collection of carpets. His children and about twenty to thirty others attended the Kindergarten. The Landhaus Göring was the residence of Göring, his wife, Emmy,[3] and their small daughter, Edda. A family called Ziczka did the housekeeping. The Adjutantur Göring accommodated the Reich Marshal's personal staff when he visited the Obersalzberg. Those living there permanently or for much of the time included his Chief of Staff, Luftwaffe General Karl Bodenschatz. The building also housed the third telephone exchange on the estate.

The Haus Speer was the residence of Albert Speer (1905–81), the Armaments Minister and head of the Todt forced-labour organisation. He rarely visited the house, but his wife, children and a nurse lived there. It was a Nazi claim that the Atelier Speer housed about forty children from bomb-damaged areas. The Beckstein Haus (formerly the Hess Haus) lodged Hitler's more important occasional visitors before and during the war. They included Mussolini and Boris III, the King of Bulgaria who died in mysterious circumstances – probably either through assassination or having a heart attack – after meeting Hitler in August 1943.

The Berghof estate's theatre, the Theaterhalle Obersalzberg, was a wooden structure whose gabled roof collapsed under the weight of snow in the winter of 1943/4. The building, seating 2,000 people, was due to have been repaired in August 1944. Stage shows and Nazi ideological meetings were held there. A flat behind the stage was occupied by a Nazi named Fillhuber. The Lager Antenberg was a camp for manual workers, mostly Czechs employed on repairing and improving roads and on snow clearance. Behind the camp were a wooden shed and piles of timber – possible hiding places for a would-be assassin of Hitler. The Klaushöhe was a German workers' settlement (Arbeitersiedlung) consisting of twenty-two houses

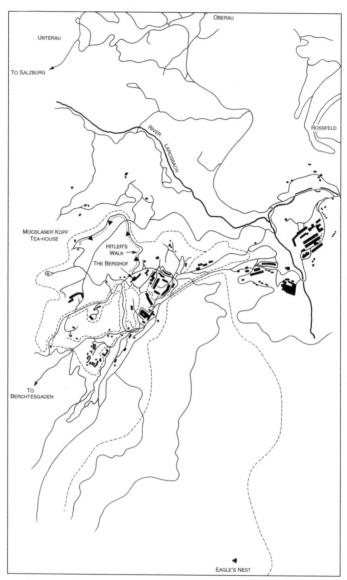

*A sketch-map of Hitler's huge estate on the Obersalzberg, showing the Berghof villa, the Mooslaner Kopf tea-house and the Eagle's Nest. These were but a few of the many buildings, amenities and military installations dotted around the estate. The broken lines on the map represent the wire fences encircling the principal buildings. Much of the area was covered by woodland and undergrowth.*

arranged in three rows. Section X knew how each building was used. For example, House Number One was a grocery shop, House Six was occupied by women working in the SS barracks, and a doctor with the SS rank of Hauptsturmführer (captain) was in House Eighteen. The Gutshof Obersalzberg, the Berghof estate's farm, produced milk, butter, honey, pig meat and other food. In addition, there was the Gärtnerei, which grew vegetables and fruit for the SS barracks.

The Mooslaner Kopf tea-house was where Hitler walked to from the Berghof villa on most days during his long stays on the Obersaltzberg. He took little other physical exercise. The Foxley papers also describe the Eagle's Nest as a tea-house, but one that the dictator had lost interest in by the summer of 1944. A stone building, it was approached by a zigzag road, steep towards the mountain summit and requiring the use of two lifts, one for passengers and the other for vehicles, during the last 100 metres of the ascent.

Other buildings on the estate included the Kampfhäusl, where Hitler completed writing *Mein Kampf* (the building was empty in April–May 1944); the Hintereck, three or four houses accommodating various functionaries; housing for civilians; the Meisterlehen, a derelict house; a sawmill; a restaurant with bar; a coffee shop, with five or six waitresses and three or four French waiters; and a post office, with six employees, including a one-armed postman. Section X sought detailed information about everybody on the Berghof estate, resident or visitor, regardless of his or her status in Nazi society. The more that was known about such people, and about everything on the estate, the greater chance there was of planning achievable operations to kill Hitler and selected other members of his regime.

Section X strove to find out as much as possible about the dictator's day-to-day life at the Berghof and about his health and physical appearance, both thought to be badly affected by the trauma of the July Bomb Plot explosion. When and where did the prematurely aged and apprehensive Führer appear out of doors on the estate? Who were his daily companions? Who visited him? What uniforms or civilian clothes did he wear? Did Hitler have one or more doubles, such as officials or actors made up to look like him? These questions were being asked by Section X. Without satisfactory answers to them it would be impossible to plan an assassination scheme that had any hope of success.

An entry in the Foxley papers made in the summer of 1944 referred to photographs of the then 55-year-old Hitler which 'often show such changes in [his] appearance that one is tempted to credit the popular belief that he has one or more doubles'. To staff officers who visited the Rastenburg FHQ in 1943 Hitler seemed to be in good health, calm and self-possessed. In contrast, officers then stationed at Rastenburg, and therefore seeing him often, considered that he looked ten years older than his actual age. One of the photographs, taken in his train in 1943, bore out a report in May 1944, that Hitler was looking 'grey and bent'. Yet others of the photographs, taken after Colonel Count Claus von Stauffenberg's nearly successful assassination attempt two months later, make him appear in good physical and mental condition. The Foxley papers comment on this: 'How much these changes in appearance are to be ascribed to the frequent [drug] injections given the Führer, who is generally known to [be in] poor health, or to the employment of a double, it is impossible to say, evidence to the latter point being particularly conflicting.'

Section X's assessments of the state of Hitler's health were based in part on reporting by the American OSS and Britain's SIS. In a report from Switzerland shortly after Stauffenberg's failure to kill Hitler, the OSS quoted an agent as saying that the dictator had serious throat trouble, which prevented him from speaking, and had had a nervous collapse. The agent added that Hitler's periods of depression and elation were so unpredictable that his entourage could not tell half an hour in advance how he would behave in a given situation. An SIS report dated 11 December 1944 said that several members of the German Embassy in Madrid had received information that Hitler was seriously ill or even mentally deranged. (See Appendix E for assessments of the dictator's health not mentioned in the Foxley papers.)

According to Section X's information, from the summer of 1944 Hitler usually wore a greenish khaki jacket and breeches when attending formal occasions; but, when surrounded by members of his entourage at the Berghof, he dressed in a brown or grey double-breasted jacket and black trousers. The only military decoration he wore was the Iron Cross.

Section X was far from being convinced that Hitler had any doubles. In its view the only confirmation of what it called the 'popular rumour' of their existence came from a Gestapo member and from a soldier belonging to the Wachkompanie of the SS-Leibstandarte Adolf Hitler. The Gestapo man was quoted as expressing surprise at having seen 'Hitler' in the Reich Chancellery in Berlin walking past him twice in the same direction within a few minutes. According to the Wachkompanie soldier, the look-alike was a junior member of the Reich Chancellery staff who wore the appropriate uniform of brown jacket and black trousers and was so like Hitler in appearance that he was often mistaken for him by SS guards, who promptly gave the Nazi salute. However, another Leibstandarte soldier, who reportedly had been one of the dictator's three principal personal servants from 1936 to 1940, denied that there were any doubles.

Even today, decades after the Second World War, it is still not known for certain whether such impersonators existed. However, it seems probable that there was at least one – a junior Reich Chancellery official named Gustav Weler. His body (with a gunshot wound in the forehead) was filmed by the Russians in May 1945, shortly after they took control of the Chancellery and its gruesome contents. (That film footage, also showing the corpses of Goebbels, his wife and their children, was kept in store by the Soviet authorities throughout the Cold War. However, that length of the film, together with other historically important material, was made available in 1992 to Ada Petrova, a Russian television journalist and co-author (with British writer Peter Watson), of *The Death of Hitler: The Final Words from Russia's Secret Archives.*)

Section X also thought it necessary to discover as much as possible about everything the dictator did at the Berghof. Information on even the seemingly most unimportant details of his daily routine was actively sought. The Foxley papers state that he was a late riser, never getting up before 9 a.m. and sometimes an hour later than that. After being shaved and groomed by his barber, he walked unaccompanied to the Mooslaner Kopf tea-house, omitting that constitutional only if he had a conference or similar engagement. (That was not how Hitler took exercise in less stressful times. For example, in 1940, when the war was going well for him and he was luxuriating in his illusions of political and military infallibility, he would set off for the Mooslaner Kopf as late as 3 p.m., accompanied by his principal adjutants and aides-de-camp; the party seldom numbered fewer than twelve and was followed by six to ten guards at a discreet distance.)

Hitler had a breakfast of milk and toast at the tea-house; in 1944 this took place between 11 a.m. and 11.30 a.m. The Foxley papers emphasise that he never walked back to the Berghof villa, instead always travelling in his motorcade past two SS pickets. He then might see Dr Theodor Morell (1886–1948), his personal doctor, and in the afternoon would receive carefully vetted visitors. These would be all sorts of people who personally interested him, ranging from artists to fellow holders of the Iron Cross.

Whenever Hitler had appointments outside his mountain retreat, he left by road at noon. If he remained at the Berghof, he had a late lunch (vegetables only) at 4 p.m. He sometimes invited Göring or the Bormann family to eat with them. After lunch Hitler worked until 10 p.m., generally with the help of a clerk or Eva Braun. He would then chair a conference on the military situation – for him an increasingly grave one. The generals and other officers who attended would arrive by car, entering the Berghof estate at picket number three, where they were given thorough security checks. Hitler had supper between 1 a.m. and 1.30 a.m. and went to bed at about 3 a.m., 4 a.m. or even later.

When travelling to or from the Obersalzberg he always went by road and rail. On the outward journey his motorcade almost always took him to Schloss Klessheim but sometimes nearby to Berchtesgaden town. He then transferred to the Führerzug, his Special Train.

The Foxley papers also show which members of Hitler's entourage lived much of the time on the Berghof estate and which were only occasional visitors. Judging from these papers, Section X had become well informed about the movements and habits of several of these leading Nazis, subordinate staff and hangers-on.

Together with Hitler, the regime member who spent most time at the Berghof was Bormann. Described in the papers as Chief of Staff of the Chancellery of the Party, a War Cabinet member, and a Gruppenführer (major-general) of both the SS and the SA, he was in command of the Obersalzberg in Hitler's absence. Bormann's unpopularity was reflected in his local nickname, the 'black shadow on the mountain' ('Schwarzer Schatten am Berg'). He rarely left the estate and nearly always wore civilian clothes – a soft hat, grey jacket and grey trousers tucked into boots. He was often seen in a three-axle touring car, usually with children in the back. He drove the vehicle himself, never at more than 30 mph – a speed limit that he himself set for the Obersalzberg.

Göring (1893–1946), described in the Foxley papers as 'successor-designate to Hitler, Chairman of the War Cabinet, member of the Privy Council, Reich Minister for Air, etc.', was a 'fairly frequent' visitor, sometimes staying for long periods at his residence on the estate, the Landhaus Göring. He was accompanied by a Luftwaffe sergeant, and his chauffeur was a Luftwaffe lieutenant. Although General Bodenschatz was his frequent companion, Göring often walked about the estate alone and did not appear to be carefully guarded. As the head of the Reichsmarschall's personal staff, Bodenschatz lived at the Adjutantur Göring, usually wearing civilian clothes. He drove his own Mercedes, in which he was willing to give 'anyone' (Section X's word) a lift.

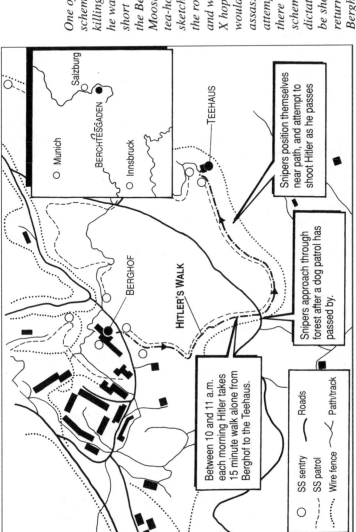

*One of the Foxley schemes envisaged killing Hitler when he was taking his short walk from the Berghof to the Mooslaner Kopf tea-house. This sketch-map shows the route he took and what Section X hoped snipers would do. If this assassination attempt failed, there was another scheme to kill the dictator: he would be shot when returning to the Berghof in his car.*

Salzburg

BERCHTESGADEN

Munich

Innsbruck

TEEHAUS

BERGHOF

HITLER'S WALK

Snipers position themselves near path, and attempt to shoot Hitler as he passes

Snipers approach through forest after a dog patrol has passed by.

Between 10 and 11 a.m. each morning Hitler takes a 15 minute walk alone from Berghof to the Teehaus.

○ SS sentry
--- SS patrol
···· Wire fence
— Roads
⌐ Path/track

Eva Braun, quaintly described in the Foxley papers as 'Hitler's secretary', scarcely ever left the Berghof estate. According to SOE's informants, she was a 'brunette,[4] attractive and unconventional in her costume, sometimes wearing Bavarian leather shorts'. Always shadowed by RSD men when she went out of doors, she took two black dogs for walks, often accompanied by Fräulein Silberhorn, the telephone operator at the Gästehaus. She was described as 'unapproachable' and by 1944 almost certainly had only a platonic relationship with the ailing dictator. The Foxley papers say that she did not wear make-up, as 'Hitler, it appears, cannot tolerate the use of cosmetics'. However, according to Reinhard Spitzy,[5] who visited the Berghof in January 1937, she lacquered her nails and wore a discreet amount of make-up. He described her as 'a nice person, who provided Hitler with all the cosy trappings of a bourgeois home life. Although she was easygoing and likeable, she did not seem to possess any particularly striking qualities. She could just as well have been a cheerful shop assistant.' Born in 1912, Spitzy was in the 1930s a member of the Viennese SS unit, the Standarte 89, and later a diplomat. During the war he worked in intelligence but turned against the Nazis and aided the German Resistance.

Eva Braun (born in 1912) was totally dominated by the much older Hitler from 1932 when she became his mistress until they committed suicide together in the Reich Chancellery bunker on 30 April 1945. By all informed postwar accounts, this Bavarian wife of the Nazi tyrant for only the last few hours of her life was a simple soul who had little interest in politics and no inkling of her master's evil character. Never given any public role, and probably incapable of performing one, she had but one objective: to please Hitler at all times regardless of the cost to herself. That cost was high: countless hours of isolation and boredom in the gilded cage of the Berghof. Erich Kempka (1910–75), the dictator's chauffeur, said of her after the war: 'She was the unhappiest woman in Germany, spending most of her life waiting for Hitler.'

The Foxley papers describe Dr Morell as the dictator's 'personal physician' on the Obersalzberg, 'age about sixty, corpulent, medium height with grey hair standing up like a brush'. From the mid-1930s this fanatical misuser of drugs had unintentionally hastened the decline of his gullible patient's health. Having earlier in his career made a name for himself by treating rich actors and artists for venereal and skin diseases, Morell had regularly given Hitler dozens of different pills and injections. These included harmful amphetamines and so-called 'miracle medicines', some of them claimed by him to have been made from material taken from bulls' testicles or from intestinal bacteria 'raised from the best stock owned by a Bulgarian peasant'. Under Hitler's patronage, Morell amassed great wealth from manufacturing patent medicines and from the compulsory use in the German army of 'Morell's Russian Lice Powder'. Göring and Eva Braun loathed Morell. He called him 'Herr Reich Injection Master' and she reportedly said that he lived like a pig.

Others often seen on the Berghof estate in the summer of 1944 included Dietrich, the Nazi Party's Press chief, who, as State Secretary in the Propaganda Ministry, represented Goebbels; Brigadeführer Rattenhuber, who, being responsible for Hitler's safety, rarely left his side; and Hauptsturmführer Müller of the RSD and formerly of the Waffen SS (Section X had detailed information on his personal appearance: aged about thirty and 1.87 metres tall, he had a dark complexion and short hair and still wore Waffen SS uniform, with a Wiking armband on his left cuff).

The Foxley papers name others holding key positions on the Obersalzberg[6] and two leading members of the Nazi regime – Himmler and Ribbentrop – who, for reasons unknown, seldom visited the Berghof. Himmler paid only two one-day visits between August 1943 and May 1944. The papers record that he moved about everywhere without a guard. He would have been an easy target for an assassin, such as a disillusioned Nazi. Ribbentrop, who had a villa at Fuschl, rarely went nearer the Obersalzberg than Schloss Klessheim.

With Morell in residence on the Berghof estate, it is understandable that his principal rival for Hitler's favour, Dr Karl Brandt (1904–48), was another infrequent visitor. As the dictator's physician in Berlin, Brandt had the grandiose title of Plenipotentiary General for Health and Medical Services and held the ranks of SS-Brigadeführer and General-major der Ordnungspolizei. Slim and 1.7 metres tall, he often wore his major-general's uniform.

Hitler lavished military and counter-intelligence resources on protecting himself. Section X knew he was especially heavily guarded on the many occasions that he stayed at the Berghof, and though the German army was being increasingly crippled by manpower shortages on all fronts in the final twelve months of the European war, the Nazi dictator never reduced the strength of the forces allocated solely to preserving himself and his inner circle from assassination or from attack by Allied air and land forces.

By the summer of 1944 Section X had become well informed about most aspects of the Berghof estate's complex defence system. For instance, it had Top Secret intelligence on the

Reichssicherheitsdienst personnel in charge of security on the Obersalzberg, the passes issued to visitors to the estate, the four units of SS troops stationed there, their weapons, the air-raid precautions, and the system of military and civilian guards. Section X had also studied in depth the topography and climate of the Obersalzberg. (See Appendix F.)

The RSD men, led by Brigadeführer Rattenhuber (a Gruppenführer from 24 February 1945) and with Hauptsturmführer Müller as second-in-command, numbered only about twenty. Most of them were Bavarians. They usually wore civilian clothes, but sometimes Waffen SS uniforms with the shoulder straps of the Ordnungspolizei (intertwined threads coloured silver and brown or green). Those RSD personnel who had been recruited from the Waffen SS wore its uniform without these shoulder straps. RSD men ranked Unterscharführer (sergeant) – the most common rank on the Obersalzberg – wore above the left cuff the Rante, a diamond-shaped black patch decorated with the letters 'SD' in silver embroidery. In winter, RSD, Begleitkommando and Wachkompanie personnel wore SS-Gebirgsjäger (mountain troop) uniform. To have any chance of killing Hitler, a Foxley agent would have had to recognise the uniforms of all the different sorts of troops and police on the Obersalzberg and he might himself have had to wear an imitation of one of the uniforms.

RSD men patrolled the whole Berghof estate, including the area around the Eagle's Nest. They usually took dogs, of which they had three, each with a handler. Section X believed that one or two RSD personnel were always in the Eagle's Nest, which was very difficult to reach except by its two lifts. There was also an RSD detachment in Berchtesgaden town, where RSD men were, as the Foxley papers say, 'always hanging about' its 'carefully watched' railway station.

All passes issued to visitors to the Berghof estate were coloured dark blue and had to be renewed each week with a numbered stamp. The passes usually bore the imprint of Bormann's or Rattenhuber's signature, although temporary passes might be signed by somebody less senior. Personnel of the SS-Wachkompanie Obersalzberg had special passes showing that they belonged to that company and were allowed on the estate only when on duty. As these privileged and trusted men were known to the guards at the entrance gates, their passes were never checked. Similarly – surprisingly – nobody looked at the pass issued to the milkman, who was employed by the Gutshof, or that of a woman who regularly delivered secret letters.[7]

The combatant troops stationed on the Obersalzberg were divided into these SS units: the Führerbegleitkommando, the Wachkompanie Obersalzberg, the Sonderkolonne and the Nebelabteilung. There was also a solely administrative unit, the SS-Kommando Obersalzberg, led by Sturmbannführer (Major) Frank. All his thirty or so men were clerks.

The Führerbegleitkommando was made up mainly of officers and NCOs. Some of its personnel were permanently stationed at the Reich Chancellery in Berlin. Twenty were on the Berghof estate (most of them Bavarians) and a few were at Hitler's personal headquarters – the FHQs, such as Rastenburg and his Special Train, the Führerzug, whenever he was travelling on it. These highly privileged troops were better dressed than other SS personnel; the NCOs, for example, had officer-style uniforms. They were distinctive also because they wore an armband inscribed 'Adolf Hitler' above the left cuff. In winter and on informal occasions all ranks wore Gebirgsjäger trousers stuffed into ski boots and a Bergmütze (mountain troops' woolly hat) with the Totenkopf (death's head emblem) on the front.

Section X was particularly well informed about the SS-Wachkompanie Obersalzberg. Formed in 1938, it was nominally under Himmler's direct control. However, in reality it was led – at least in April–May 1944 – by Obersturmführer (Lieutenant) Ubart, but he was answerable 'for administrative purposes' to Sturmbannführer Frank. Seventy per cent of the estimated 180 members of this guard company had been on the Obersalzberg since the start of the war. Most of them were Austrians or Bavarians but there were some ethnic Germans from the Sudetenland, Upper Silesia and Romania. The company included a mountain rescue patrol (the Bergwacht) and a fire-fighting platoon (the Feuerlöschzug), one of whose additional duties was to check that the blackout precautions were being strictly observed. This dull task was carried out at various times but not later than 2 a.m. Evidently even the reputedly fanatical Nazis belonging to this platoon were not prepared to lose more than a few hours' sleep in the service of their Führer! Reveille was at 7 a.m. In the unlikely event that the Wachkompanie men failed to get out of bed then, Section X would, of course, have been delighted. However, it did know exactly how to wake them up and give them misinformation. It had obtained the company headquarters' telephone number.

The SS-Sonderkolonne (or SS-Dienstwagenhalle) provided motor transport for Hitler and his entourage. One of its three platoons was stationed on the Obersalzberg. Commanded by Obersturmführer Kreiderer, it had between sixty and eighty men and eight Mercedes cars. The SS-Nebelabteilung was responsible for creating smokescreens if these were judged necessary in the event of the Berghof estate being attacked by Allied land or air forces. The unit comprised three troops, each with eighty to a hundred men. They were dispersed, two to a hut, all over the countryside on and around the Berghof estate. Their smoke-making equipment, consisting of a gas flask, stove pipe and small holders, was operated by turning a handle, or electrically if the equipment was within the estate.

By 1944 Section X had assembled a mass of detailed intelligence on the many pickets and patrols operating all over the Führergebiet. The SS controlled most of these respectively static and mobile guards, but there were also a few civilian pickets and patrols. The SS pickets were numbered one to ten and G1 to G3, with one unnumbered picket. Picket 1 was stationed at the Haus Türken. Picket 2 stood a short distance in front of the Berghof, but only at night, when he was closely watched by RSD men. Picket 3 was nearby at the entrance to the villa. He had access to alarm devices to alert staff at the Haus Türken. When Hitler was at the Berghof there was an Untersturmführer at this post. When the dictator arrived his chauffeur gave one toot on the horn and the driver of Bormann's car, often accompanying Hitler's, gave two toots. Only then was the gate at this post opened. Picket 4 was stationed behind the servants' quarters at the villa. Picket 5 guarded the Gästehaus; Section X envisaged the possibility of a would-be assassin entering and passing through that building to get into the back of the Berghof. Picket 6 stood between the Gästehaus and the Berghof at a high point where he had a good view; Section X believed that Picket 7 was no longer being mounted in the autumn of 1944. Picket 8 guarded the loading ramp at the start of the Führerstrasse, the special road used by Hitler and his henchmen when travelling by car to and from the estate. Picket 9 was at the Maierhaus, the home of a family called Forz. Picket 10 comprised a team of six men stationed inside the Theaterhalle; when a show was being staged the guard contingent also included RSD men and the Wachkompanie's entire Bereitschaft, a squad liable to be called out at any time of day or night.

Picket G1 was stationed at the gate to the Gärtnerie; according to the Foxley papers, he exercised 'strict control' when Göring was in residence. That perhaps meant that he was rather lax at other times. Picket G2 guarded the front of Göring's house night and day, largely to prevent unauthorised persons entering its air-raid shelter. However, Picket G3, positioned behind the house, was on duty only at night. The unnumbered picket was stationed at the Gutshof. His main task was to keep as close a watch as possible on Hitler during his walks to the Mooslaner Kopf tea-house. But he could see him, at a distance of 800 to 1,000 metres, for only part of that time.

In the autumn of 1944 Section X was not totally certain that this system of pickets had not been modified since the spring when more air-raid shelters were being built. In the section's opinion, some sentries might have been redeployed to guard these shelters. Some of the pickets had automatic or machine pistols. Others had rifles and G3 had a machine-gun mounted on a tripod.

With one exception, the SS operated one-man patrols. All carried rifles and were relieved every two hours. Section X's knowledge of the routes taken by these patrols was incomplete. However, it did have potentially useful scraps of information: Patrol 1's beat was from the Berghof to the Mooslaner Kopf, where he chatted for a long time to a civilian picket. Patrol 5 walked from SS Picket 3's post (at the entrance to the Berghof) to a civilian's picket's post at Teugelbrunn. The patrol crossed a bridge over a stream until he was within sight of the civilian picket but did not go right up to him. At night the patrol went on to the Mooslaner Kopf, where there was a telephone for use in an emergency. There were also bells on trees, presumably to be rung as another means of raising the alarm. Patrol Gästehaus went from there to Picket 3's post (Posten). Patrol Posten Antenberg walked beside a wire-mesh fence to Posten Rodelbahn. He could see down to the Führerstrasse except where it was hidden by trees. Patrol Bienenhaus operated only when Hitler was in the Berghof. So did Patrol Kehlstein, made up of two men. They covered the area north of the Kehlstein mountain in winter.

The civilian pickets were mostly Bavarians or Austrians. As described in the Foxley papers, they looked like ordinary workmen of 'a very mixed type', but in reality were 'reliable Nazis' of high status. Although they stood in sentry boxes like soldiers, they wore civilian clothes without any distinguishing marks. They were apparently unarmed. One-man civilian pickets guarded posts named Teugelbrunn, Auerstrasse, Rodelbahn and Antenberg, and – oddly – there were two civilian sentries at the SS barracks. The Foxley papers note that it was easy to pass the picket at Posten Rodelbahn 'if approached in the [unspecified] right way'. The only civilian patrols were lumberjacks and a gamekeeper who roamed around the Kehlstein.

Section X was also well informed about the fences, anti-aircraft guns, air-raid precautions and air-raid shelters on and around the Berghof estate. The fences inside and surrounding the estate were made of wire-mesh. They were 200 to 220 centimetres high and were supported by steel tubes places at intervals of three to five metres.

The tops of the tubes were bent over inwards and held three or four strands of barbed-wire. The many gates in the fences were also made of wire-mesh and were locked, except those being guarded. Surprisingly, the wire-mesh did not carry electric current and, as far as Section X knew, there were no trip wires or automatic alarm devices.

The Foxley papers list the locations of no less than six detachments of anti-aircraft troops protecting the Berghof.[8] Most of their artillery was of 8.8-centimetre calibre but there was also a battery of four-barrelled AA guns. Again surprisingly, there were no searchlights. But, according to the Foxley papers, all the Führergebiet buildings were treated to resist fire and were reported to be sprayed with paint in 'a disruptive pattern' which was changed every three months. Section X's knowledge of the Obersalzberg's air-raid precautions was remarkably extensive. Warnings of the approach of hostile aircraft were received direct from Warnkommando, Travenstein, and from the Nazi Party Chancellery in Munich. The officer commanding the Führergebiet's warning system, Untersturmführer Bredow, had his office in the second house of the Vordereck – and Section X even knew the number of his telephone extension (202).

Sirens on the Berghof estate gave two sorts of warning signals: The 'Alert' – three deep blasts lasting a total of one minute; this meant that a single plane was in the vicinity or that one or more aircraft were flying straight towards the Berghof estate but were still some distance away. And the 'Flieger Alarm' – a wailing sound signifying that more than one aircraft were in the area; this alarm was given even when a few planes became detached from formations bombing nearby targets, such as in Munich. There were also two sorts of 'all clear' signals. While an 'alert' was being sounded on the sirens a special warning was being given by telephone (three short rings repeated twice) to various personnel concerned with fire fighting and other tasks associated with air raids. Section X knew all the relevant telephone extensions.

Even early in the war, when his strategy was bringing him a seemingly unendable line of military and political successes, Hitler severely rationed his contact with the general public. Whatever he did, his own safety was always paramount in his thinking. When Winston Churchill and King George VI were visiting bombed areas of London and other cities, the cowardly Führer never undertook any similar humanitarian task in Germany. As the war continued increasingly to his disadvantage, he became more and more reclusive. He spent long periods in the Berghof, isolated from everybody except the small band of diehard Nazi sycophants whom he chose as his companions. Thus cut off from painful realities, Hitler spent much time fantasising, reminiscing about the early days of the Nazi movement, watching films and admiring the mountain scenery. He was living in a fool's paradise, feeling he was safe – at least as safe as he could be anywhere. Hitler would perhaps have been less confident if he had known how much Section X knew about his Bavarian alpine retreat.

# Chapter Four
## *The tea-house and road plots*

Section X carefully examined the possibility of killing Hitler during one of his frequent visits to the tea-house on the Mooslaner Kopf. It acknowledged that the scheme would be as perilous as any of its other assassination plans. However, as the Foxley papers say, 'Action here is nevertheless worthy of consideration in view of the fact that whereas a considerable interval of time may elapse between Hitler's visits to Schloss Klessheim and other FHQs, the Führer rarely misses his daily walk to the tea-house. . . . Thus from the middle of March 1944, before which date the snow was too thick, Hitler went to the Teehaus nearly every day.'

According to Section X's information, Hitler set out from the Berghof for the tea-house between 10 a.m. and 11 a.m. Walking alone, he was watched throughout this 15–20 minute stroll by an SS patrol. He was also within view of the SS picket at the Gutshof for about 1,000 yards (914 metres) of the walk. In addition, Hitler was seen by the SS pickets at the Theaterhalle and Göring's house as he crossed what the Foxley papers describe as a 'concrete by-pass' – presumably a footbridge or path – from the Oberau road to the Führerstrasse. These sentries were, however, well over 500 yards (457 metres) away. During this walk the dictator could not bear to feel that he was being watched. If he spotted an SS man following him, he looked back and shouted sarcastically, 'If you are frightened, go and guard yourself.'

Section X visualised one or two snipers being entrusted with the assassination. Assuming two were chosen, they would make their way through woods beside the River Larosbach to a part of the wire-mesh fencing near the concrete by-pass. They would then be between 100 and 200 yards (about 91 to 182 metres) from where Hitler walked. The snipers needed to be at their destination after 10 a.m. to give the RSD dog patrol time to have passed by. Each man would be equipped with a Mauser sniper's rifle, explosive bullets in the magazine, a telescopic sight (not to be fixed in position until needed), wire-cutters, and a haversack full of grenades, needed for self-protection, particularly to make a quick escape.

The explosive bullets are only mentioned in passing in the Foxley papers. As they are not described, it is impossible to identify them. However, they might have been one of the sorts of ammunition outlawed by the 1899 Hague Peace Conference – bullets which expand or flatten easily in the human body. Snipers used such ammunition on a few occasions in earlier conflicts. Such an occasion would have been when the sniper had only a single opportunity to hit his target and so needed to do maximum damage with that hit – like blowing off a man's head. The explosive effect was achieved by including a small quantity of dense liquid metal in the nose of the bullet. When this ammunition hit its target the nose cap collapsed and the liquid metal was projected as a high-speed jet through the target's body. The bullet was not, however, fused and did not explode in the sense that a cannon shell does. One of the liquid metals used in these bullets was mercury fulminate – $Hg (ONC)_2$. A fictional illustration of the huge amount of terrible damage done by this ammunition can be seen in the film *The Day of the Jackal*.

The snipers in the Foxley operation would wear the uniform of mountain troops (Gebirgsjäger). This would be a sensible disguise, as the overwhelming majority of the patients in the Platterhof military hospital were mountain troops. In wintertime the Führerbegleitkommando, the SS-Wachkompanie Obersalzberg and the RSD (when not in civilian clothes) all wore this type of uniform, with minor modifications. So, as the Foxley papers explain, 'impersonation on these lines would obviously facilitate approach to within striking distance'. A mountain troop's uniform could be quickly converted into that worn by SS personnel on the Obersalzberg. All that had to be done was to move the national markings (Hoheitsabzeichen) from above the right breast-pocket to the left sleeve above the elbow; remove the red, white and black rosette and Hoheitsabzeichen from the front of the cap (Bergmütze) and put in their place the death's head emblem (Totenkopf); and change the Wehrmacht collar patches for the SS flash and badge of rank, worn respectively on the right and left sides of the collar. Section X thought it might also be necessary to remove the edelweiss emblem from the left side of the cap.

If the sniper or snipers failed in their mission and Hitler reached the tea-house unharmed, Section X had another idea about how to kill him while he was still in the area. As the Foxley papers explain '. . . it might be possible to retrieve the situation, and even to regard the sniper's attempt as a diversion, by attacking Hitler in his car on the return journey to the Berghof'. Section X envisaged this attack being made by two agents firing a PIAT gun or a Bazooka[1] from inside the woods near the tea-house. Having seen that the dictator had survived, these men would not take up their own firing positions until the arrival at the tea-house of his motorcade (the Kolonne). Section X hoped that the operatives would thus not risk being spotted by any pickets and patrols in the Mooslaner Kopf area, as these guards' attention, it was reasonably supposed, would be drawn in the opposite direction towards the concrete bypass. Section X also expected that the motorcade would be sent for immediately after the first assassination attempt. The Foxley papers explain: 'Whether Hitler returned alone to the Berghof or took his breakfast at the tea-house before returning, the guards would hardly expect a second attack to be made.'

The Foxley documents describe these alternative plans to kill Hitler near the Mooslaner Kopf tea-house as only 'possibilities of action in the Berchtesgaden area'. That was indeed what they were. They were tentative schemes, devised in the summer of 1944 without receiving first-hand information on the Obersalzberg since May of that year. In those circumstances, as the Foxley papers emphasise, 'it is not possible to say whether security and safety measures have been tightened of late, or whether extra precautions are being taken at FHQ only'.

Clearly, Section X's first need was to obtain an accurate up-to-date picture of what was happening on the Obersalzberg. The acknowledgement in the Foxley papers of the lack of this essential Top Secret intelligence did not mean that it was unobtainable. Indeed, with even some well-informed Nazis beginning to lose confidence in Hitler's baseless claims to military brilliance, it was likely that more and more valuable information about his movements and about the Führergebiet in general would become the subject of insider gossip, which would soon reach the ears of Allied intelligence agents. Though there were important gaps in Section X's knowledge of the elaborate system of guarding the dictator, these gaps were remarkably few and were probably fillable. The jigsaw was gradually being completed.

By the autumn of 1944 Section X had solved many problems relating to the 'possibilities of action in the Berchtesgaden area'. But there was one problem it never had. Section X always knew when Hitler was making one of his frequent visits to the Obersalzberg. Whenever he was there, and at no other time, a large swastika flag was flown in the car park in front of the Berghof. One of Section X's informants, a prisoner of war who had belonged to the SS-Wachkompanie Obersalzberg, emphatically confirmed that that was so. The flag was visible from several places, including the Schellenberg–Unterau road, and the Café Rottenhöfer and the Doktorberg, both in Berchtesgaden. Another indication that Hitler was staying at the Berghof, or was about to make a visit, was the presence in the neighbourhood of various Sonderzüge – the Führerzug at the Schloss Klessheim sidings, Keitel's train at Bischofswiesen, the Gästezug (the train reserved for important visitors) at Berchtesgaden and Ribbentrop's train at Salzburg. That Hitler was visiting the Berghof was also evident from overheard conversations between patrons of a Berchtesgaden tavern much frequented in the evenings by off-duty members of the Führerbegleitkommando.

Section X also knew where would-be assassins of Hitler could hide safely in the Berchtesgaden area. For example, two of the town's inns could provide them with lodgings, despite one of these taverns being patronised by members of the SS-Wachkompanie. Two other inns and three cafés were also visited by these troops. Section X was evidently confident that its agents, if properly trained and disguised, could mix safely in crowded bars and eating places with some of the most brutally fanatical of their enemies. Another hiding place was the Haus Brandtner on the Berchtesgaden–Obersalzberg road. Section X thought it possible to stay there without arousing suspicion despite its being near a police post, or perhaps because it was so sited. Operatives might also hide in several sheds on the Hoch Lenzer. These could be reached from Berchtesgaden or from the Königsee, if some distance were kept from a camp at Dürreck. Many other empty sheds were to be found between Oberau and the Obersalzberg.

Section X's information on hiding places near the Berghof on the Obersalzberg itself was a little out of date, being based on intelligence reports dating from May 1944. These showed the existence of several abandoned habitations, including the Kampfhäusl, the Jugendverpflegungsheim and the Meisterlehen. However, all three of these were difficult to reach because of the wire-mesh fence surrounding the Führergebiet, and the Jugendverpflegungsheim was uncomfortably close to the Führerstrasse. Also both the Meisterlehen and the Jugendverpflegungsheim were on open land. But the Kampfhäusl was partly surrounded by pine trees and, if, as reported in May 1944, it was never visited, it seemed to be the best potential hideout on the Obersalzberg. It would, moreover, be a place to meet Czech workmen from the Lager Antenberg who might be drawn into the conspiracy to assassinate Hitler. Section X agents might first contact such Czechs at the Trimbacher tavern in Berchtesgaden, at which many of them drank.

The section also knew how operatives could stealthily make their way across country from Berchtesgaden to the Obersalzberg. This would involve taking a path through two 1.8-metre-high tunnels and along the south bank of the River Larosbach, and then going uphill through woods towards the Mooslaner Kopf tea-house in an area reportedly not patrolled either by the RSD or the SS.[2]

Section X agents might also use the public bus service between Berchtesgaden and the Obersalzberg. But, as described in the Foxley papers, on some buses this would be 'rather risky', as passes might be inspected. However, on workmen's buses the security was slack. The conductor merely shouted 'Everyone got passes?' and, on hearing a chorus of 'Jawohl', he allowed everybody to get on board. Section X knew the timetables and routes of all the bus services, and was informed about the use of one service to carry mail, as well as passengers, except important letters which were delivered in a red postal vehicle driven by an elderly man wearing a gold Nazi Party badge. No detail of daily routine on the Obersalzberg, such as this seemingly commonplace piece of information about the Nazi postman, was considered too unimportant to be imparted to potential assassins.

Another of Section X's 'possibilities of action in the Berchtesgaden area' was a scheme to kill Hitler when he was travelling in his motorcade (the Kolonne) from the Berghof to Schloss Klessheim. In the autumn of 1944, when the outline of this plot was recorded in the Foxley papers, the dictator was thought to be still using the Schloss as one of his alternative personal headquarters as a result of the threat to the Rastenburg FHQ from the advancing Soviet army.

The route taken on this journey of little more than 30 kilometres was through Oberau, Unterau, Schellenberg and Grodig, and then on the Autobahn to Salzburg. Finally the motorcade circled that city, skirting the suburb of Maxglan. Almost the whole distance from the Berghof to Grodig was wooded. Apart from about 500 yards (457 metres) before reaching Oberau and about 100 yards (91 metres) on the other side of that village, the Führerstrasse was heavily wooded all the way except for a few clearings. On a kilometre-long stretch near Unterstein the woods were particularly thick and came right down to the road. Section X saw from aerial photographs that a length of the route near Schellenberg – a stretch on which the Führerstrasse rejoined the Berchtesgaden–Salzburg highway – appeared to have woods close to both sides of the road.

It was judged from all this information that there would be 'adequate cover' for an assassination party armed with PIAT guns or Bazookas. The agents would also carry explosive and smoke grenades for what the Foxley papers describe as their own 'close protection'. In other words, they would be equipped to have a good chance of escaping after completing their mission. It was believed that the assassination party should, if possible, fire at Hitler as his car turned a sharp bend in the road where the motorcade would be forced to reduce its usually fast speed.

Unfortunately, Section X's information on the guarding of the route dated only from May 1944, so more intelligence on this would be needed before the start of any detailed planning of the operation. Remarkably, until 1940 the road on the dictator's then different route from the Berghof to Salzburg was unprotected. However, it was a verified fact that the 1944 route was guarded by both SS and RSD personnel, almost certainly chosen from Nazis thought to be savagely loyal to their Führer. That was as much as Section X knew in the autumn of 1944. As the Foxley papers say, 'No details are available as to the spacing of sentries along the route or whether they are only placed at dangerous points. Intervals between guards (who must in any case be few in number) must be considerable.' It may seem strange that there was a manpower shortage here – one of the few places where Hitler, reclusive during much of the time and always anxious about his own safety, was vulnerable to attack.

Section X's information on the vehicles comprising the motorcade was probably more up to date, judging from the absence in the Foxley papers of any reference to the need to obtain more intelligence on that subject. Before the war and until well into 1940 the Kolonne usually totalled about ten cars, Hitler's being the leading one. This luxurious limousine was followed by four cars, each carrying six SS guards. Members of his entourage travelled in the remaining five cars. However, since 1940 the motorcade was shorter, though it never consisted of fewer than three Mercedes-Nurberg six-seater cars. The latest vehicles of this model were reportedly armoured and had thick bullet-proof windows. In 1944 the Kolonne was, unlike in the past, preceded by a RSD man on a motorcycle or motorcycle combination. He rode about 200 yards (more than 180 metres) ahead of the leading car and was armed with a machine-pistol. When travelling to Schloss Klessheim Hitler usually rode in the second car rather than the leading one. He always sat in the front beside his chauffeur, SS-Sturmbannführer Erich Kempka, with Eva Braun or Brigadeführer Rattenhuber, or both of them, in the back of the car. It was only when accompanying a foreign leader, like Mussolini or the Hungarian Regent, Admiral Horthy, that Hitler sat in a back seat. His limousine was distinguishable from the other cars in that it had a large swastika emblem on its right-hand front mudguard. As recorded in the Foxley papers, Kempka drove 'very fast in order to minimise the chance of being hit'.

On the relatively few occasions that Hitler got on his Special Train at Berchtesgaden, rather than at the Schloss Klessheim railway sidings, the motorcade would go along the Führerstrasse and cross a bridge over the River Ache. This brief local drive was also through heavily wooded country, providing adequate cover for an assassination party armed with PIAT guns or Bazookas. However, as this route was much shorter than the journey to Schloss Klessheim, it was easier to guard. Section X therefore thought it unsuitable for the sort of operation it had in mind.

Even the proposed assassination on the Schloss Klessheim route would have been more complex to plan in detail and more dangerous to execute than the similar schemes to kill Hitler near the tea-house. As the Foxley papers explain, 'The question of timing is considerably more difficult than in the case of the Mooslaner Kopf.' From 10 a.m. the car park in front of the Berghof would need to be kept under constant observation, this being possible from the road between Schellenberg and Unterau. However, there were many empty huts near Unterau that were usable as hideouts.

Lacking up-to-date information from the scene of the proposed action, by the autumn of 1944 Section X could make only preliminary plans on how to kill Hitler on the journey to the Schloss Klessheim railway sidings. However, it was thought that there was a possibility of attacking the motorcade when it was making an involuntary wait between tunnels on the Führerstrasse between the Obersalzberg and Berchtesgaden. The members of a PIAT party engaged on such an operation might hide in empty huts on the Hoch Lenzer. They would wear imitations of German uniforms, either those of mountain troops (Gebirgsjäger), as in the Mooslaner Kopf assassination projects, or those of members of the Nebelabteilung (the smoke unit), who were distributed in pairs all over the Obersalzberg and surrounding areas.

The Foxley papers mention 'recent' newspaper reports (probably in September 1944) that Hitler had 'taken up his quarters on the Führerzug', but Section X believed that he would still spend much of his time at the Berghof. It was also expected that the train would try to escape into a tunnel if attacked from the air or land. The tunnel nearest the Berghof was one on the Berchtesgaden–Bad Reichenhall line, and another tunnel had reportedly been built nearby. With the Führerzug hiding in either of these tunnels, the motorcade would have to wait for it to come out after the emergency had passed.

Some officers of SOE's German Directorate, formed on 30

October 1944 as an enlarged and reorganised version of Section X, thought then that Hitler might be killed in a combined operation by air and land forces. However, this was little more than an idea – one for which less preparatory staff work had been done than for the other 'possibilities of action in the Berchtesgaden area'. To undertake such an operation its planners, who would include air force and army commanders as well as the German Directorate, would have to learn some hours ahead of the dictator's presence on the Obersalzberg. The scheme envisaged an aerial bombardment of the Berghof and the SS barracks accompanied by the dropping of a paratroop battalion and men of Britain's crack Special Air Service.[3] The Foxley papers express the view that this two-pronged attack would be 'well worthwhile' as it offered the 'best chance' of eliminating Hitler as well as other leading Nazis on the Obersalzberg, such as Bormann.

These papers add: 'Apart from the Wachkompanie, the Begleitkommando and the RSD with a total of about 260–280 all ranks, there would be little opposition, since the smoke and AA [anti-aircraft] personnel are scattered over a very wide area. Most of the Begleitkommando and the RSD would moreover take to the air-raid shelters in all probability, so that the Wachkompanie need alone be reckoned with.' Continuing in this optimistic manner, the Foxley papers assert that opposition would, in fact, be offered only by men on stand-by duty (Bereitschaft), by the fire-fighting platoon, by the pickets and patrols, and by the 'residue of the Wachkompanie' specifically allocated for anti-paratroop duties. According to SOE's information, this guard unit's weaponry consisted only of rifles, machine-pistols, twelve machine-guns, 'two old 8-cm mortars and a few 5-cm mortars'.

Based on all this intelligence, it was believed that a paratroop battalion could 'swamp' any resistance from the troops guarding the Obersalzberg. It was also thought that the nearby Salzburg and Bad Reichenhall garrisons would be unable to 'send help in time' and it was even doubted whether they still existed, as they might already have been 'sent to man the Western defences' against the advancing Allied forces.

The German Directorate was probably justified in believing that a combined operation would achieve its declared aim of 'eliminating' Hitler and other leading Nazis. It is therefore anticlimatic that the part of the Foxley papers concerned with this imaginative proposal ends lamely with this declaration: 'It was hoped at one time that this operation might be planned to take place in conjunction with a revolt by the foreign workers of the Salzburg area, in particular by French deportees and prisoners-of-war, and Poles and Ostarbeiter, whose first action would have been to seize the arms depots in the Salzburg area. . . . There appears, however, little possibility of cooperation at the present time with foreign governments in this connection.'

Many of SOE's proposals to organise special operations, not just this one backed by a hoped-for revolt of foreign workers, depended on permission for them being obtained from the exiled governments of Nazi-occupied countries. At various times during the war such permission was either refused or given only after long negotiation.

As part of their research into the possibility of killing Hitler in a combined operation, SOE staff officers re-examined the mass of information they had on the potential recruits for the revolt mentioned in the Foxley papers – the estimated 100,000 to 150,000 slave labourers and other foreign workers living, usually in miserable conditions, in and around Salzburg. The papers say of the situation in 1944: 'Except in the case of domestic servants, workers in hotels, restaurants and cafés, and labourers on isolated farms, it is likely that all foreign workers are now housed in communal camps (Gemeinschaftslager) in the Salzburg area.' Ostarbeiter, namely Russian, Ukrainian and other deported 'workers from the East', comprised the great majority of these people. They included a significant number of women and girls, many of them domestics in Salzburg itself. Others were cleaners of railway carriages, such as at the Berchtesgaden station. Second in number to the Ostarbeiter were the estimated 15,000 Poles in the Salzburg area. They worked in agriculture, road construction, textile mills, salt works and hydro-electric plants and on the railways, including in the Salzburg and Berchtesgaden stations, where, again, the women cleaned the carriages. Like the Ostarbeiter, the Poles were accommodated in camps, being fed separately from other inmates. Poles and Ostarbeiter wore the 'Ost' badge on the left breast of their overalls, and were forbidden to speak to Germans in cafés.

The next most numerous nationality were the French, including deportees and certain privileged prisoners of war (prisonniers de guerre transformés). According to the Foxley papers, they were much better treated than the Ostarbeiter and Poles and were allowed out at night until 10 or 11 p.m. In Salzburg they had welfare offices and the exclusive use of a 'foyer' in the Nussdorferbar in Franz-Josef Strasse. French men and women were employed at Salzburg railway station, the women washing the Special Trains. Czech workers included a few at the Salzburg station but the Foxley papers particularly note: 'There are two Czech camps on the Obersalzberg, almost within a stone's throw of Hitler's residence.' Among the other foreigners were Croats, Serbs, Bulgarians and Greeks. There were also some Italians (railwaymen, waiters and factory workers) who, like the French, received 'favoured treatment'.

The Foxley papers end their descriptive piece on the foreign workers in the Salzburg area by quoting 'Russian sources' saying that many foreigners in Austria had fled from their places of employment and formed themselves into guerrilla bands. In July 1944, Baldur von Schirach, the Gauleiter and Defence Commissioner of Vienna and former Hitler Youth leader, had reportedly ordered every Nazi Party member 'to hunt out the thousands of foreign workers who had joined the guerrillas'.

SOE had other information that might be useful if any detailed planning of a combined operation were undertaken. For example, according to an Austrian prisoner of war captured at Brest in September 1944, many bombed-out people from various parts of Germany had settled in Salzburg. In July 1944, when the PoW visited it, it was not overcrowded. However, its food situation was very bad. He also said that there was no organised anti-Nazi movement in the city but most people there were disillusioned about National Socialism. On the other hand, he once saw a demonstration in the streets against a captured Royal Canadian Air Force officer. The PoW, a 31-year-old Austrian nationalist and a lawyer before the war, also readily gave his interrogators various other information about the Salzburg area. He believed that Salzburg aerodrome had no anti-aircraft protection and was not heavily guarded, and he estimated that there were about 15,000 prisoners of war, mostly Russians, in camps in the Schwarach area, south of Bischofshofen.

If the Obersalzberg combined operation had become anything more than just a promising idea generated by SOE staff officers, special forces' personnel for the paratroop battalion would have had to been chosen from exceptionally brave, tough and resolute men. Almost certainly some of them would have been Germans and Austrians living in Britain as fugitives from Nazi persecution. About 75,000 Germans and Austrians, mostly Jews, fled to the UK between 1933 and 1939. About 10,000 of them served in the British armed forces in the war. It is reasonable to assume that all these people were strongly hostile to Hitler personally as well as to the Nazi regime in general, and thousands of them and former German prisoners of war served in the Allied armed forces during the war.

The Foxley papers, however, say nothing about who would be picked for the proposed paratroop battalion. However, it has been reported since the war that some German and Austrian refugees were infiltrated by SOE into Nazi-occupied Europe. Those captured were put in concentration camps or executed, usually after torture by the Gestapo.

According to research by Captain Peter Leighton-Langer (born Langer), himself a refugee from Austria when he arrived in the UK in 1938[4], aged 15. In the spring of 1943 many German and Austrian soldiers serving in the Royal Pioneer Corps were transferred to other British units: 216 went to armoured regiments, 221 to the Royal Artillery, 174 to the infantry, nearly 1,000 to the Royal Engineers and other technical regiments, and about 220 into Intelligence. Others joined the Royal Navy or the RAF, nearly 100 became parachutists and 120 were recruited into No. 3 (Miscellaneous) Troop of the 10th Inter-Allied Commando, also known as X Troop. Men of that rigorously trained unit engaged in various risky reconnaissance operations and other special missions. On D-Day soldiers of X Troop were part of the vanguard of the Normandy invasion.

With so many German and Austrian refugees serving in Britain's armed forces, why was it that Section X found such difficulty in recruiting agents? Was the section's method of 'talent spotting' flawed? Did it put enough resources into finding the right men?

# Chapter Five
## *Foxley thoroughly re-examined*

An improbable report from Algiers was received at SOE's London headquarters on 20 June 1944. It said that 'a source whose reliability was being checked has put up an immediate project for killing Hitler. . . .' The source was a French colonel who claimed that the dictator was hiding in a château at Perpignan until 24 June. To put it mildly, this would have been an extraordinarily odd place for Hitler to stay, even briefly, at that critical time, as it was then only fourteen days after D-Day and the Allies were already establishing their foothold in Normandy. The Americans, for example, were on the brink of liberating Cherbourg. A secret location, perhaps a holiday retreat, in a town in the far south of France, only a short drive from the Spanish frontier, was scarcely the best site for Hitler to establish a field headquarters, even a temporary one. Or perhaps he was fleeing to Spain, the Perpignan château being the last hiding place on the way there?

Despite the improbability of the report, SOE acted on it swiftly, partly because it had been sent at the instigation of Alfred Duff Cooper,[1] who, with ambassadorial rank, was Britain's link with the Algiers-based French Committee of National Liberation. In a letter marked 'Top Secret' and 'Please destroy after reading', General Gubbins, the SOE Chief (CD), requested General Sir Hastings Ismay,[2] Churchill's principal channel of communication with British and other Allied military leaders, to 'ask whether the Chiefs of Staff would approve the immediate execution of Hitler if this should prove to be practicable'. Gubbins added: 'It may be argued that to kill Hitler would turn him in the eyes of the Germans into a martyr. On the other hand, I feel that his removal would certainly shorten the war considerably. I am naturally giving instructions for the project to be investigated in the greatest detail but if meanwhile you could obtain for us a decision on the question of principle whether we should be allowed to carry out this project or not, I should be most grateful.'

Ismay replied to Gubbins on 22 June in a 'Top Secret and personal' letter and with a telephone conversation. The letter enclosed a minute which Ismay had sent to Churchill on the previous day. 'The Chiefs of Staff', the minute said, 'were unanimous that, from the strictly military point of view, it was almost an advantage that Hitler should remain in control of German strategy, having regard to the blunders that he has made, but that on the wider point of view, the sooner he was got out of the way the better'. The minute also noted that approval, in principle, for the project had been given by the Foreign Secretary, Anthony Eden. Churchill's approval was confirmed with his initials 'W.S.C.' written near Ismay's signature. Authority for the immediate go-ahead of the assassination plan had been obtained from 'all concerned', as Brigadier E.E. Mockler-Ferryman (AD/E), the co-ordinator of SOE operations in north-western Europe, noted in a telegram.

The sanctioning in principle of the unnamed French colonel's scheme to kill Hitler did not mean that any of the Allied political and military leaders, or their staffs, thought it had more than a remote chance of being successful. The plan was vaguely described. The colonel had reportedly said that the château in Perpignan, or 'house' as Ismay called it in his letter to Gubbins, needed to be 'bombed quickly' as Hitler was due to leave it on 24 June. Ismay commented in his letter: 'I do not know whether this means bombing from the air, or by your people [SOE operatives], but in any case the story is so fantastic that I don't think we need expect very much!' Similar scepticism was expressed by SOE staff officers. In an internal minute they had to be assured that this assassination scheme was not a joke.

Hitler, of course, never visited any château or house in Perpignan in June 1944. He was more than a little busy elsewhere, giving his generals unwise orders on how to halt the start of the liberation of France.[3]

Although the Perpignan affair deservedly came to nothing, it stimulated the SOE leadership into resuming the in-depth study of everything related to the possibility of assassinating Hitler. How, where and when could the deed be done? Or even should it be done, bearing in mind that by the middle of 1944 he had on countless occasions manifested his incompetence as a military strategist, mainly through giving his generals criminally foolish orders? Asking these and similar questions, Section X began a thorough re-examination of the various Foxley schemes which lasted until near the end of the war in Europe.

In his 'Perpignan' letter to Ismay on 20 June, Gubbins had recalled that 'in 1941 SOE had a project for eliminating Hitler and that this received the approval of all departments. Actually circumstances suddenly changed and the operation had to be abandoned.' The Foxley papers do not say what this project was and do not in this context mention the Polish railway saboteurs' attempt to assassinate Hitler in the autumn of 1941. However, it is clear that the project had the blessing of Britain's War Cabinet, Chiefs of Staff and Foreign Office, that is 'all departments' whose permission would have been needed then, shortly before the United States entered the war.

As recorded in a minute by Gubbins, Air Vice-Marshal A.P. Ritchie (AD/A – SOE's Air Adviser) 'raised very pertinently' at an SOE Council meeting on 27 June 'the question of a deliberate and continuous effort to try and liquidate Hitler'. This, Gubbins added in a disparaging reference to a great amount of work already done on the Foxley project, was 'a matter which has in the past been dealt with (if at all) on a very ad hoc basis'. However, it was now time to 'make this a matter of particular study' by a 'group' which he intended to set up. Gubbins explained:

> The points to be discussed [by the group] will be how best to obtain knowledge of Hitler's movements, how to induce him, if necessary, to come to some locality at our instigation, how to deal with him there, etc. At some time or other in the near future Hitler must in any case disappear from the scene, even if we [SOE] should not be the direct agents for his elimination, and we can at least prepare such action to be taken on his disappearance as will contribute best towards the situation most favourable to the Allied Nations.

On the following day Gubbins chaired a meeting at which the head of Section X, Lieutenant-Colonel Ronald Thornley, declared that personally he was opposed to Operation Foxley as he believed that Nazi Germany's strategy and conduct of the war might improve if Hitler were assassinated. After discussion, however, it was generally agreed that the killing of the dictator was desirable. Thornley then said that this being so, he thought that the blame for the assassination must be put on the German armed forces, as this might result in a 'clearly desirable' civil war. Patrick Murray (D/CD), SOE's Director of Organisation and Staff Duties, said that the most important thing was not only that Operation Foxley should succeed but that 'we should decide on what conditions we wished to strive for in Germany, and a concerted plan should be drawn up with this in view'. Air Commodore Archibald Boyle (A/CD), SOE's Director of Security, said that the 'very difficult' problem of how to kill Hitler had been studied by both the Russians and the Poles, but presumably to no avail.

Gubbins decided that a small team would begin preliminary work on Foxley immediately and would report to him from time to time. He added that he would ask the head of SIS, Major-General Sir Stewart Menzies (C), to appoint a member of his staff to join that team.

In a minute to Gubbins on 8 July, Boyle reported that Menzies had instructed that every piece of information about Hitler's movements, well-being, habits and related matters be sent to SOE immediately (to Boyle personally, he being the main channel of communication with SIS and MI5). The minute also noted that the Air Ministry had been asked to make a detailed survey of Hitler's travels in aircraft.

In addition, Boyle advocated that Himmler and Hitler should be regarded jointly as assassination targets. He believed that the killing of Himmler 'would in many respects be more advantageous' and that 'preparation of the necessary intelligence regarding the pair will be no more difficult than for individual treatment'. Concerning the recruitment of a team of potential assassins, Boyle declared that this was not easy but 'Poles, Russians and Czechs provided the best field'.

Three months later Thornley was still expressing opposition to Operation Foxley. He wrote in a minute on 9 October:

As a strategist, Hitler has been of the greatest possible assistance to the British war effort . . . his value to us has been equivalent to an almost unlimited number of first-class SOE agents strategically placed inside Germany. Although the military situation has been temporarily stabilised on the western front and the German army appears to have regained cohesion, Hitler is still in a position to override completely the soundest of military appreciations and thereby help the Allied cause enormously . . .

To remove Hitler from the wheel at a time when he and his fanatics have pledged themselves to defend every street and every house on German soil, would almost inevitably canonise him and give birth to the myth that Germany would have been saved if he had lived. If, as is almost inevitable in my view, the assassination was traced to Allied sources, the repercussions would probably be grave. It would be disastrous if the world came to think that the Allies had to resort to these low methods as they were otherwise unable to defeat the German military machine. From every point of view, the ideal end to Hitler would be one of steadily declining power and increasing ridicule.

Similar opposition to Foxley was expressed on 12 October by Miss E.B. Graham-Stamper (X/AUS) and Mrs Marguerite Holmes (X/AUS.1). Miss Graham-Stamper thought Hitler 'should be permitted to live – until he dies of senile decay before the eyes of the people he has misled. Rob him of his halo! Make him a laughing stock!' Mrs Holmes declared: 'Any attempt by the Allies, successful or otherwise, to assassinate Hitler would be simply playing into Germany's hands. We should immediately have a modern version of the Kyffhauser nonsense, offering every incentive to [Nazi] German rebirth.' She was referring to a legend that the twelfth-century Emperor Frederick the First (Barbarossa) is asleep inside the Kyffhauser mountain in Thuringia but will one day wake up and lead the German people to victory in battle.[4] Mrs Holmes also doubted whether Hitler could be correctly identified, as some people thought he had several doubles. She asked: '. . . how do we know that we assassinate the right Hitler? There are said to be at least three of them.'

Air Vice-Marshal Ritchie had no old-fashioned qualms about using what Thornley described as 'low methods' of killing Hitler. His view that planning Operation Foxley should continue was accepted as SOE policy at a Council meeting held on 10 October, the day after Thornley's minute.

In a memorandum discussed at that meeting Ritchie mentioned that 'a section of the Germans themselves' (a reference to Colonel Stauffenberg and the other officers in the 20 July Bomb Plot) had tried to carry out Foxley 'for us'. He suggested that German reactions to that assassination attempt should be studied to see more clearly what results might be expected from a successful Foxley. Although acknowledging that 'a large body of opinion' was unconvinced of the importance, or even of the advisability, of mounting the operation, he himself was more than ever certain that it was 'vitally necessary' and that now was the time to 'reap the full benefits from it'.

Ritchie quoted from an assessment by SHAEF on the morale of the German armed forces, based on interrogations of prisoners of war. This document showed that most prisoners were glad to be out of the war and that 'a great majority' of senior officers considered that for them it was lost. However, junior officers 'generally still exude an air of optimism based, apparently, on their faith in Hitler'. A successful Operation Foxley, Ritchie continued, would have both long-term and short-term consequences. Under the heading 'Long Term', he claimed that there was 'abundant evidence to prove that Hitler is regarded by a large section of the German population as something more than human'. It was this 'mystical hold' over the German people that was largely responsible for keeping the country together. 'As long as Hitler continues to live among them, the people will have faith and, having faith, they will remain impervious to logical argument or demonstrated fact.'

Air Vice-Marshal Ritchie then took a gloomy look into the future. Mercifully, the postwar Germany that he envisaged never materialised, although, from time to time, small and vicious neo-Nazi groups have emerged there (as in several other countries), but they have never seriously threatened the democratic process, despite, or because of, their extremism. 'After the war,' he asserted, 'Hitler will undoubtedly be regarded in Germany as the greatest man who ever lived. There may be a short period immediately succeeding hostilities during which it becomes fashionable to vilify him, but this will not last long and his ultimate position in Germany as the greatest German is assured.' Earlier, Ritchie had made another unsupported assertion: 'To the Germans the might of their country is manifested in the strength and success of their armed forces.' He continued in his memorandum:

There are already signs that reasons are going to be found for Germany's defeat which do not lay the blame on the army, thus preparing the way for its comeback. To start with, the military disasters may be attributed to Hitler's misdirection, particularly by the generals and General Staff, but this is likely to change rapidly as the Hitler legend grows and the 'Party' or some other scapegoat will be found. Everything will be done to prevent the German people's faith in Hitler and their belief in the infallibility of the directors of the German army from clashing. Our purpose must be to ferment [sic] the incompatibility of these two beliefs.

Under the headline 'Short Term', Ritchie wrote: 'It has been held that Hitler has proved himself to be so incompetent as a director of military operations as to be a positive asset to the Allies and that, were he removed, control of the military machine would pass into more competent hands and thus make the defeat of Germany more difficult.' However, he added, the military situation had reached a point where it mattered little who was in charge as it was 'almost inconceivable that any individual could at this stage retrieve the situation for Germany'. Any advantage that the German army might get from Hitler's removal would be 'more than offset by the tendency for the people and army to drift apart and for internal dissention within the Wehrmacht to increase'.

Ritchie also commented on what he thought would happen if power passed to Himmler. He doubted whether the SS leader could by 'ruthless suppression' keep either the people or the army with him. If the army 'became supreme' it would 'come to terms' with the Allies as soon as possible, having recognised that, from the military viewpoint, the war was already lost. 'In either case the jealousy between the army proper and the SS would probably grow to such proportions as entirely to nullify any advantage that might be obtained from sounder strategy.'

On the question of preventing an assassinated Hitler becoming a 'martyr', Ritchie wrote: 'From the short-term point of view this is unlikely to have any appreciable effect; from the long-term point of view, whatever happens, it is obvious that Hitler will become a legendary figure and his mode of death will not materially alter the situation. On the other hand, as long as Hitler remains alive, he will retain the outward loyalty of the majority of the generals and General Staff owing to the oath they have taken to him personally.' Ritchie concluded:

> Although the majority of senior officers of the German army now recognise that they have been defeated in the military field, and the vast majority of the population are utterly weary of the war and have more than an inkling that the military situation is nearly desperate, they still believe, or at least attempt to reassure themselves, that there is yet still hope. This belief, illogical though it may be, is based entirely on their faith in the genius of Hitler. Remove Hitler and there is nothing left.

Only a little more than six months after Air Vice-Marshal Ritchie had written his memorandum, Hitler killed himself. By taking that coward's way out he also destroyed the bogus 'legend' about himself in the minds of the German people, that is all of them except a tiny minority of fanatics. Democracy, common sense and civilised standards are more enduring than SOE's pessimistic Air Adviser had thought.

Each of the various schemes to assassinate the dictator was re-examined during the last months of the war in Europe. This led to yet more debate by the SOE staff officers dealing with operations in Germany. Some of their thoughts are revealed in the Foxley papers. For example, in a minute written on 17 October 1944, Major William Field-Robinson (X/GER), expressed his cautious belief that 'the only remotely feasible operation which might eventually be carried out would be for a first-class marksman to shoot Hitler from a distance during his constitutional walk' to the Mooslaner Kopf tea-house on the

Berghof estate. He added that the agent would have to conceal himself at a place within firing range of his target, in the period between the routine passing through the area by the dog patrol and the arrival of the Führer. The agent would also need 'a cover which would enable him to have a plausible reason for hanging about the neighbourhood' and he would have to be a first-class marksman even before receiving special training.

Field-Robinson rejected all the other suggested methods of assassinating Hitler. Concerning a proposal to poison the milk supply needed for coffee-making, he commented: 'The whole day's delivery would have to be poisoned and there is no means of ensuring that someone else would not have had a taste of it before the Führer. Besides, without being an expert chemist, I can safely say that: (a) Milk is a well known antidote to most poisons. (b) I doubt whether there is a poison which would not affect either the flavour or appearance of the milk'.

On the proposed 'doctoring' of the Führerzug's drinking water, Field-Robinson recalled his own frequent rail journeys in Germany before the war. 'In all my travels, which have meant making my "home" in the rolling stock of the International Sleeping Car Company and that of the Mitropa, I have never yet found anybody to drink water from the taps.' He added that he was certain that Hitler would drink bottled mineral water only, and to poison 'one or a number of bottles would mean such complicity [sic] as to render it impossible to carry such a thing out'. He presumably meant that the deed could not be done because of unacceptable security risks when seeking the necessary cooperation of large numbers of people, the reliability of at least some of whom would be uncertain.

Field-Robinson was similarly dismissive of the idea that the foreign cleaners of the Special Trains could place a time-bomb in the Führerzug or wreck it any other way. He believed that it would be impossible to ensure that the agent selected by SOE would be picked as a member of the train-cleaning gang on the day that the operation was planned. Besides, he added, there would be a time-lag between the placing of the bomb and Hitler boarding his train, during which he felt sure the device would be discovered.

Field-Robinson quoted Captain Francis Boothroyd (X/DOC. 1 when in Section X) as believing that only three Foxley schemes were worth studying. These were the Mooslaner Kopf tea-house project; the parachute attack on the Berghof, which Boothroyd envisaged as being rather like Skorzeny's rescue of Mussolini in September 1943; and an attack on the Führerzug by foreigners used as slave labour locally.

Recently gathered intelligence relevant to assassination planning was being evaluated by SOE all the time. For example, on 31 October 1944, in a minute to Boyle, Major H.B. Court (L/BX) reported new information from a strongly anti-Nazi prisoner on war and from SIS. The PoW, Unteroffizier Deiser of the Luftwaffe, had said that Schloss Klessheim seemed to have been used, at least until the end of 1943, mainly as a 'reception place'. Court noted that this tallied with later reports that Admiral Horthy, the Hungarian Regent, was 'received' there by Hitler in March 1944, and might still be there – as a prisoner. SIS reported that a small station, camouflaged with dark green paint, was being built at the Schloss sidings, and that Hitler, Himmler and Ribbentrop were, in October 1944, the only leading Nazis visiting the Schloss itself. SIS also revealed that 'several barracks' were being constructed in a wood beside the railway line near Berchtesgaden, that overhead telephone wires were being installed in an area of about 18 kilometres radius around Schloss Klessheim and the Obersalzberg, and that air-raid precautions were being tightened in the Berchtesgaden area, which could be blanketed in a cloud of smoke emitted from 200 points.

Similar miscellaneous information was provided by Deiser. He had said that foreign workers were employed in the Siezenheim area (his uncle employed two of them, one French and the other Russian). There was also a French prisoner-of-war camp, with about 250 to 300 internees, near Siezenheim and the River Saalach. These men worked on farms and left the camp at 6 a.m., returning at 10 p.m. in winter and 9 p.m. in summer. When being interrogated Deiser had observed drily that the camp's guards were 'ready to talk about anything for a packet of cigarettes'. Deiser had also said that 'very anti-Nazi' railwaymen operated the signal boxes at and near Freilassing station. No special measures were taken when a train passed through the station but when one stopped the platforms were cleared of everybody except railway staff.

The information given by Unteroffizier Deiser – eagerly, it seems – was obviously valued by the planners of the never-to-be Operation Foxley. However, his extended family, like that of many others in Germany and Austria, was divided into mutually hostile camps of haters and idolisers of Hitler. Although Deiser's uncle, Friedrich Haidenthaler, a former member of the then-outlawed Austrian Social Democratic Party, is described in the Foxley papers as 'a most reliable anti-Nazi', his estranged wife and his adopted daughter were 'rigid Nazis' and welcomed every opportunity of doing him down. Haidenthaler was a businessman (owner of the

Kunstmuhle Haidenthaler at Siezenheim) and had many friends in the neighbourhood, mostly shopkeepers and employees of the railway administration in Salzburg who would be reliable anti-Nazis. He also owned a shoot at Henndorf, about 16 kilometres north-east of Salzburg, where he often went at weekends with his friends, but never accompanied by his wife. An SOE agent could contact him there or through Deiser's mother.

Even with his familial predicament, Haidenthaler would probably have been an excellent link-man in one or more of the Foxley plots. However, the existence of German and Austrian families bitterly divided in their attitudes towards the Nazi dictatorship was one of the many factors that Section X and its successor, the German Directorate, had to take into account in all their operational planning, not only that relating to the proposed assassination of Hitler.

On 8 November the head of the German Directorate, Major-General Gerald Templer (AD/X), the future field marshal, acknowledged that there was still 'a grave divergence of views' on the 'desirability and feasibility' of Operation Foxley. He minuted that 'all experts on Germany' with whom he had discussed the matter had agreed with him that Foxley was 'unsound and would not be in the interests of the Allied cause'. But, he added, 'among certain members' of the SOE Council and 'among the highest in the land in England' there were 'several strong advocates' of the proposed operation. It is tempting to speculate that Churchill was among these, bearing in mind his reaction to the Perpignan affair and his frequent strong support for bold and imaginative actions.

However, all this debate was theoretical, as SOE had not yet found a potential assassin of Hitler. It would have to wait until near the end of the war in Europe before such an extraordinary candidate unexpectedly offered his services. In contrast to the indecision and all the other difficulties relating to Operation Foxley, the German Directorate was confident that Foxley II, the proposed killing of one or more of Hitler's principal henchmen, would have 'everyone's backing' and should be 'very carefully studied'. The production of a research paper on Foxley II was ordered.

# Chapter Six
## *Chemicals, bacteria and Hess*

Writing on Christmas Day 1944, in reply to questions asked by colleagues, the head of the German Directorate, General Templer, declared that he had no objection to an assassin of a leading Nazi (a Foxley II candidate) using chemical or biological weapons. 'If we get permission to do the job,' he commented in his minute, 'I cannot believe that anyone will boggle at the use of chemicals. Let us say straight away that they are allowed. . . . The same remarks apply as to the use of bacteria.' It seems that Templer was implying that Hitler and his principal henchmen were so bestially evil that any means of killing them, even those internationally outlawed, would be sanctioned by the Allies' highest political and military authorities. He was, of course, expressing his personal assessment of what would be acceptable, and permission to use chemical or biological weapons was never sought.

Templer recalled that he had personally ruled out the 'infiltration of a body [a would-be assassin] into the apartments, kitchens or whatnot of the person concerned. In view of the very high standard of security precautions which are undoubtedly carried out among the entourage, I cannot believe that we shall have any success along this line.' However, he did believe (but did not give any reasons for doing so) that an agent might manage to get into an office inside a private house, one or two other people probably being present in the room.

General Templer also thought that 'some affair à la Heidrich' presented 'no particular difficulty, certainly not on the equipment side'. The only snag was the 'production of the body to do the job'; one was always being sought. The 'Heidrich' whom he mentioned was SS-Obergruppenführer (Lieutenant-General) Reinhard Heydrich, the Reich Protector (governor) of Bohemia and Moravia, who was fatally wounded in Prague on 27 May 1942 by a grenade thrown at him as he rode in his open Mercedes limousine. This operation, codenamed Anthropoid, was mounted by two Czechs who had been trained by SOE in Britain and parachuted into their homeland by the RAF.

Templer also declared that he could not say whether the proposed assassination would be a suicide operation and, provided the death of the target Nazi was achieved, he did not mind whether it was attributed to 'natural causes or attack'. He explained: 'If the body [the agent] is going to use some method which will do the trick more or less instantaneously and which he will be spotted doing, then it is obviously a suicide.' But this might not necessarily be the case. Wryly, Templer ended his minute, which was addressed to Colonel F.T. Davies (AD/Z), the Director of Research, Development and Supply: 'In view of the date [Christmas Day], I should like to add "peace on earth and to all men of good will".'

In addition to discussing chemical and biological weapons, the Foxley II research paper rejected the use of poisons; Templer had already indicated his lack of confidence in them. According to the research paper, poisons had been much overrated by popular belief and popular fiction. Many of the so-called 'scientific' facts in modern crime stories were 'quite inaccurate', and it was not established beyond doubt that Alexander VI, the Borgia Pope, 'ever poisoned a cardinal'. The paper added: 'We [SOE] have at our disposal, nevertheless, a number of first-rate poisons for use in a variety of ways. The difficulty lies, not in finding the toxic substance but in getting it to the spot where it can do its work.' The four 'routes of administration' were:

(i) By mouth. This involves access to the victim's food at some stage, not necessarily during or after its preparation for the table. (ii) By inhalation. We have one substance (W) very effective by this route; and N, a bacterial substance, is lethal by this route in a minute dose (perhaps something like a millionth of a gram). This is a fruitful method if access can be gained to living quarters or to clothing. (iii) By injection. The important thing here is that it is necessary to get the substance into the body, not merely to apply it to an abraded surface: thus 'Borgia rings' and the like are excluded. The biggest practical use of this method is probably the poisoned bullet. By this means it is possible to make any bullet wound fatal. (iv) Absorption through the skin is theoretically possible (e.g., the poisoned gloves of the Valois), but in practice no poisons are sufficiently rapidly absorbed by this route to make it worthwhile except in unusual circumstances. It has, however, slight possibilities if bacterial attack is not excluded. Access to the possessions of the intended victim is, of course, necessary.

The research paper, which did not identify the toxic substances with the initials W and N, added these warnings: 'If the operator is likely to be searched any "gadget" had better be avoided. Guns and hypodermic syringes disguised as fountain pens are usually not a bit convincing, and are likely to lead to the death of the operator before he has had any opportunity of making his attack.' The paper ended: 'There is often a tendency for the non-scientist to be rather bemused by the power of science: this may be flattering to the scientist, but it is the enemy of clear-headed planning. Let us therefore remember that a strong, determined and properly trained man can kill an unsuspecting adversary in a few seconds with his hands. This may perhaps prove the most profitable line of thought.'

Should Rudolf Hess, the former deputy leader of the Nazi Party, be asked to help the German Directorate in plotting the assassination of a prominent Nazi? That question – perhaps the most bizarre one ever asked by an SOE staff officer – was pondered for about three weeks by General Templer (AD/X). It seems that he, as head of the directorate, or some political or military authority senior to himself, decided in January 1945 that Hess could have no such part to play. It can be deduced that that decision was made in that month, as the matter ceased to be mentioned in SOE internal correspondence on 8 January. However, on 18 December 1944 Major L.H. Manderstam (X/PLANS from October 1944) had asked Templer: 'Has the possibility of using Hess for Foxley II ever been considered?' He had added that 'Hess might either be bluffed into doing it with the reason given to him that it might open the way for peace negotiations or, alternatively, [he might] be hypnotised into doing it.' Hess was 'known to be an extremely nervous individual' and should be 'very susceptible to hypnotic treatment'. Manderstam also asked whether hypnotism had ever been considered in SOE operations, mentioning that 'an American officer stationed in Ireland', whom he did not name, had claimed success as a hypnotist.

On 8 January 1945 Manderstam asked Templer these and other questions:

Has Hess come to this country as Hitler's emissary, [as] a representative of a group, or on his own initiative? Is Hess sane? If insane, is he subject to fits of insanity or is it of a more permanent nature? Is Hess physically fit? . . . Does Hess still believe in Germany's victory? What is Hess's present attitude towards Hitler and Himmler? Is Hess genuinely afraid of the Bolshevisation of Europe? Does Hess believe in the possibility of co-existence of a strong and prosperous Germany with the British Empire? Who, in Hess's opinion, stands in the way of an Anglo-German understanding? What is Hess's attitude towards the Allies, and Great Britain in particular? Who, in Hess's opinion, is to blame for the present conflict? Can Hess be psychologically induced, by producing the necessary 'evidence', into believing that Himmler, or any other Nazi leader, is the only person who prevents the possibility of re-approachment [sic] between Germany and Great Britain? What are Hess's reactions to the German Liberation Committee in Russia? What are Hess's views as to his fate should he return to Germany as an escapee or as an 'emissary' of this country? What are Hess's views as to what will happen to him after the cessation of hostilities?

Today, with the benefit of the mass of information about Hess that has been published since the Second World War, it is easy to see that he could never have played any sort of Foxley II role, either as an adviser to the German Directorate or as an 'escapee' or 'emissary' between Britain and Nazi Germany. However, during the war, any knowledge of what he was really like was restricted to a small group of politicians, government officials and others who dealt with ultra-sensitive State affairs.

Born in 1894, Hess served in the First World War, initially as a soldier but near the end as an air force officer and pilot. After that conflict, in which he was wounded twice, he became totally under Hitler's spell, remaining so for the rest of his long life. His devotion to his master was expressed in blind obedience and fulsome eulogies.[1] Alongside Hitler he participated in the 1923 Munich Putsch and together they later spent some not uncomfortable time in Landsberg prison; there Hess assisted the future Nazi dictator in writing much of *Mein Kampf.*

From 1925 to 1932 Hess was Hitler's private secretary and confidant – one of the few people who was addressed by him as *du*, the intimate form of 'you' in the German language. In 1933 Hess became deputy leader of the Nazi Party (but not deputy Head of State), a Reichstag member and a Minister without Portfolio. From February 1938 he was also a member of the Secret Cabinet Council that 'advised' Hitler on foreign affairs, a euphemistic way of saying that it helped him plan his future war of aggression. In August 1939 with the conflict about to begin, Hess joined the Ministerial Council for Reich Defence.

However, he had serious temperamental weaknesses as a prominent politician and was a less important member of the Nazi dictatorship than his State and Party offices suggested and as some contemporary commentators supposed. By the time Hitler and Stalin were carving up Poland in September 1939, Hess's status was even further diminished; by then Hitler was listening mainly to men whom he found more useful, such as Göring, Himmler, Goebbels and Ribbentrop.

It was probably with the aim of regaining his old place as the dictator's right-hand man that Hess flew to Scotland in a Messerschmitt 110 aircraft on the night of 10 May 1941. For him this was his greatest act of devotion to his Führer, his idealised father-figure. He genuinely believed that he would be able to negotiate the United Kingdom's withdrawal from the war, giving Nazi Germany a free hand to conquer the Soviet Union. As part of this self-appointed 'peace mission' he made various demands that he had expected would be granted immediately. These included Churchill's resignation as Prime Minister of the coalition government, as, in Hess's opinion, he had been planning the war since 1936; the requirement that Britain make peace with Fascist Italy; and the demand that Germany be given back its former colonies. He also revealed his belief that the Duke of Hamilton, then an RAF wing-commander, belonged to a British 'opposition party' with which he needed to negotiate. Hess said much else in the same dotty vein and asserted that Hitler had no wish to destroy a fellow 'Nordic' country, Britain, which had 'no hope of winning the war'.

Hess's ignorance of foreign affairs and of the political scene in Britain, together with his general naivety and arrogance, was breathtaking. He demanded to meet King George VI and to be treated with the dignity due a cabinet minister. But, to his dismay, he found that he was a mere prisoner of war. Although a thoroughly uncooperative patient, he was given many psychiatric examinations and was detained successively in a military hospital in Scotland, the Tower of London, a location near Aldershot and a former hospital at Abergavenny.

Hitler was enraged by what Hess had done and reportedly ordered that he be shot immediately if he ever returned to Germany. An official press bulletin said that Hess had become 'a deluded, deranged and muddled idealist, ridden with hallucinations'. This was one of the few accurate Nazi pronouncements.

In preparation for Hess's appearance as a defendant at the Nuremberg Trials he was examined by British, American and Russian doctors. Their separate national reports, which tallied in matters of substance, said that he was legally sane but was suffering from hysterical amnesia, an escape from uncomfortable realities.

The British report, by Lord Moran, Churchill's personal physician, Brigadier Dr J.R. Rees and Dr George Riddoch, stated:

> ... He is an unstable man, what is technically called a psychopathic personality. The evidence of his illness in the past four years, as presented by one of us who has had him under his care in England, indicates that he has had a delusion of poisoning, and other similar paranoid ideas. Partly as a reaction to the failure of his mission, these abnormalities got worse, and led to suicidal attempts. In addition he has a marked hysterical tendency, which had led to the development of various symptoms, noticeably loss of memory, which lasted from November 1943 to June 1944, and which resisted all efforts at treatment. A second loss of memory began in February 1945 and lasted until the present [November 1945]. . . At the moment he is not insane in the strict sense. His loss of memory will not entirely interfere with his comprehension of the proceedings, but it will interfere with his ability to make his defence, and to understand details of the past, which arise in evidence.

The American report, by Drs D. Ewen Cameron, Jean Delay, Paul L. Schroeder and Nolan E.C. Lewis, declared that Hess was 'suffering from hysteria characterised in part by loss of memory'. There was 'a conscious exaggeration' of this amnesia and 'a tendency to exploit it to protect himself against examination'. He was not insane in 'the strict sense of the word'.

During the Nuremberg Trials the gawky and hypochondriacal Hess often slept or seemed to be asleep, spoke incoherently or refused to speak, and generally acted in an inappropriate manner. He was once seen reading *Grimm's Fairy Tales* in the dock. On 1 October 1946 Hess was found guilty of 'conspiracy to wage aggressive war' and of 'crimes against peace'. He was sentenced to life imprisonment. Delivering the judgment, Lord Justice Lawrence said: 'Hess was a willing participant in the German aggression against Austria, Czechoslovakia and Poland. He was in touch with the illegal Nazi Party in Austria throughout the period between the murder of Chancellor Dollfuss [in July 1934] and the Anschluss [in March 1938], and gave it instructions. . . He proposed laws discriminating against the Poles and Jews.'

From the earliest days of the Nazi movement Hess was viciously anti-Semitic. When a student at Munich University shortly after the

First World War he spent much time distributing pamphlets inciting hatred against the Jews.

In Spandau prison, Berlin, his conduct continued to be bizarre. He committed suicide there in 1987.

Clearly, Hess had none of the qualities of an SOE agent. Imagine him as an adviser to the German Directorate or as an 'escapee' or 'emissary' between Britain and Nazi Germany! Also, there is no evidence that he, a die-hard Nazi, ever wished to play any sort of secret service role on the Allies' behalf.

# Chapter Seven
## *Four Little Foxleys*

Ever hopeful, the German Directorate never gave up planning the assassination of a few carefully chosen members of the Nazi dictatorship. Indeed, it persisted even when it was obvious to every informed commentator that the war in Europe would not last much longer. On 16 March 1945 the Directorate began studying a document by Major H.B. Court (L/BX), which suggested four possible targets for a Foxley II operation: Goebbels, Lieutenant-General Bruno Ritter von Hauenschild, Major-General Otto Ernst Remer and SS-Obersturmbannführer Otto Skorzeny.

By then Goebbels, a glutton for hard work, was Gauleiter of Berlin and commander-in-chief of the huge contingent of armed forces defending it, as well as being Propaganda Minister and the holder of lesser posts. The other three men were subordinate to him in his military appointment – one which he was ill-equipped to hold. He had no experience in any of the armed forces, either in command or even in the ranks, having been rejected for First World War service in the Kaiser's army because of his deformed foot.

Court viewed Goebbels, Hauenschild, Remer and Skorzeny as less difficult targets than many other prominent Nazis who, he believed, were no longer in Berlin. However, as had so often happened in the past, the already well-informed SOE needed yet more Top Secret intelligence before it could begin any detailed planning of an assassination. The matter-of-fact language of the Foxley papers does not disguise the German Directorate's exasperation over having to wait for Section V, the counter-espionage branch of SIS, to give it permission to interrogate a number of captured SD agents.[1]

With Section V seemingly slow to cooperate and with no certainty of more German intelligence personnel falling into Allied hands in the near future, Court suggested that SOE ask its American counterpart, the Office of Strategic Services, to let it interrogate three SD agents in US custody.[2] He believed that all these agents, held either by the British or the Americans, knew much about Skorzeny. They might, he thought, also have intelligence on the SS leadership and on the RSHA (the Reichssicherheitshauptamt – the Reich Security Main Office).

Created by Himmler in the autumn of 1939, the RSHA unified the bureaucracies of all the organs of repression in Nazi Germany. It was the umbrella organisation coordinating the activities of the Gestapo, the SD and the Kripo (the criminal police) and provided the central office for both the SS and the Interior Ministry. Supervised by Himmler, the coarse and drunken Ernst Kaltenbrunner headed the RSHA from January 1943 until the end of the war in Europe.

Of the four Foxley II (or Little Foxley) targets, the German Directorate knew least about Hauenschild. He was Goebbel's second-in-command and commander of Wehrkreis III, a military district of more than 39,000 square kilometres which covered the city of Berlin and the whole of Brandenburg province and had a population of well over 7 million. A Bavarian, he was an efficient tank general with previous service in the artillery. He participated in the invasion of Russia in June 1941 as commander of 4 Panzer Brigade and was awarded the Knight's Cross in September that year. In April 1942 he was moved from the Eastern Front to Rennes, France, to command 24th Panzer Division. However, in the autumn of 1942 he was so severely wounded that he was judged unfit to remain in a fighting command. The Oak Leaves award was added to his Knight's Cross, and in October he was put in charge of motorisation at the OKH (Oberkommando des Heeres, the Army High Command). On 2 February 1945, he was given the Wehrkreis III appointment with headquarters at Charlottenburg, Berlin, making him the militarily incompetent Goebbels' right-hand man in undertaking the impossible task of defending the capital.

As with every other of its Foxley II targets, SOE tried to learn as much as possible about Hauenschild's physical appearance, daily routine and general background. He had, according to the Foxley papers, 'always been on good terms with the Nazis' – meaning, presumably, that, although never failing to support them, he was perhaps not a Party member. These papers have this less than complete description of Hauenschild: 'big built' with 'heavy' face, 'strong chin, well shaped ears, straight nose, hair turning grey at [the] temples'.

Lieutenant-General Hauenschild was always a poor candidate for assassination. The German Directorate's information on him was scrappy, and he was small fry compared with most other Little Foxleys. On 21 March 1945, shortly after he had been relieved of his Berlin post, his name was removed from the Directorate's list of possible targets.

SOE similarly lacked sufficient intelligence on Otto Remer,

although he apparently remained a Little Foxley candidate until the end of the war in Europe, as the Foxley papers do not say that he was ever struck off the assassination list. In February 1945 at the age of thirty-two Remer became the youngest major-general in the German army when he was put in command of the forces defending Berlin's eastern approaches. This appointment was a reward for his Hitlerite zealotry, manifested both then and until his death in October 1997, aged eighty-five. A venomous inciter of racial hatred and street violence after the war, he co-founded in 1950 a neo-Nazi group called the Sozialistiche Reichspartei.

Remer played a key part in the bloody suppression of the Bomb Plot attempt to overthrow the Nazi dictatorship on 20 July 1944. He was then only a major (and not yet an over-enthusiastic Party member) commanding the Wachbataillon Grossdeutschland, the guard unit stationed in the Berlin suburb of Döberitz. At 4 p.m. the city's military commandant, General Paul von Hase, who was one of the anti-Hitler conspirators, ordered Remer to prepare his troops to occupy government offices and the Berlin radio station and to arrest Goebbels and leading SS officers. Wishing to ensure that whatever happened he would be on the winning side, Remer put his company on a state of alert and made troop movements in obedience to Hase's orders. However, shortly afterwards, influenced by one of his lieutenants who was a fanatical Nazi, he switched his allegiance. In a telephone conversation with Goebbels, the only regime member in Berlin, he learned that Hitler was still alive. The dictator himself then telephoned Remer from the Rastenburg FHQ, ordering him, under Himmler's command, to 'suppress all resistance with ruthless energy'. This he did. As described in the Foxley papers, Remer 'marched the Berlin Wachbataillon . . . to the Kommandantur and subsequently arrested the rebels, some of whom he shot on Hitler's instructions'. So began a massive bloodbath of actual or suspected members of Der Widerstand, the German Resistance.

The Foxley papers also mention the award to Remer of the Knight's Cross and Oak Leaves in 1943 for his service in Russia and France, but say nothing else of significance about him. SOE was evidently ignorant of his daily routine and knew little about his physical appearance, having only a head-and-shoulders photograph of him. Like Hauenschild, he was a poor candidate for assassination.

Much more was known about Skorzeny and, although junior in rank to Hauenschild and Remer, he had a far more important position of influence than theirs. The Foxley papers say of him: 'SS-Obersturmbannführer Otto Skorzeny, energetic, bold, ruthless and fanatically devoted to the Nazi cause, may be described without exaggeration as the most dangerous of the younger Nazi chiefs.' Born in Vienna in June 1908, he was at the end of the war in Europe not quite thirty-seven years old. Nominally subordinate to SS-Brigadeführer Walter Schellenberg, head of the RSHA's foreign espionage and sabotage department (Amt VI), Skorzeny not only had Kaltenbrunner's active support, but was in practice responsible only to Himmler. According to the German Directorate, Himmler had reportedly given Skorzeny the command of 'all sabotage and subversive activities, including *coup de main* and irregular methods of warfare'. He trained, equipped and largely directed the Nazi underground movement abroad, drawing on both the SS and the Wehrmacht for recruits.

However, in March 1945, when the Foxley papers' biographical piece on Skorzeny was written, he would have had little opportunity to direct clandestine operations of the kind mentioned above. The Russians were advancing towards Berlin and what was left of the Third Reich was in disarray. In that desperate situation almost all his time must have been spent in commanding Hitler's bodyguard, an additional responsibility given him by the dictator after the Bomb Plot, and in being in 'charge of all security measures in Berlin', the Foxley papers' description of a task even more recently added to his already heavy workload.

SOE had much information on Skorzeny's daily routine, but not enough to make him an immediate target for assassination. As the Foxley papers say, his 'multifarious activities' showed that he was unlikely to remain for long in one place. The papers add: 'Friedenthal, near Oranienburg [north of Berlin], is probably the address at which he might most frequently be found. This headquarters (where Skorzeny is said to keep his files and have his office) is reported to be located in a small hunting lodge called Jagdschloss or Schloss (Gut) Friedenthal.' The Schloss included Skorzeny's living quarters, a telephone exchange and an officers' mess and bar. A note in the Foxley papers that the crockery used there was marked 'SS Schloss Friedenthal' is an example of the sort of detailed information which the German Directorate gathered as possible briefing material when training agents.

The Schloss was near Sachsenhausen concentration camp, next to which were barracks accommodating SS personnel and agents being trained for sabotage and special intelligence operations. According to one of SOE's informants, guards at the barracks gate would allow anybody to enter as long as they had a soldier's paybook and travel documents (Marschbefehl – marching orders). However, in Major Court's view, this applied only to members of the SS and to those Wehrmacht personnel on training courses at Friedenthal; other Wehrmacht troops, he believed, would be treated with suspicion.[3]

Skorzeny also had a Berlin headquarters. But where exactly? Court believed it might be in two buildings in the Grunewald district: Delbrückstrasse 10, which formerly housed SS sabotage personnel, and number 6 in the same street, which had been used by these men as an equipment store. These buildings were near the RSHA Amt VI headquarters at Berkaerstrasse 32. The German Directorate also believed that Skorzeny might occasionally be seen at FHQ, Hitler's personal headquarters. But there was no up-to-date intelligence on its location, only a two-month-old report that it was at Zossen. With the dictator probably often on the move, such information was useless.

In the past Skorzeny had frequently visited the various establishments where the irregular forces under his command were trained in secret. For example, on 20 April 1944, he was at the Leibstandarte Adolf Hitler barracks at Berlin-Lichterfelde, selecting men for training as swimming saboteurs, and three months later he was inspecting trained swimmers in Venice. He also visited Gravenwoehr, headquarters of 150 Panzer Brigade, and Deersheim, near Wernigerode, an SS training school, as well as reportedly having addresses in Vienna and Döbling.

The German Directorate was well informed about Skorzeny's physical appearance and other personal characteristics. It knew that he was more than 1.9 metres tall, weighed about 88kg and was of 'very powerful build'. However, its information about his hair was contradictory, it being described by different informants as 'brown', 'dark', 'short and brushed back' and 'wavy'. His face was 'round-oval' with 'scarred heavy cheeks, large nose, very strong chin, sunburnt (brown) complexion'. His hands were 'coarse'. He spoke with a 'slight Viennese accent', sometimes lapsing into broad dialect. He wore SS uniform or civilian clothes.

Skorzeny's career, attainments and character were also well known to SOE. An admirer of Hitler when a schoolboy, he joined the Nazi Party in 1932 shortly after graduating in engineering from Vienna's Technische Hochschule. In 1934 he set up in business as a motor engineer and joined the Allgemeine SS. At the start of the war he was called up for service in the Luftwaffe but transferred in January 1940 to the Waffen SS. As an officer in the Das Reich Division, he fought in Western Europe, the Balkans and Russia. (Appendix G gives other biographical information on Skorzeny, including on his leadership of the glider-borne special detachment that rescued Mussolini from captivity in Italy in September 1943.) An Alpine climber, skier and strong swimmer, Skorzeny could also speak Italian and knew some Arabic. Said to be an inspiring personality to his admirers, he was, however, described by a Wehrmacht officer (quoted by Court) as a 'typical evil Nazi' with 'fantastic notions and a predilection for dirty methods'.

Not knowing his whereabouts at any one time, the German Directorate never made any detailed plans to assassinate Skorzeny, but it kept his name on its list of Little Foxleys until the end of the war in Europe.

Foxley II also focused attention on Goebbels. He was occasionally vulnerable to attack. Much detailed information about his daily routine – frantic in the last months of his life – was on the files of the German Directorate. It had, for instance, up-to-date Top Secret intelligence on his idiosyncratic personal habits, on his many official and private addresses, on some of his travel arrangements, and on those of his subordinates with whom he mainly associated. Most importantly, the Directorate knew the few occasions when Goebbels was not closely guarded. Certainly by March 1945 when Major Court (L/BX) wrote a five-page biographical piece on him for the Foxley papers, and probably much earlier than that, it was clear that he was an excellent candidate for assassination. He remained on the list of possible targets until he, like his idol, Hitler, committed suicide.

As energetic as he was evil, Dr (Paul) Josef Goebbels had accumulated an assortment of dissimilar posts towards the end of the Third Reich. The most important of these were: Minister of National Enlightenment and Propaganda, the Nazi Party's propaganda chief; Plenipotentiary for Total War (a job he had from July 1944, making him second only to Hitler in terms of real power in the regime); Gauleiter and City President of Berlin, with responsibility for its defence; and Chairman of the Inter-Ministerial Air Damage Commission.

Rumours that Goebbels had left Berlin in February 1945 were disproved shortly afterwards by a German radio report that he was 'busy showing himself to Berliners and organising the defence of the capital'. Commenting on this broadcast, Court recalled reports that Goebbels had been similarly energetic in trying to boost public morale during the first large-scale air raids on the city in 1943. Court believed that he was now likely to remain there 'until the very last', as it was Berlin that he had 'won for Hitler with so much effort in the early days of the Party'.

An assassin would have had no difficulty in identifying Goebbels. As the Foxley papers say, 'with his diminutive stature and club foot', he needed no description. He either wore Nazi Party uniform, on which since December 1944 he had had added the Grossdeutschland black and silver armband, or civilian clothes. During his morale-boosting meet-the-people trips he wore a grey hat and overcoat with green scarf.

Goebbels usually arrived at one or other of his offices between 9 a.m. and 10 a.m. However, in summer he would sometimes arrive as early as 6 a.m. but would lie down for a rest at 10.30 a.m. after drawing the curtains on his office windows. Persons wishing to visit him would have to submit written applications to do so. These would be vetted by his personal adjutants, the leader of whom was Ministerialdirektor Bermdt. Only people whom the Foxley papers describe as 'celebrities' – presumably leading Nazis and other prominent figures trusted by the regime – did not have to follow this procedure. They could make appointments by telephone. When in Berlin Goebbels was always closely guarded. His chief personal detective was SS-Untersturmführer Wilhelm Kruse. Aged about thirty-five, he was a burly man with a small moustache and a scar on his right cheek.

Self-controlled in public, Goebbels was clearly scared on the frequent occasions that he had to take cover in the Befehlsbunker, his personal air-raid shelter in the Propaganda Ministry. According to SOE informants, he carried a flask of brandy in his hip-pocket during air raids and would take a nip from time to time. Elsewhere, the only alcohol he usually drank was champagne.

An assassin would have found it difficult to locate Goebbels, as he had many addresses, official and unofficial. Four were official. Three of these were in Berlin: the Propaganda Ministry; the Gauleiter headquarters; and his office as Plenipotentiary for Total War. His fourth official address was his office in Munich as head of Nazi Party propaganda.[4] The German Directorate realised that there was little or no chance of assassinating Goebbels at any of these official addresses. However, it believed he might sometimes have been less well guarded elsewhere. Even during the hectic final months of his life he probably at least occasionally made brief visits to one or other of his five off-duty haunts known to the Directorate. These were: the Kunstlereck am Zoo, a café patronised by a select few from the Propaganda Ministry; the Jockey Bar, commandeered by that ministry; a private room at the Hiller Restaurant; and two journalists' clubs, the Auslands-Presseklub and the Haus der Deutschen Presse.

Like other members of Hitler's inner circle, Goebbels owned or had sole control over many residences. These – acquired by all manner of fair or foul means – included: state apartments in Berlin's Hermann Göringstrasse (now Ebertstrasse); villas at Cladow and Pfaueninsel; two castles at Gatow; a villa at Bad Reichenhall, near Berchtesgaden, where he was said to have lodged his mother; and the Villa Hohenwarte, in Vienna. However, there is no hint in the Foxley papers that the German Directorate ever regarded any of these residences as settings for a Little Foxley.

Some of Goebbels's homes were by 1945 inaccessible to him. For example, Schloss Rheydt was in American hands, and SOE had an unconfirmed report that he had bought a property in Majorca, the Casa San Vicente. Perhaps he envisaged this as a postwar refuge from international justice, a remote rural retreat from which he was unlikely to be extradited as long as General Franco ruled Spain.

Over the years Goebbels met his many mistresses in various locations, including at least three houses in suburban Berlin. From time to time he was particularly attracted to bathing belles from the UFA film studios. He reportedly had a swimming pool built for them and entertained them at another of his homes, Schloss Schwanenwerder, when his wife, Magda was absent. All this caused Major Court to comment in the Foxley papers: 'It is not known whether Goebbels now finds time for the pursuit of the fair sex to which he has always been so much addicted. It appears that Magda Goebbels, sickened with the doctor's infidelities, consented to a divorce in July 1944, so that, now untrammelled in any way, Goebbels may pursue these affairs with even greater zest than in the past.' However, there was not a chance of him doing that. In the fraught and action-filled final weeks of his life, when the end of the Nazi dictatorship was clearly imminent, Goebbels had little or no spare time for sexual adventures. The German Directorate never seriously regarded his love nests as places where he might be assassinated.

But Court, and probably others, did think that a Little Foxley might be mounted in yet another of his residences, the Sommervilla Waldhof am Bogensee, or when he was travelling between there and Berlin. This house, standing within a large estate surrounded by coniferous woodland, had several advantages for Goebbels. It was near a six-hangar 'get-away' airfield between Bockow and Schonwalde and had good road and rail links with Berlin. His not infrequent use of this pleasant country retreat, especially after the start of heavy air raids on the capital in 1943, was one of many Nazi state secrets about which SOE was well informed.

The estate, on the western shore of Bogensee lake and about 8 kilometres from the nearest railway station at Bernau, was ringed by a wire fence 2 metres high and topped with barbed-wire. The approach road to the estate was only 4 metres wide and was reached from another road running between two highways, the Prenzlauer Chaussee and the Berlin–Stettin Autobahn. When viewed from a distance, the wire fence was largely hidden by conifers. The entrance gate to the estate was secured only by a Zeis Ikon patent lock and, surprisingly, was not guarded. Visitors had to ring a bell to summon servants who would let them in. However, the house and estate as a whole were protected by security personnel, albeit by a total of only about six men – uniformed members of the SS armed with revolvers and Gestapo in civilian clothes. The nearest large military presence was at Bernau.[5]

A well-briefed assassin, such as one trained by SOE, would have had no difficulty in recognising the Sommervilla Waldhof, a single-storey white house with a grey-blue, V-shaped roof and exceptionally high ceilings. Goebbels' study in the main wing had a glass wall facing the lake, making him a not too difficult target for a water-borne attacker. Buildings near the summer villa included a guesthouse (known to be unoccupied in 1943 and perhaps still unused in 1945), an air-raid shelter, a blockhouse and a ten-door garage block containing the estate's central heating plant.

To get to Berlin by train Goebbels would have had to be taken in his car to Bernau railway station and from there travel 35 kilometres southwards on the line from Stettin (now Szczecin in Poland). However, he was thought to favour doing this journey solely by road. He reportedly left the Sommervilla Waldhof between 9 a.m. and 10.30 a.m. and returned there between 6 p.m. and 7 p.m. These times did not tally with his usual work schedule, already mentioned, but he did occasionally vary his working hours – often because of Allied bombers overhead.

On his road journeys from the summer villa Goebbels travelled as the single back-seat passenger in a Mercedes limousine, which, unlike Hitler's similar cars, bore no distinguishing symbols, such as the swastika. A guard sat beside the chauffeur. Both were members of the SS. Goebbels had no other protection on this publicly exposed car ride, much of the route on the Prenzlauer Chaussee. Rarely did leading Nazis take such risks with their personal safety.

Even late in the war, Goebbels was an excellent candidate for assassination. His death in dramatic circumstances would have been a fine propaganda coup for the Allies. However, SOE did lack a few pieces of Top Secret intelligence essential to the planning of such an operation, particularly the dates and times of his occasional car journeys between the Bogensee estate and Berlin.

Goebbels remained on the Little Foxley list until 1 May 1945, when, the day after Hitler's suicide, he too ended his ignoble life. So did Magda, who shared her husband's fanatical beliefs. Earlier, Goebbels had arranged to have their six children murdered; they were playing together until shortly before they were given lethal injections.[6]

As the dictator of the mass media, of the arts and of every other means of influencing public opinion in Nazi Germany, Goebbels made his practice of systematic deceit into a pseudo-science. He was – as described by a German general[7] quoted in the Foxley papers – a 'master of the spoken word and a phenomenally clever and intelligent man who can play any part'. Goebbels was also the Nazis' most voluble promoter of anti-Semitism. But it was not only hatred of the Jews that obsessed him. By his own admission, he detested humanity as a whole. He wrote in his *Diaries*, published after the war: 'I have learned to despise the human being. . . After I have been with a person for three days, I no longer like him; if I have been with him a week, I hate him'.

The son of a factory foreman, the physically small Goebbels was widely read in philosophy, literature, art, history, Greek and Latin – putting him intellectually head and shoulders above the other members of Hitler's inner circle. Born in the Rhineland town of Rheydt in October 1897, he rejected all the values of his devout Catholic family at an early age. When only twenty-four years old he was awarded a doctorate by Heidelberg University after studying there and at seven other universities. However, in his immediate postgraduate years he failed to make a living as a novelist, journalist and writer of plays in verse. This experience exacerbated his already deep bitterness over his all too obvious club foot, the result of unsuccessful surgery on his left thigh when he was a boy. It was during one of his periods of despair that he heard Hitler speak at a public meeting in Munich in 1922. 'At that moment I was reborn!' Goebbels later declared. He joined the Nazi Party in 1924 and quickly rose to prominence in its ranks. No other member of Hitler's inner circle had his great talents as an orator, publicist and administrator – talents that he prostituted every day of the twelve years of the Third Reich.

# Chapter Eight
## *The Himmler problem*

Himmler, Kaltenbrunner, Bormann and Göring were yet more Little Foxleys. However, as SOE never learned much about their day-to-day movements and lifestyles, how they might be assassinated remained only a discussion topic until the end of the war in Europe. Of these four leading Nazis, Himmler alone was the subject of analytical minuting by officers of the German Directorate.[1] They, together with many other members of the Allied intelligence community, realised that he was engaged from at least the middle of 1944 in important new sorts of clandestine activity. But exactly what these were was unclear.

Was the militarily incompetent Himmler – since July 1944, the Reserve Army's commander-in-chief as well as leader of the SS – plotting to seize power from Hitler? Did he want a negotiated peace settlement with both the Western and Eastern Allies rather than the 'unconditional surrender' demanded by them?[2] Or did he hope to make a separate peace with the Western Allies and then continue fighting the USSR? Did he believe that a small and heavily fortified Nazi state might be set up in some mountainous location, say the Bavarian Alps, as a successor to the Third Reich? Did he intend from such a supposedly impregnable enclave that die-hard National Socialists might prolong the war indefinitely?

It was these and similar questions that the Allied political and military leaders were asking (and requiring answers to from the intelligence community) in the final months of the European war. Although it may seem absurd more than half a century after the event, there was real concern at the time that such an enclave (what the Allies called a 'National Redoubt') might be created. That anxiety was particularly felt by General Eisenhower, the Supreme Commander, Allied Expeditionary Force.[3]

Although important, SOE's information on Himmler, mainly provided by SIS and OSS, was much too fragmentary to be the basis of any assassination plan. An OSS report, undated but probably written shortly after the July Bomb Plot, said: 'The main authority in Germany is . . . being exercised for the moment by a triumvirate – Himmler, Goebbels and Bormann – of course, in the name of the

Führer. Himmler, profiting by Hitler's illness, has been working to divide the generals. Both military men and even certain high government officials who are suspected of oppositional tendencies are being sent to work in munitions factories.' Among Foreign Ministry officials reportedly so treated was von Grobba, former head of the Near East Department. The report added:

> With the generals who are prepared to go along with the [Nazi] Party, led by von Rundstedt, as commander of the Western Front, and Guderian, as commander of the Eastern Front, Himmler is reported to have made a pact along the following lines: Territory disposition is to be directed solely by strategic considerations. If necessary, withdrawals can be effected independently of prestige considerations or any wild orders of the Führer. On the other hand, the military will participate with the SS in perfecting the Nazi underground organisation.

It reportedly consisted of 200,000–300,000 members of the SS, the Hitler Jugend (Hitler Youth) and the Bund deutscher Mädel (the League of German Girls). 'It is Himmler's idea that the present stubborn military resistance will provide time for organising the [Nazi] underground. At the same time, Hitler is still speculating on tiring out or dividing the Allies. The Germans hope to raise the figure of Allied losses to such an extent that Allied public opinion will be alarmed. . .'

Himmler, who knew nothing about naval strategy, was also allegedly proposing that some Allied convoys be attacked by large numbers of one-man submarines operating from mother ships. The report added that the Germans were reportedly accumulating a reserve of fighter aircraft, including 'a high proportion' of jets.[4] Though lacking the fuel supplies required for continuous large-scale air operations and for meeting 'other vital needs', the Nazi authorities proposed to hold this reserve for 'certain mass attacks'. For example, when countering '2,000-plane' bombing raids.

The OSS report ended: 'The [Nazi] Germans are allegedly basing their estimates on the theory that not only Germany but also England [sic] has really lost the war. They expect de Gaulle at Moscow to secure backing, not only against a German revival, but also against Anglo-Saxon predominance in Western Europe. The Russian–French alliance, in the long run, would eliminate British and American influence.' OSS's London office, which issued the report, commented that the information in it did not 'on the surface appear improbable' and that its author, an agent in Switzerland, was 'reasonably honest'.

In October 1944, SIS sent SOE a French intelligence report that Himmler had appointed SS-Obergruppenführer Eric von dem Bach-Zelewski as 'supreme commander-in-chief' of the Nazis' 'German resistance movement' intended to operate – it did not say where – after the Third Reich's capitulation. The report claimed 500,000 members of this 'movement' were given identity cards made out by the Gestapo in the names of persons reported missing after air raids. Himmler by then, the report asserted, commanded not only the 'army of the interior' [the Reserve Army], but also controlled the 'army at the front'. He had appointed two, or possibly three, SS generals to conventional military commands. Although the report did not say so, one of these generals, Bach-Zelewski, led the SS forces that crushed the Warsaw Uprising in August.[5]

An SIS report on 8 December 1944 said that several diplomats at the German Embassy in Madrid had expressed anxiety over the power being exercised by Himmler now that Hitler was stated to be seriously ill or even mentally deranged. These diplomats had recently received orders direct from Himmler, causing them to believe that he had gained supreme command. Himmler was 'cordially disliked' by members of the embassy, who said that under his leadership German military resistance would be 'more fanatical' and the Gestapo's repression of the civilian population would become even harsher.

On 11 December SIS thus assessed German public opinion of Hitler and Himmler: 'As to the question of Hitler's responsibility for involving the Reich in a lost cause, the issue is confused because Hitler's prestige has gone to such an extent that the ordinary German hardly gives him a thought, everybody hates Himmler, and people are too depressed and tired to argue about the responsibility of the Party or Hitler or the German people as a whole for involving Germany in the war.' The SIS report added that it was now the custom in Germany to classify people under three headings: '120 per cent Nazis', 'Nazis' and 'Germans'. There was 'mild animosity' against Nazi Party bosses, but 'real animosity' was reserved for Himmler. Germans refused to discuss him publicly. However, one brave individual described him as the 'most frightful monster who has ever been on earth' and 'a thousand times worse than Ivan the Terrible could ever have been'.

Towards the end of the war in Europe the German Directorate investigated whether it should or could contact Himmler's personal masseur, Felix Kersten, who was then living in Sweden, evidently with the SS leader's active approval. According to Swedish press reports in February 1945, Kersten had visited Sweden several times during the war, ostensibly as a businessman, and currently had a 'manual therapy' practice in Stockholm. He also allegedly had a luxurious flat there. One newspaper, *Trots Allt!* wondered whether he had come to Sweden to put out peace feelers on the Nazis' behalf or to defect from Germany. Another press report noted that he had a German exit permit and had been allowed into Sweden because he had done the country 'certain great services'.

In an exchange of telegrams with British diplomats in Stockholm, SOE asked on 8 February whether, if required, Kersten could be flown to Britain or questioned in Sweden. However, the diplomats were wary about approaching him, pointing out that he was suspected of being 'an extremely dangerous person and entirely unreliable'. Two days later, the German Directorate decided against trying to contact him – so perhaps losing a chance of obtaining valuable Top Secret intelligence on Himmler's activities and intentions.

Much more was learned about Kersten after the war. If that additional information had been available to the Allies early in 1945, the Directorate might have made a different decision. Born in Estonia, he trained in agriculture and briefly managed a large farm. Then, in 1919, he fought in the Finnish army in the war against Russia, after which he took Finnish citizenship. He discovered his skill as a masseur when in a Finnish military hospital and was later professionally trained in Berlin. In 1925 he took over a lucrative practice, which he expanded by opening other clinics in Holland as well as Germany. He treated Himmler for the first time in March 1939, giving him relief from his frequently recurring stomach cramps. His other patients included Hess, Ribbentrop and Robert Ley, head of the German Labour Front – all of them thoroughly neurotic and Ley a dipsomaniac. A Swedish citizen from 1953, Kersten (1898–1960) declared after the war that he had persuaded Himmler to save the lives of many Jews.[6]

As well as acting through Kersten, the SS leader hoped to put out peace feelers to the Western Allies through the Berlin representative of the Swedish Match Company, a man named Möller. SOE was informed of this move by the Foreign Office's Political Intelligence Department (PID). In a report dated 22 November 1944, the PID recalled that in 1942 five Swedes had been arrested in Warsaw and condemned to death in Berlin, but their sentences had been reduced to life imprisonment as a result of the King of Sweden writing to Hitler. Without any reason being given by the Nazi authorities, two of the five were in 1944 freed and allowed to return to Sweden.

Möller meanwhile was informed through an intermediary that if he visited Himmler in Berlin he might be able to negotiate the release of the other three Swedes. However, he feared that if he accepted the invitation, the SS chief might interrogate him to discover the considerable amount he knew about some of the July Bomb plotters. Apart from that and other intimidating factors, Möller, who had had earlier discussions with one of Himmler's close associates over the imprisoned Swedes, had no intention of being 'used' by the Reichsführer-SS.

The German Directorate had little information about Himmler's whereabouts. He was 'continually on the move', Major Court noted in a minute on 4 December 1944. This key member of the Directorate added that as Himmler was by then 'to all intents and purposes the Führer', he might be using Hitler's Special Train, the Führerzug. Court made that reasonable speculation from recent intelligence reports pointing out that certain matters specifically relating to the SS had been telegraphed to that train.[7]

There were also gaps in the information the Directorate knew about the residences owned or otherwise acquired by Himmler. It had an incomplete list that included a house in Berlin's Dahlem district, possibly his headquarters in March 1945, and a villa in Aigen, Austria. The villa once belonged to Baron von Trapp, a retired naval officer who, even after the Anschluss, made little or no attempt to hide his anti-Nazi feelings. The Foxley papers say laconically that he 'emigrated to the USA in 1939'. That he indeed did, but not until after he had fled to Switzerland with his children and their governess – a fine feat of bravery and endurance told in the 1965 film *The Sound of Music*.[8]

If SOE had known the occasions when Himmler visited the villa, the possibility of assassinating him there might at least have been considered. In December 1944, Court quoted a report describing Aigen as 'a hotbed of communism, particularly among the railwaymen living there.' Whatever their politics, these men had a special reason for detesting Himmler, for many local rail workers had been beheaded as a direct or indirect result of his orders. Might a potential assassin have been found in Aigen? None was ever sought.

The Foxley documents do not mention Himmler's frenzied and contradictory activities in the last weeks before he killed himself on 23 May 1945. Long before then he had lost what little sense of reality he had ever had. As part of his efforts to approach the Western Allies, he met Count Folke Bernadotte of the Swedish Red Cross, proposed the surrender of the German armies on the Western Front and in Denmark and Norway, and ordered the ending of the mass murder of Jews. All this he did without telling Hitler. Simultaneously, he and other die-hard Nazis still dreamed of having their fortress enclave in the Bavarian Alps or thereabouts; he even also briefly fancied Schleswig-Holstein as the location for such a rump republic of National Socialism. Almost to the end of his life the Reichsführer-SS – the architect of the 'Final Solution' and the overseer of all the repressive organs of the Nazi dictatorship – held the mad delusion that the Western Allies would regard him as a dependable politician with whom they could meaningfully negotiate.

However, he did eventually realise that his cause was lost. But that disillusionment came only after Hitler had dismissed him from all his posts on discovering his 'treachery', and Admiral Dönitz, briefly Head of State after the dictator's suicide, had also condemned him.

In disguise and carrying a dead man's identity papers, Himmler left Dönitz's headquarters near Flensburg on 10 May. Shortly after being captured by British troops he killed himself by crushing a phial of potassium cyanide hidden in his mouth.

Never short of new ideas, Major Court suggested in February 1945, that ten of Himmler's principal subordinates be considered as candidates for assassination. They were, he minuted, 'potentially more dangerous' than other Little Foxleys because of 'their comparative youth and the active part they might play in any Nazi underground movement'.

All these men were high-ranking SS officers in charge of central offices of the SS or of RSHA departments. Most of them were believed to be still in Berlin and, according to Court's assessment, offered a 'considerably easier target than Hitler, Himmler or Goebbels, for example'. He considered that the elimination of at least some of these SS men would probably have 'an immediate and marked effect' on Nazi Party morale.

The German Directorate had photographs, personal descriptions and the home or office addresses of most of the ten. It hoped shortly to obtain all information on their daily routines and lifestyles that would be needed if any assassinations were planned. Court commented: 'In view of the apparent tardiness in withdrawing FHQ [Hitler's personal headquarters] from East Prussia it is possible that SS and RSHA offices may remain in Berlin and only be withdrawn to South Germany at the last moment, although there is already evidence that archives were removed some time ago.'

The Foxley papers list the ten possible targets. They were: Brigadeführer Walter Schellenberg, the foreign intelligence chief, heading the RSHA's Amt VI and Militärisches Amt; Gruppenführer Heinrich Müller, head of Amt IV of the RSHA, the Gestapo; Brigadeführer Professor Otto Ohlendorf, head of the RSHA's Amt III, which supervised SD activities within Germany; Obergruppenführer Gottlob Berger, in charge of the SS's central department (Hauptamt) from 1940 and of the prisoner-of-war administration from January 1944; Obergruppenführer Hans Jüttner, head of the SS's operational headquarters (Führungshauptamt); Obergruppenführer Oswald Pohl, a member of Himmler's personal staff and controller of the SS's economic and administrative department, the WVHA (Wirtschaftsverwaltungshauptamt); Gruppenführer Richard Glucks, head of the WVHA's Amtsgruppe D, the department administering the concentration camps; Gruppenführer Dr-Inz Kammler, described in the Foxley papers as being 'now in charge of rocket sites in the West', having formerly been responsible for a WVHA department; Brigadeführer Hermann Fegelein, Himmler's liaison officer at Hitler's personal headquarters, the FHQ; and Obergruppenführer Wünnenberg, head of the Ordnungspolizei, who as well as his SS rank was a conventional police general. All ten belonged to the Allgemeine SS, the main (or 'general') part of the SS and some also had high ranks in the Waffen (military) SS.

The Foxley papers say nothing about what progress, if any, was made in finding out more about these 'easier targets'. However, judging from what is known now, SOE played no part in what happened to any of them. This is particularly well exemplified in the case of Schellenberg, Müller, Ohlendorf, Berger and Fegelein.

Schellenberg (1910–52) had recently arrived in Sweden when the Dönitz regime surrendered. Extradited back to Germany in June 1945, he gave evidence at the Nuremberg Trials and was himself tried by an American military court. After fifteen months of hearings he was, in April 1949, sentenced to six years' imprisonment but was released in June 1951, because of ill health. He then lived in Switzerland and Italy until his death.

Schellenberg was recruited into the SS when a young law student with an uncertain future. For him the thrill of intrigue, rather than enthusiasm for Nazi ideology, was his chief motivation. In November 1939 he staged the Venlo incident, which resulted in the kidnapping on the Dutch–German border of two SIS officers, Captain Sigismund Payne Best and Major Richard Stevens. But in July 1940 he failed during a visit to Spain to kidnap the Duke and Duchess of Windsor, who had recently escaped from France and were on their way to the Bahamas. In the last years of the war, while still energetically serving

Hitler, Schellenberg urged his patron, Himmler, to seek a negotiated peace with the Western Allies. To this end he secretly contacted the OSS office in Switzerland, the Swedish Red Cross, the World Jewish Congress and other intermediaries, and tried to persuade Himmler to moderate his persecution of the Jews.

Müller (born in 1900, or 1896, according to some records) disappeared without trace in the dying days of the Third Reich. He was last seen in Berlin and there was some postwar speculation that he had fled to Latin America or the USSR. An admirer of Soviet police-state methods, he was so closely identified with the Gestapo that he was known as 'Gestapo Müller'. Like Himmler, he was mild mannered and painstakingly polite on social occasions. This was borne out by a British officer prisoner of war who described him as 'a very decent little man'. For Müller, organising terror on a vast scale was an administrative matter to be considered coolly. His efficiency in his job was never in doubt.

Ohlendorf (1907–51) was a desk-bound official in the last days of the Third Reich. Extraordinarily brutal even by SS standards, he had a doctor's degree in jurisprudence and was deeply versed in philosophy, sociology and economics. For a while he was a professor at the Institute of Applied Economic Science. Joining the SS in 1926, he was typical of a certain sort of tunnel-visioned German intellectual of that time. During the invasion of the USSR he led an 'action group' murdering Soviet Jews, partisans and communist officials behind the German line of advance. He was convicted of war crimes and hanged in 1951.

Berger (1896–1975) was one of the last visitors to Hitler in the Reich Chancellery bunker. A simpleton, he genuinely believed in National Socialism. In 1940 he persuaded his hero and patron, Himmler, to try to recruit 'properly Aryan' SS divisions in Holland, Norway and other occupied countries.

Fegelein (1906–45) was shot dead on 28 April, two days before Hitler killed himself. On 26 April he had quietly slipped out of the Chancellery bunker. On the following afternoon the dictator noticed his absence and demanded that he be returned to duty. A telephone call located him at his apartment in the Kurfürstendamm area (one of the minority of addresses of the so-called 'easier targets' that SOE did not know). An SS search party found him there, but he was too drunk to be moved and was with his mistress. On a second visit to the apartment shortly afterwards, the SS men arrested him after discovering clear evidence that he was preparing to flee. Still drunk but tidily dressed in civilian clothes, he was packing a suitcase with jewellery, gold watches and other valuables, and he also had in his possession several forged passports and a large sum of money, including Swiss francs. His mistress had disappeared.

Although a deserter, Fegelein – one of Hitler's favourites – would probably not have been killed by the SS if the circumstances had been different. As it was the Führer had only recently learned about the absentee Himmler's attempts to make peace with the Western Allies. How else could Hitler take revenge on the man he had for long called 'der treue Heinrich' than by ordering the execution of his personal representative?

Fegelein was unscrupulous in all his personal behaviour. A drop-out from Munich University, he was a police officer cadet and then a groom in his father's riding school before joining the SS in 1933. Apart from being an accomplished horseman (he commanded the SS's Central Riding Academy in 1937), Fegelein owed his subsequent swift career advancement solely to patronage. His place in Hitler's inner circle had seemingly been made secure in June 1944 by his marriage to Eva Braun's sister, Margarete (Gretl). But when the dictator ordered his death, Eva said nothing in his defence.

Although the advancing Allied armies were making it plain that the European war would not last much longer,[9] Major Court minuted on 16 March that Berlin still appeared to 'offer considerable scope for action' for the planners of Little Foxleys. However, the exact whereabouts of the proposed assassination candidates at any one time were still unknown. And even the headquarters (FHQ) then being used by Hitler had not yet been located. Court speculated about all this in his minute. It was, he stated, 'perfectly possible' that Hitler and Himmler were in Berlin. He explained: 'Hitler's photograph has already appeared in the press addressing German troops on the Odor front, whilst Himmler, as GOC there, may well have his HQ in Berlin.' A recent interrogation of a prisoner of war, Hauptmann (Captain) Gaum, who had guarded Hitler at Rastenburg after the July Bomb Plot, revealed that the guard contingent had been split up on leaving East Prussia in November 1944. Members of the guard had been sent to Zossen, the Reich Chancellery and Berlin-Dahlem. Court added: 'Zossen is definitely the nearest FHQ to Berlin. It is possible that Hitler, when in Berlin, uses the Reichskanzlei (or what is left of it) as an office by day, and sleeps in Berlin-Dahlem at night.' Possible locations were Am Dohnenstieg, 8a, 10 and 10a. The last of these properties belonged to Himmler and might be used by him as a headquarters. Jüttner, 'as Himmler's right-hand man', might well be there too.

All this was speculation – made less than two months before the end of the war in Europe. In these circumstances, it is difficult to believe that SHAEF would have sanctioned any of the assassination projects that Major Court had in mind. He was, however, probably right in thinking that the ten prominent and comparatively young subordinates of Himmler whom he named were 'potentially more dangerous' than other Little Foxleys because of the part they might have played in forming 'any Nazi underground movement' of the sort envisaged by General Eisenhower. But Court was wrong in believing that the killing of any of these ten – all well down the Hitlerite regime's pecking order – would have had an 'immediate and marked effect' on Nazi Party morale. In these final months of the Third Reich, there must have been scarcely any such morale left, and most individual senior Nazis must have been thinking mainly about saving their own skins.

# Chapter Nine
## *Searching for the unfindable?*

An assassin of Hitler, if not a member of the dictator's own entourage, would have had to possess an extraordinary combination of disparate qualities. He would have needed to be boundlessly brave and resourceful in this most exacting of assignments. Capable of quick and effective thinking in a tight corner, he would also have required Job-like patience, being prepared to rethink his plan of action time and time again if changing circumstances demanded that he did so. A Foxley agent would also have had to speak German fluently and mix easily with all sorts of Germans, ranging from die-hard Nazis to those hating and despising the regime. Never could he risk causing anybody to suspect what he intended to do. However, most daunting of all for the agent would have been the realisation that his attempt on Hitler's life might well have involved his own death, either at the scene of the action or later through torture and execution.

With all these factors in mind, Section X and the German Directorate searched for some time for the right person for the Foxley 'job'. Occasionally the 'talent-spotters' commented woefully that no candidates had yet been found. Then, in January 1945, when they must have begun thinking that they were searching for the unfindable, they were told about Captain Edmund Hilary Bennett, a 25-year-old intelligence officer.

The Foxley papers do not say how he came to the German Directorate's notice. These documents also contain no biographical information on him, and his SOE personal file reveals only that he was born in Stockport on 10 May 1919, and had been working since 23 December 1944, in the Military Research Section of the British Defence Attaché's staff in Washington. However, Bennett must have had exceptional qualities, for the German Directorate examined in depth his candidature for the assassin's assignment.

This process involved consulting various specialist advisers, notably Dr Dudley Maurice Newitt (1894–1980), SOE's Director of Scientific Research (DSR) since 1941 and a Fellow of the Royal Society since 1942. A distinguished chemical engineer and the son of a ballistics expert, Newitt supervised the invention, manufacture and supply of the many devices used by SOE agents. Awarded the MC during First World War service in the Middle East, he was an hospitable man of great physical as well as intellectual energy; his peacetime joy was travelling rough on long journeys by land and sea. On completion of his SOE service in 1945 he was appointed to a professorship at Imperial College, London.

Dr Newitt and the other boffins, who at least initially were not given Bennett's name, asked whether 'the man who is going to carry out this operation' normally wore glasses, or if he did not do so, could he be persuaded to wear them. They also asked if he had false teeth or any 'physical peculiarity such as wearing a truss or a false limb'. Replying in a minute dated 16 January, General Templer guaranteed that the agent would wear glasses and was 'extremely unlikely' to have any of the mentioned peculiarities. On the question of false teeth, he suggested that Colonel Davies (AD/Z) – to whom the minute was addressed – might 'pursue the line [with the boffins] as we can give him [the agent] some false teeth even if he does not want them'. Although dental health standards in the 1940s were markedly lower than those today, even in those dark wartime days there must have been few robust young would-be secret agents with any false teeth. It therefore seems that Templer was at least briefly toying with the gruesome idea of having some almost certainly healthy teeth extracted for an unspecified operational reason – perhaps to enable poison to be hidden in one or more hollow artificial teeth.

The general's minute did not name Bennett and was in other ways imprecise. But there was no ambiguity from 8 February when, according to SOE personnel records (but not the Foxley papers), the question of whether to employ this mysterious young captain as an agent was being studied by Major Leslie Montgomery Smith (X/AQ),[1] the German Directorate's officer dealing with documentation, travel and quartermaster supplies.

Then on 16 March Templer telegraphed SOE's New York representative:

1. For your private information we are considering using this man for a high-priority assassination task which would require his lying low in Germany for [a] considerable period, collecting [the] necessary intelligence to enable him to do [the] job. 2. Before making official application for him [we] would greatly appreciate your advice as to his suitability. 3. Can you possibly give us this without divulging to him [the] real nature of the task we have in mind?

This last sentence indicated that, even at this late date in the selection process, Captain Bennett had not been told exactly what was expected of him.

However, he seemed fearless. SOE's man in New York cabled back on 22 March:

A. Have seen subject. . . . B. He, far from being discouraged by my intimidations [sic] of possible toughness of [the] assignment, showed even greater keenness. C. He however wishes to make one stipulation which is that he will not find himself out of a job on completion of [the] assignment or if [the] German war ends before [the] operation takes place, since his present interesting and specialised employment is good for the duration of both wars. D. He would like to get a permanent clandestine job and says [he would] be happy to live in Germany after [the] war.

Anticlimatically, Colonel Thornley (AD/X.1), acting on Templer's behalf, telegraphed New York four days later: '1. Under present circumstances do not feel justified in applying for this officer. 2. May revert later.' But the German Directorate did not revert. By then – 26 March – it was obvious to all that an Allied victory in Europe would come soon, as indeed it did only six weeks later. Even the greatest enthusiast for Operation Foxley would have had to admit that the fighting would be over before an agent had been trained and placed in Germany to wait and wait and wait for the right moment to strike Hitler down.

How long did SOE search for this operative? How diligent was that hunt? Was it conducted only within the intelligence community? Or was the trawl wider? Did it, for instance, extend to the German and Austrian refugees, mostly Jews, who had fled to Britain from Nazi persecution before the war, and some of whom were serving in the British armed forces? The Foxley papers have no answers to any of these questions. However, it is reasonable to suspect that, apart from examining the possibility of employing Captain Bennett, the German Directorate did not put much effort into its belated 'talent-spotting'.

Much earlier in the war, in 1941, one other man, a Macedonian with a record of violent crime, volunteered to kill Hitler. He had nothing in common with the undoubtedly sincere and blameless Bennett, and the only purpose of recounting the bizarre events involving him is to show some of the problems that SOE encountered when selecting agents for its more exacting operations.

The Macedonian was known only by his assumed name, Vilmar.

He was recruited by SOE's Middle Eastern representatives in Cairo, possibly without the organisation's headquarters in Baker Street, London, being informed. That sort of undisciplined decision-making, which occasionally occurred, reflected the not always good relations between Cairo and Baker Street. It is perhaps significant that there is no mention of Vilmar in the Foxley papers.

Apart from being a crack shot, he had little to recommend him for any clandestine operation. He was fat, middle-aged and often drunk. At social functions he soon became maudlin, sometimes crying like a child, and delighted in startling total strangers by showing them the gunshot scars pitting one of his legs.

In fairness to the staff officers of SOE, Middle East, it must be emphasised that it was not without misgivings that they accepted Vilmar as an agent. It seems that they did so largely because of the enthusiasm of the anti-Nazi Bulgarians who recommended him. The Bulgarians said he had once been a 'terrorist' but revealed nothing else about him. Having a criminal past was not always a disqualification for service in SOE, as some offenders had useful skills like safe-breaking and expressed a wish to atone for their misdeeds through acts of patriotic heroism. Or perhaps they just wanted to get out of jail!

Carrying forged documents representing him to be a Bulgarian businessman, Vilmar was infiltrated into Portugal. From there he went to Switzerland, a good country in which to monitor the German press and radio to discover when Hitler would appear in public. After travelling on to Germany and Austria, he called at the Bulgarian consulate in Vienna two days before the Führer was due to visit that city. In an interview with the consul, Vilmar praised Hitler lavishly and requested an audience with him or, if that were not permitted, to be allowed to see him at a function. The consul replied that the most he could do was to take Vilmar to a diplomatic reception attended by the Führer.

However, nothing like that happened. On the eve of Hitler's visit to Vienna, Vilmar went to a nightclub, ordered champagne and invited several girls to join him. It was not long before he was drunk, and following his usual practice on such occasions, he rolled up a trouser leg and showed the girls his gunshot scars. A little later, with even greater pride and joy, he revealed that he was carrying a pistol. That was too much for one of the girls. She called the police. Vilmar was arrested and, although his forged passport and other documents were accepted as genuine, he was deported to Bulgaria a few days later. He was never heard of again. Claiming to be terminally ill with cancer, Vilmar had wanted no payment as an agent except living expenses.

But he did request a commission, presumably in one of the British armed forces, and a posthumous decoration if he were killed in his attempt on Hitler's life.[2]

Could SOE have organised the assassination of the Führer if more time and resources had been put into planning Operation Foxley and finding the right man for the job? Or was it a mistake even to think that he should have been removed from the scene, with or without bloodshed? As it had become evident by 1943 that he was an incompetent supreme commander, temperamentally incapable of making sensible strategic decisions, should the Allies by then have abandoned all thought of trying to have him assassinated? Could or should any of the other leading Nazis on the Little Foxley hit-list have been killed? What would have been the cost in reprisals – probably more bloodbaths like those conducted by the Gestapo after Heydrich's assassination in 1942 – if Hitler or one of his principal henchmen had been liquidated? These questions were not easy to answer in SOE's Baker Street headquarters during the war. Neither are they now by ourselves in peacetime more than half a century after the event.

It was always acknowledged by Section X and the German Directorate, as well as in Whitehall and Washington, that all the members of the Nazi regime were usually so heavily guarded that it would have been extraordinarily difficult to assassinate any one of them. As the Führer was by far the most closely protected of them all, the final version of the plan to kill him, containing much detail, would have been especially hard to devise. The man given the assignment would have had to be aware, like Captain Bennett, that the mission might result in his own death.

To try to understand what motivated Hitler, and to help what-might-have-been speculators to decide whether Operation Foxley could or should have been attempted, it is necessary to look at what is now known about Hitler's formative early years, his personality and his lifestyle as dictator.

Adolf Hitler was the fourth child of the third marriage of an Austrian customs officer, Alois Hitler (1837–1903), who had been born illegitimately and given his mother's surname, Schicklgruber (sometimes spelt 'Schickelgruber'). It was only when Alois Schicklgruber was in his thirties that he had himself renamed Hitler, the surname of his probable father. As a boy, Adolf was deeply embarrassed by any mention of his father's original surname, which sounded rather like that of a minor character in a comic opera. From the future dictator's point of view, it was fortunate that the name change had been made. 'Heil Schicklgruber!' might well have raised more than a few laughs among the world's newspaper readers if Berlin correspondents had reported it as having been the rousing declaration of loyalty by the regimented masses at the Nuremberg Rallies.

Hitler was born on 20 April 1889, in the little Austrian border town of Braunau-am-Inn; Bavaria was on the other side of the River Inn. The ancestors of both his parents lived in the Waldviertel (woodlands) of Lower Austria where many of the people were dour and suspicious of outsiders and where mental illness and inbreeding were common. His mother (née Klara Pölzl) was pallid, hardworking and almost illiterate. She was twenty-three years younger than her husband and before marrying him had been successively his domestic servant and mistress. She was also his niece. She adored Adolf, although she did admit that he was 'moonstruck', and she indulged him as much as she was able to. In contrast, his father was a tyrant within the home and, at least from shortly after his early retirement from the customs service in 1895, was a heavy drinker. As well as making liberal use of corporal punishment, he had a waspish tongue, which was directed mainly at humiliating Adolf and his half-brother Alois, junior. At an early age the future Führer developed his never-modified belief that life was a constant struggle in which the strong had the undeniable right to dominate the weak. (This belief he was to express in a speech made at Kulmbach on 5 February 1928: 'The idea of struggle is as old as life itself. In this struggle, the more able win while the less able, the weak, lose. Struggle is the father of all things. . . . It is not by the principles of humanity that man lives or is able to preserve himself above the animal world, but solely by means of the most brutal struggle.')

When Adolf was eleven years old he declared his wish to be an artist when he grew up, and, according to his version of what happened, his father countered by harping on the benefits of a civil service career. Hitler later wrote in *Mein Kampf*: 'I did not want to become a civil servant, no, and again no. All attempts on my father's part to inspire me with the love or pleasure in this profession by stories from his own life accomplished the exact opposite. I . . . grew sick to my stomach at the thought of sitting in an office, deprived of my liberty, ceasing to be master of my own time and being compelled to force the content of my whole life into paper forms that had to be filled out. . .' The future dictator reacted to his dictatorial father by refusing to study at the high school in Linz which he then attended.

In Munich in 1923, when Hitler was on trial for treason because of his part in the Beer-hall Putsch, one of his former teachers at the high school, Professor Eduard Huemer, gave evidence for the defence. 'Hitler', he said, 'was certainly gifted, although only in particular subjects. However, he lacked self-control and, to say the least, he was considered argumentative, autocratic, self-opinionated and bad tempered, and unable to submit to school discipline. Nor was he industrious. Otherwise he would have achieved much better results, gifted as he was.' Hitler's examination marks at the high-status Linz high school were so low that he was made to transfer to the less prestigious high school at Steyr. His stay there was brief. His last school report, in September 1905, gave him 'adequate' or 'satisfactory' marks in seven subjects and 'excellent' in free-hand drawing. He was so exhilarated by the prospect of leaving school that he got drunk.

In a private conversation when he was Führer, Hitler recalled his school days and heaped puerile abuse on almost all his teachers. For example, he said on 7 September 1942: 'Our teachers were absolute tyrants. They had no sympathy with youth; their one object was to stuff our brains and turn us into erudite apes like themselves.'[3] He did, however, lavishly praise one of his former teachers, Dr Leopold Poetsch, a German nationalist whose extreme views and demagogic oratorical style he found inspiring. He wrote in *Mein Kampf*:

> . . . he was able not only to hold our attention by his dazzling eloquence but to carry us away with him. Even today I think back with genuine emotion on this grey-haired man who, by the fire of his words, sometimes made us forget the present; who, as if by magic, transported us into times past and, out of the millennium mists of time, transformed dry historical facts into vivid reality. There we sat, often aflame with enthusiasm, sometimes even moved to tears. . . . He used our budding national fanaticism as a means of educating us, frequently appealing to our sense of national honour. This teacher made history my favourite subject. And indeed, though he had no such intention, it was then that I became a young revolutionary.

In his late teens Hitler idled away much of his time, day-dreaming and taking long walks by himself. A joyless youth, pale and often ailing, he saw enemies everywhere and frequently picked arguments with all and sundry. His only solace was in reading books on German history and mythology, borrowing large numbers of them from libraries. In October 1907 he failed the entrance examination to the Vienna Academy of Fine Arts – the first of two demoralising blows to the would-be artist. 'Test drawing unsatisfactory,' the examiners' report said. In 1908 he again tried to enter the academy. This time he was not even allowed to sit the examination. At a preliminary viewing his drawings were dismissed as unacceptable.

His mother having died of cancer in December 1907, Hitler's morale was at rock bottom until the start of the First World War. Although unquestionably poor during this period, he refused opportunities to learn a trade or to take any sort of regular employment. He also rejected a suggestion that he should apply to train to be an architect. Instead of accepting any of these offers, he did all manner of casual unskilled work, such as carpet-beating, portering and shovelling snow. He claimed that he was often destitute and hungry. 'Hunger was then my faithful bodyguard; . . . My life was a continual struggle with this pitiless friend,' he was to write in *Mein Kampf.* But his 'hunger' – probably occasionally real – never caused him to accept regular manual work, which he despised with a lower-middle-class scorn. However, he did often earn small sums through drawing sketches of important buildings in Vienna. He also produced posters for shopkeepers advertising goods such as 'Teddy's Perspiration Powder'. Despite his anti-Semitic passion, he readily accepted gifts from individual Jews who befriended him.

In May 1913, Hitler left Vienna and settled in Munich, but his lot did not improve. However, with the outbreak of war in August 1914, he joined the German army. This was one of the few occasions when this hater of religion prayed, even mentioning his doing so in *Mein Kampf.* He was exhilarated by the thought of joining in the conflict and by his deliverance from poverty and from a long run of personal failure that had seemed to have no foreseeable end.

Hitler's war record was outstanding. He was awarded two Iron Crosses. Wounded twice and attaining corporal's rank, he was a brave soldier but an odd one. He never requested leave. He never received personal letters and gifts. He never spoke about women. Most extraordinary of all, he never complained about the filth, rats and lice in the trenches, or indeed about anything. While others cursed their predicament, he kept silent, speaking out only to make stilted declarations of patriotism.

After 1918 Hitler was angered by what he regarded as various unexpected outcomes of the Armistice. All the targets of his hatred, particularly the Jews, seemed to him to be having their own way. Everything appeared chaotic, as much indeed was. In Bavaria, to which he returned at the end of November 1918, the

King had abdicated and there was a short-lived 'people's republic' led by a Jew, Kurt Eisner.

Countering all this, extreme right-wing elements in the army were soon violently into politics. To his delight, Hitler was retained by his Bavarian regiment to investigate the activities of political parties. In a routine assignment, he visited a small group of nationalists calling themselves the German Workers' Party. He joined the party in September 1919. Within two years he was its leader and had changed its name to the National Socialist German Workers' Party, abbreviated to Nazi. He found he had a talent for rabble-rousing oratory and, for the first time in his life, he felt self-confident – brashly so. By January 1933, he was Chancellor of Germany.

Hitler was an extreme example of one sort of mixed-up person to be found nowadays dominating the scene in many a German beer-hall, British pub or American bar. Such a man, regarded by most people as a bore to be ignored if possible, was an under-achiever at school but has subsequently read widely about one or two subjects about which he has an obsessive interest. However, although he has no real depth of intellect, there is nothing that this wearisome fellow will not express an opinion on. He preaches stridently on all manner of subjects that he knows little or nothing about. He oversimplifies issues that are complex and is intolerant of those who try to correct his misconceptions. He mistakes his own unverified assertions for established fact. He has a set of prejudices that he has held since childhood and is determined to retain, despite cast-iron evidence that they are baseless. Whole countries, ethnic communities, social classes, professions and interest groups he denounces with relish. He thinks entirely in black-and-white terms; for him there are no shades of grey. He is sometimes excitable and always tries to use his forceful personality to browbeat, mesmerise or cajole his listeners into accepting his opinions.

As the boy Adolf had hated school, so the adult Hitler hated routine office work and the reading of official documents. In his view, that sort of thing should be done by lesser mortals, not by great strategic thinkers like himself. Although presented to the world by Dr Goebbels as the quick and infallible maker of decisions, the Führer was in reality often indecisive. Sometimes he agonised for weeks or even months over fairly unimportant matters. When circumstances demanded swift action, he was often influenced unduly by the last member of his entourage who spoke to him or by one who grabbed his attention through making an obsequious remark. There was an art in knowing the right time to speak to him. As Alan Bullock, the historian, writes in *Hitler: A Study in Tyranny*: 'Ministerial skill in the Third Reich consisted in making the most of a favourable hour or minute when Hitler made a decision, this often taking the form of a remark thrown out casually, which then went its way as an "Order of the Führer".'

Throughout his twelve years as dictator Hitler never knowingly issued an instruction that would undermine his personal authority or diminish him even slightly in the eyes of the German people and armed forces. His own survival at the top was always his paramount concern. He was a believer in divide and rule. In his book *How We Squandered the Reich*, Reinhard Spitzy describes how Hitler played off one regime member against another:

> He never allowed any of his colleagues to become too big for his boots, and it was only with the utmost reluctance that he permitted the others to ostracise one of their number who had fallen into disfavour. A balance of power was more important to Hitler than anything. Hitler saw to it that there were two occupants for every post and every position. There was a Reich Minister for Justice and a Reich Law Führer; there was a Reich Foreign Minister, but also agencies such as the Dienststelle Ribbentrop, the Auslandsorganisation der NSDAP and Rosenberg's Aussenpolitisches Amt whose heads concerned themselves with questions of foreign policy. It pleased Hitler immensely to see organisations which dealt with similar issues engage in feuds with one another. For only in such circumstances, so he believed, would he be able to maintain his independence from the specialised ministries. . . . Those who had become too powerful he gladly cut down to size; to those who were stranded out on a limb he extended a hand and helped them back onto their feet.[4]

Clearly, Hitler knew how to show restraint when it was the means of preventing any challenge to his leadership. Equally clearly, his idiosyncratic style of government was grossly inefficient. At least when staying at the Berghof, he was a late riser and generally had a routine that did not encourage hard work. Herbert Döhring, major-domo at the Berghof for seven years, said that in the mid-1930s the Führer gave as little as two to three hours a day to running the Third Reich.[5]

In view of all that was known about Hitler, it is unsurprising that there were differing opinions at SOE headquarters in 1944 about whether to continue planning Operation Foxley. According to one school of thought, an assassination of the Führer might have devastated the Nazis and shorted the European war. The opposite view was that Hitler, the great strategic blunderer, was making a valuable contribution to the Allied war effort and should therefore be allowed to continue doing so.

Do you, the reader, think that Operation Foxley or any of the Little Foxley projects should have been attempted? In answering that question you would, of course, have to bear in mind that everybody on the Allied side, civilians as well as military, realised by the autumn of 1944 that the end of the European conflict was in sight. There was clearly not much war left in which to gather intelligence for any particular assassination scheme and to find and train the agents who would be given the assignments.

If a Foxley or Little Foxley project had ever been authorised, SOE headquarters would have had the terrible responsibility of deciding whether the death of one leading Nazi could be politically, militarily and morally justified, bearing in mind that, even near the end of the war, the Gestapo might react to the assassination by massacring all and sundry.

Gestapo revenge was savage, even for the killing of Nazis less important than the principal Little Foxley targets. The most ghastly bloodbath was that which followed the assassination of Heydrich in 1942, SOE's Operation Anthropoid. The first to be executed were 1,331 Czechoslovaks. The actual assassins, together with 120 Czechoslovak resistance members who were hiding in a Prague church, were besieged there and killed. Three thousand Jews from the Theresienstadt ghetto were deported for extermination; and 152 Berlin Jews, some of the few remaining in the city, were executed on Goebbels' orders. The bloodbath was completed with the destruction of the small Czech villages of Lidiče and Lezaky. Lidiče's 198 male inhabitants and 7 of its women were executed; 184 other women in the village were sent to Ravensbrück concentration camp, and 98 children were abducted.

The only assassinations that did not result in massive reprisals were those of people in the occupied countries who had appalling records of collaboration with the Nazis. At the request of Norway's government-in-exile, SOE planned to destroy the Rinnan-Grande Group, comprised of notorious collaborators who operated between Oslo and Nordland in the service of the Gestapo. In October 1944, SOE headquarters in London persuaded Ivar Naes, who had taken part in previous SOE operations, to assassinate Ivar Grande, co-leader of the group. For several nights Naes hid outside Grande's house in the Alesund area, hoping to kill him as he arrived home. However, that plan was abandoned when it was learned that Grande always returned home in daylight, following an incident in which he had been threatened at night. Naes then tried to break into the house and throw handgrenades at Grande. But the collaborator escaped to a safe place when his dog barked, warning him that a would-be intruder was in the garden. It was then proposed to shoot Grande with a silenced pistol as he left Gestapo headquarters in Oslo. This plan had to be dropped too because the collaborator reportedly wore protective armour. Finally, in December 1944, two other SOE agents in a stolen car chased Grande as he cycled home in the late afternoon. They riddled him with bullets from a silenced Sten gun.

Grande was, of course, extremely small fry compared to Hitler and the other leading Nazis targeted by Section X and the German Directorate. But killing this unguarded Norwegian traitor proved to be far from easy, showing that even the seemingly simplest assassination project needed careful planning. Foxley-style operations often failed for all manner of reasons. The 'target' might cancel an appointment or change his travel plans at short notice, as Hitler often did. He might be even more effectively guarded than the plotters had expected. Other unpredictable difficulties might occur, like those described in Appendix B, 'No shortage of would-be assassins'. The planning of Operation Foxley and the Little Foxleys had nothing in common with the fantasy world of James Bond.

**Tailpiece:** Independent of SOE and SIS, a few American intelligence officers were in 1943 beginning to consider whether Hitler might be killed. They thought it worth at least briefly examining an offer by Egon Hansfstaengl to be the assassin. This young man, the refugee son of the Führer's former foreign press chief, suggested that he might be allowed into the Berghof if he said he was bringing a message from his father, also in exile. He thought that, as Hitler's godson who had often met him in the past, he might be granted the privilege of a private audience with the Führer. He would kill him – and presumably be arrested and executed. However the young man's proposal was soon dismissed as unrealistic. There was also, in 1944, a similarly bizarre plan by several OSS research officers to drive Hitler mad. These officers, dubbed 'the choirboys' suggested that American aircraft should drop around the Burghof a quantity of pornographic literature discrediting the Führer. This proposal was also soon rejected.[6]

# Chapter Ten
## *The SOE plotters*

Section X, responsible from 18 November 1940, for SOE activities in Germany and Austria, gets scant coverage, or none at all, in most of the many books and press articles on the Special Operations Executive written since the 1950s. Some of the authors of this still burgeoning literature acknowledge that SOE operations in Germany were often thwarted by the omnipresent Gestapo's systematic and ruthless persecution of every expression of opposition to the Nazi dictatorship. In that dire situation and with Goebbels in total control of all official means of influencing German public opinion, Section X (or the German Directorate as it was called from 30 October 1944) has been assessed by even some authoritative historians and journalists as having achieved little or nothing.

However, judging from biographical information provided by the Foreign and Commonwealth Office,[1] the members of Section X and the German Directorate, together with other SOE staff working closely with them, made a much bigger contribution to the war effort than was hitherto believed.

For example, Lieutenant-Colonel Ronald H. Thornley, was highly praised in a confidential report on his leadership of Section X from January 1941, until the formation of the German Directorate, of which he became deputy head.

The report says:

. . . Colonel Thornley has had an extremely difficult task but he has given to it abounding energy and his work has certainly borne fruit. He has been responsible for undermining the German will to resist in a number of ways and his ingenuity and resourcefulness have enabled SOE to put into operation a great variety of plans, all of which have contributed to the disorganisation of the German regime. In addition to a continuous campaign of forged documents and forged instructions to members of the German armed forces, propaganda campaigns and other subversive attacks, agents have been collected, trained and despatched to carry out sabotage and establish communications.

Perhaps the best tribute to the work that Colonel Thornley has done can be found in many captured German documents which have shown that the subversive attacks which have been launched from this country have caused the German authorities the greatest possible annoyance and dislocation.

In a long and very often thankless task Colonel Thornley has kept up the pressure and never flagged in his determination to bring his work to a successful conclusion.

Washington publicly recognised Thornley's – and indirectly his department's – significant contribution to defeating the Nazi tyranny. In 1948 he received the United States's Bronze Star and Medal of Freedom with Bronze Palm.

Born in December 1909, Thornley (1909–1986) graduated from Cambridge University in 1931 in modern European history, French and German. From then until the outbreak of war he gained an extensive knowledge of Germany, Austria and other European countries through his work as a businessman. He volunteered for military service in 1939 and at an SOE staff training course at Brickendonbury Manor (Station XVII) scored the higest marks. After being demobilised on 1 October 1945 he returned to the commercial world, completing a successful career as managing director of Ideal Standard, Hull.

Unfortunately, SOE's far from complete personnel records reveal little or nothing about many of the other staff of Section X and the German Directorate. However, from the patchy information from the SOE archives and from other sources, it is clear that this secret organisation's specialists on German and Austrian affairs were astute and well informed.

In addition to Thornley, the long-serving officers of Section X included Major William Field-Robinson and Captain A. Kier, both of whom joined it in July 1941. SOE's surviving personnel records say nothing about Field-Robinson. But a file on Kier (born in August 1910) shows that he was a 'conducting officer', having joined SOE from Intelligence Corps field security. In March 1942 he took a group of Germans to Cairo, and in September 1944, when back in Britain, he organised unspecified *coup de main* operations. In July 1945, he joined the Foreign Office's Political Intelligence Department.

By 1944 Section X had fifteen officers and a few other staff. When formed in 1940 it was run by only five people, including its then leader, Lieutenant-Colonel Brien Clarke.

With the symbol AD/X, Major-General Gerald Templer, the future field marshal, headed the German Directorate. He had twenty-six officers, together with secretaries, on his central staff, with others contributing to the work of the Directorate when needed. The most important officers included Templer's deputy, Thornley (AD/X.1), Field-Robinson (X/GER), Kier (X/GER.1), Captain A.H. Campbell (X/GER.2), Miss E.B. Graham-Stamper (X/AUS), Mrs (Clara) Marguerite Holmes (X/AUS.1), Major John Forrest Hayward (X/INT), Major G. Prentice (X/S, formerly X/PLANS), Major Leopold Herman Manderstam (X/PLANS), Captain Francis Boothroyd (X/DOC) and Mrs Diana Davenport (X/DOC.1), a lieutenant (by March 1945 a captain), who for cover purposes was a member of the First-Aid Nursing Yeomanry (FANY).[2]

Templer joined SOE after convalescing from serious wounds inflicted in Italy in extraordinary circumstances. As commander of the 6th Armoured Division leading the advance towards Florence in August 1944, he was driving up to the front when a lorry, carrying a looted piano, pulled off the road to let him pass and ran over a mine. Debris from the resulting explosion struck Templer's back, crushing one vertebra and damaging two others. In great pain he was given emergency hospital treatment and in September he returned to Britain in plaster. Gubbins, an old friend of Templer's, learned of his plight and brought him into SOE. It seems this was done with the minimum of formality – as sometimes happened when staff were recruited.

However, it was an appropriate appointment, as in 1938 the then brevet Lieutenant-Colonel Templer served in the War Office's Military Intelligence Directorate. After the start of hostilities in September 1939, he was appointed Chief of Staff to Major-General F. Noel Mason-Macfarlane, the head of military intelligence at GHQ in France.

The postwar career of Field Marshal Sir Gerald Templer (1898–1976) is too well known to require recalling in detail. He is mainly remembered as the High Commissioner and Director of Operations in the former Federation of Malaya from 1952 to 1954, being the chief strategist in the defeat of the communist insurgency there. He ended his military service at the top, as Chief of the Imperial General Staff from 1955 to 1958.

The German Directorate staff under Templer's control were from various backgrounds and had special talents. For example, Mrs Holmes (born in January 1895, and briefly married to a planter in Kenya) had worked for many years before the war in Austria, Switzerland and Czechoslovakia. Her knowledge of Austria, particularly of its socialist movement, was profound.

For some months after joining SOE she helped in smuggling large quantities of forged documents and other 'black' propaganda material into Austria and Germany. This involved her making long, tiring and dangerous journeys through France, carrying heavy 'luggage' which she delivered to various contacts in border areas. When France fell this activity became impossible, and Mrs Holmes – in the words of an SOE commendation of her work – 'put at our disposal her most extensive knowledge of reliable and unreliable elements inside Austria'. This information was of 'the greatest value' to SOE in 'the difficult task of penetrating Austria from the neighbouring countries'. Mrs Holmes also played a key role in the recruitment and briefing of agents, and became an expert writer of letters in code. She was one of several female staff officers who did outstandingly efficient work for SOE – an organisation which was ahead of its time in having no sexist reluctance to give women responsible jobs.

Educated at Oxford University and the London School of Economics, Major Hayward (born in February 1916) did economic research work for Courtaulds for eighteen months. With a commission in the Royal Army Service Corps, he joined SOE's L (Intelligence) Section in April 1941. Later, he liaised with the Political Warfare Executive in the preparation of propaganda material and the compilation of a sabotage handbook for PWE. In March 1944, he joined Section X as X/DOC, that symbol being changed to X/INT eight months later. According to an SOE report on Hayward's 'most valuable service', he made himself into an expert forger of German documents and became an authority on German uniforms, travel regulations and administrative matters. His knowledge of forgery was so extensive that even SIS had come to him for advice and he had provided MI9 with the faked documents used by several British prisoners of war when escaping from Germany. In July 1945, Hayward joined the staff of the Allied Control Commission in Germany to do work related to monuments and the arts.

Major Manderstam was born in Riga in July 1901. Originally Latvian, he became a South African citizen in 1928. A scientist, he graduated from Riga University in 1924, having also studied at Moscow and Jena Universities. Between 1926 and 1941 he held posts of chief chemist, chief engineer, technical manager and consulting engineer in major companies in Johannesburg, Lourenço-Marques (today's Maputo) and London. He joined SOE in March 1941. As head of its Angola mission from June to November that year, he suborned the crew of a Vichy ship, the *Gazcon*, in Lobito harbour. This operation, resulting in the delivery of this vessel to the Royal Navy, earned him the MBE. Between September 1942 and March 1944 he engaged in special missions related to Spain, Portugal and

Portuguese East Africa, as well as infiltrating Russian agents into northern Italy (Operation Pickaxe). He served as X/PLANS from November 1944, until the end of his SOE service in August 1945. His languages included German, Russian, Afrikaans, Portuguese and French.

A Cambridge graduate in French, German and economics and the owner of a second-hand bookshop, Captain Boothroyd (born in July 1913) joined Section X in June 1943 as X/1. Later successively X/INT and X/DOC.1, he was X/DOC in the German Directorate, in charge of agents' documentation and the preparation of their cover stories. Signing off from SOE in October 1945, he was posted to the Intelligence Corps depot.

Trained in parachuting, Mrs Davenport (born in June 1918) was an officer in SOE's F (French) Section before joining the German Directorate. She had previously been a motor transport driver, including for the American army, and had worked for the Foreign Office. She signed off from SOE in September 1945.

Like the officers, the German Directorate's secretarial staff were talented and from various backgrounds, judging from the surviving personnel files in the SOE archives. For example, Mrs Paula Graham (born in July 1912) was commended for her 'first rate' service in SOE from 23 August 1941 to 30 December 1945. A member of a Scottish Jewish family of Latvian origin, her various jobs included being X/GER.C, Field-Robinson's personal assistant.

A few senior staff officers who never belonged to Section X or the German Directorate contributed regularly to the planning of SOE operations in Germany and Austria. Such men included Air Commodore Archibald Robert Boyle (1887–1949), Air Vice-Marshal Alan Patrick Ritchie (born in April 1899), Brigadier Eric Edward Mockler-Ferryman (1896–1978), William Evelyn Houstoun-Boswall (1892–1960), Colonel Francis Thomas Davies (born in December 1906) and (Malcolm) Patrick Murray (1905–1979).

Boyle (A/CD) was SOE's Director of Security, the member of its Council in charge of formal dealings with SIS and MI5. Starting his career in the army in 1907, he won two Military Crosses in the First World War. However, for about twenty years after 1918 he worked in air intelligence, initially with the RAF and later as a civilian in the Air Ministry.

Ritchie (AD/A) was SOE's Air Adviser and an ex-officio member of its Council from 24 February 1944 to 31 July 1945. He joined the Royal Flying Corps in 1917 and had a long and varied career in the RAF. He was awarded the Air Force Cross when commanding a flight in southern Russia in 1919–20. After graduating from the RAF Staff College in 1928, he had two spells of duty in Khartoum and from June 1937 to November 1939, he headed the Combined Army and RAF Intelligence Service in Palestine. Between January 1940 and his joining SOE he was briefly in charge of RAF Intelligence in France and then held staff or command posts, the last being Air Officer Commanding 93 Group, Bomber Command. Lord Selborne, Minister of Economic Warfare from February 1942, described Ritchie (in his personal file) as 'a man of outstanding ability and indefatigable in work . . . [with] an extremely quick mind and one that goes deep'.

Mockler-Ferryman, nicknamed 'The Moke', was head from March 1943 to the summer of 1944 of SOE's London Group, which coordinated operations in north-western Europe. He too was a Council member. A former artillery officer with an MC from the First World War, he was, before joining SOE, Eisenhower's head of intelligence for the landings in French North Africa in November 1942. His war service was recognised with British, US, French, Belgian and Dutch awards. Gubbins said of him in an SOE report: 'Quiet, efficient and firm, he . . . directs his operations with marked skill, enthusiasm and initiative.'

Houstoun-Boswall, created KCMG in 1949, was SOE's Political Adviser (K/POL) and an ex-officio Council member from August 1943 to the autumn of 1944. A holder of the MC and the Croix de Guerre from the First World War, he was a career diplomat with worldwide experience, including service in five European countries and Japan. In 1935 he studied at the Imperial Defence College.

Recruited from MI(R), Tommy Davies – as he was known to fellow Council members – was SOE's Director of Research, Development and Supply (AD/Z). Like his father, General Sir Francis Davies, he made his mark militarily, but in irregular warfare. In the 1930s he had travelled widely through his export work for Courtaulds. Shortly after joining the Grenadier Guards he participated with Gubbins in the British military mission to Poland in September 1939. During a flight from there to the Baltic States his plane was fired upon by both the invading Germans and the defending Poles. Later, he delivered essential stores to Romania in preparation for the planned destruction of the Romanian oilfields. This task involved him in a risky journey by flying boat from Britain via Alexandria. He was sent abroad on other secret missions early in the war. In Yugoslavia he gathered a mass of valuable information about its munitions production. He also made operational trips to the Middle East and Norway. Then, in the most hazardous of his missions, he entered

Holland during the Nazi invasion and organised the destruction of strategically important documents held by Dutch banks.

Murray (D/CD), formerly a senior official in the Air Ministry, was Gubbins's administrative deputy from November 1943 and a Council member.

Not least among the planners of operations in Germany was Gubbins himself (1896–1976). His heavy worldwide responsibilities as the last and most distinguished of the three successive Chiefs of SOE (CD), did not prevent him from keeping a close watch from 1944 on the various schemes to kill Hitler and other leading Nazis. Like Mockler-Ferryman, Gubbins was awarded the MC in the First World War when an artillery officer. After two spells in the War Office (1931–2 and 1935–7), he was the Chief of Staff of the British military mission to Poland in the summer of 1939. In May 1940, he commanded a new sort of specialist assault troops, the Independent Companies, later renamed the Commandos. Landing clandestinely in Norway, they harassed the flanks and lines of communication of the invading German army. Shortly after this Gubbins was made responsible for raising a network of small guerrilla groups, called Auxiliary Units. These would have been mobilised if Hitler had invaded England, as he indeed intended to do for a while in 1940 in his proposed Operation Sealion.

Colin McVean Gubbins served in SOE from November 1940 until it was disbanded on 30 June 1946. He was well qualified for the key posts that he held in it: initially in charge of training and operations policy, later as Vice-Chief (V/CD) and from September 1943 as Chief (CD). A student of unorthodox warfare, he was also an accomplished linguist, fluent in German and French and able to read Russian. His marked diplomatic skills served him well in his negotiations with all sorts of Allied political and military authorities, not least the governments-in-exile. A small wiry Scottish Highlander, he was an exceptionally inspiring leader.

Major-General Sir Colin Gubbins, as he eventually became, was loaded with honours, including the DSO (1940), the KCMG (1946) and similar awards from the United States, France, Poland, Norway, Denmark, Belgium, Holland and Greece. British officers were normally not allowed to accept more than four foreign decorations, but the postwar Prime Minister, Clement Attlee, waived that rule in the case of Gubbins.

# Chapter Eleven
## *Sabotage without explosions*

Shortly after the end of the war in Europe, senior SOE staff officers wrote potted histories of the Executive's country sections. The history of Section X and German Directorate has little to say about Operation Foxley and the Little Foxleys. The rest of the text describes the organisation of sabotage and the dissemination of black propaganda. It would seem, therefore, that the lively debates on how or even whether to undertake the Foxleys did not dig deep into the time spent on planning the section's less controversial projects.

SOE headquarters staff, especially those dealing with the operations in Germany and Austria, believed strongly in what they called 'administrative sabotage'. By that they meant the causing of as much disruption as possible to selected parts of the Third Reich's government bureaucracy. Section X hoped thereby to demoralise officials, undermine people's trust in the Nazi administrative system and cause chaos generally – just what Hitler did not want when waging aggressive war.

The sort of administrative sabotage considered least difficult to begin organising in late 1940 was the distribution of forged ration cards. Section X recognised, as a policy document said, that Germany had 'come to rely on its elaborate administrative system' in the rationing of both food and clothing. There was already some ration-card forging in Germany, presumably by common criminals, and at least one person had been sentenced to death for using a counterfeit card. Clearly, any cards handled by Section X agents would have to be top-quality replicas which shops and the bureaucracy would accept as genuine.

In January 1941, X officers deduced from intelligence reports that the supply situation in Germany was suffering a seasonal decline and that traffic in various sorts of forged ration cards was growing. It was therefore decided that the section should investigate how to exploit that trend. The officers reasoned that as soon as the cards began appearing on the market in large numbers, local organisers of the rationing system might find themselves overloaded with unexpected extra work. This was the least that might happen. At most, it was hoped that – in the words of a Section X minute – 'doubt might be thrown on the whole basis of rationing'.

By February the section had made a thorough study of the Nazi German rationing system and had seen examples of all the various cards in use. The X officers then began planning Operation Rosebush – a 'gift' to the Third Reich of 100,000 replicas of the clothes ration cards currently being issued in Hamburg and valid until 31 August 1941. SIS, which in February was still the producer of forged documents used by SOE, was asked to supply the cards. This it did, but only after questioning the usefulness of the operation and raising other objections, all of which took time to answer. It was then found that SOE's own channels into Germany, as yet far from fully developed, could not handle as many as 100,000 cards. The Air Ministry's help was therefore requested and RAF aircraft dropped the cards – together with their bombloads – during raids on Hamburg and the Ruhr in July and August 1941.

Despite the snags and delays encountered during its planning, the operation was successful. It was attacked in the Nazi Press and the disruption it caused to local administrations was later revealed by German prisoners of war during routine interrogations. On 25 October 1941, Munich newspapers reported that the clothing cards were now made from a new sort of watermarked paper. On 23 April 1942, a special local mouthpiece of the Nazi Party, the *Westdeutscher Beobachter* (circulation 237,000) belatedly revealed that a couple had been imprisoned for using part of a forged card. Much later still, in September 1943, Section X learned from a Norwegian student that Operation Rosebush had had a chaotic effect on the clothing trade of the targeted German towns.

In subsequent ration-card operations the PWE did the forging, sometimes with advice from SOE scientists and other specialists. Formed in the summer of 1941, PWE was perfectly equipped for this task, largely because of the fortunate accident that it had obtained a complete set of the Gothic type used by all German government departments. In the early days of the Hitler regime the Monotype Corporation had won an international competition to provide the type. The company supplied each of the government departments with a set but made an extra one for itself. By chance Ellic Howe, when a sergeant-major at Britain's Anti-Aircraft Command HQ, was shown this set. He and the Gothic type were soon transferred to PWE.

The success of Rosebush encouraged Section X to plan Operation Grog, a much bigger and potentially more damaging act of 'administrative sabotage', as it related to food rationing. For Grog

PWE printed about 250,000 forgeries of a special issue of ration cards used only by soldiers on leave. These counterfeits covered periods of two, six or seven days and were stamped as if issued by the food offices of each of the selected towns over which they were dropped by RAF Bomber Command between February and April 1943. Some while later, interrogated German prisoners of war revealed that shops in the towns targeted in February had been completely cleaned out of food by those people lucky enough to have picked up the cards. In mid-March the authorities in Essen ordered soldiers to report to local food offices to ensure that their ration cards bore official stamps which were properly dated, and retailers were instructed not to accept loose ration coupons. Similar orders were issued by the Nazi occupation authorities in Eupen, a Belgian manufacturing town near the border with Germany.[1]

Section X was becoming even more ambitious and had apparently long since abandoned any thought of using its own land-based agents to smuggle forged ration cards and coupons into Germany. In X's next operation, codenamed Pack, Bomber Command dropped about 100 million coupons (in sheets of 100) of the sort contained in food ration cards issued only to travellers. This delivery, in August and September 1943, was over a large area of Germany. Nazi Press reports in September and October described any use of such forgeries as 'tantamount to sabotage' deserving the severest punishment. According to information that eventually reached Section X, the food supply situation in Essen was seriously disrupted after the dropping of travellers' meat coupons on 30 September.

Operation Sleuth, Section X's next venture, was a fivefold enlargement of Pack. About 500 million of the travellers' food coupons were dropped between December 1943 and August 1944, but this time the United States Army Air Forces and the RAF took part. The Nazi authorities paid a back-handed compliment to the PWE forgers. As the Kripo, the criminal police, commented in documents found after the war,[2] these coupons were 'extremely dangerous forgeries' that traders found difficult to detect. In many areas Operation Sleuth completely disorganised the rationing system for several weeks.

The last five rations operations – codenamed Cleveden, Caldwell, Catfoss, Plateau and Fradswell – were organised by the German Directorate.

Operation Cleveden was unusual in that genuine documents were used. These were blank clothes-ration cards – albeit only 21,060 of them – that had been stolen or otherwise acquired from offices in

Eupen and Aachen. Stamped by PWE to make them seem valid, they were dropped by the RAF and USAAF over Düsseldorf in January 1945.

For Operation Caldwell the PWE forgers produced 2 million copies of a special issue of cards entitling soldiers returning from the front to obtain extra food rations. British and American bomber aircraft delivered these cards between December 1944 and February 1945. On 22 January newspapers in Hamburg published official announcements ordering off-duty soldiers to have their special ration cards stamped at food offices.

In Operation Catfoss, conducted between January and 9 March 1945, the RAF and the USAAF dropped 5 million sheets of forged special coupons sanctioning extra rations for selected civilians. As there were 12 coupons on each sheet, a total of 60 million coupons were delivered. After this operation Berlin newspapers reported that a man had been sentenced to two years' imprisonment for trying to use meat coupons that he had found after a bombing raid.

Plateau was another travellers' rations operation, like Pack and Sleuth. This time 16 million forged coupons (in sheets of sixteen) were dropped by the RAF, but it apparently did so a little behind schedule, as its last delivery was made only shortly before 4 March, the expiry date of the genuine issue of travellers' ration cards.

Various sorts of forgeries, together with some genuine ration documents, were dropped by the RAF in Operation Fradswell. The bomb loads included 1 million replicas of certificates that entitled bombed-out people to claim extra rations of food and clothing. About 200,000 of the certificates were dropped over Cologne, Dortmund, Hamburg and Munich from February to 9 March, shortly after these cities had been bombed. Also included in the deliveries were 2,000 genuine clothing cards, stamped by the PWE forgers as having been issued in Berlin. In other raids on Munich, Nuremberg and Berlin, the bombs fell along with 6,000 copies of cards entitling bombed-out citizens of these cities to articles of haberdashery. Yet other deliveries included some genuine special coupons allowing the purchase of hardware articles anywhere in Germany, and a few genuine clothing certificates for widows and infants. Operation Fradswell was, however, never completed. SHAEF decided that, in view of the Allied breakthrough, any further use of forged cards by the German people would seriously hinder the smooth working of the Allied government when it took over.

Under Gestapo supervision, German scientists studied every detail of the forgeries and wrote papers on how to detect the subtle differences between the counterfeit and genuine cards. One such document, written in Berlin on 12 April 1943, noted that the paper used in the soldiers' ration cards then being dropped on Germany (Operation Grog) was shown under ultraviolet light to have an intense fluorescence varying from pink to light brown. This compared with the genuine card's blue-violet fluoresence. Chemical tests showed that the forgeries did not react to chlorine bleaching agents, but genuine cards treated with sodium hypochloride turned yellow. Real cards had a lighter wood content. The counterfeits were made from machine-polished paper, between 0.13 mm and 0.15 mm thick, which was less smooth and slightly thicker than the genuine cards' satin-finished paper of between 0.9 mm and 0.10 mm. The scientists found that the watermarks on the forged and real cards were almost identical, but there were minute differences in representation of the national emblem and in the shape of the figure '6' on the six-day ration card. The Nazi authorities' problem of how to identify the counterfeits was, however, complicated by a few of their own cards bearing small imperfections. The Hitler regime never told the German people about these scientific findings. Members of the general public were only warned in general terms that forged and genuine ration cards were not identical in every respect. The scientists' Berlin document of 12 April 1943 concluded: 'The forged ration cards are such deceitfully good copies that single coupons cut from them cannot be recognised immediately as forgeries.'

One indicator of the success or the ration-card operations was that so few ordinary members of the German public were caught handling the forgeries, although there were, of course, more arrests than Section X and the German Directorate knew about. Another significant factor was that the threat of dire penalties did not prevent the widespread use of the counterfeits. This caused a great but unquantifiable amount of 'administrative sabotage', particularly in the last few months of the war in Europe when the Third Reich was in chaos for other reasons.

The unsung heroes and heroines of the rationing operations were the SOE agents on the ground. Without them the dropping of millions of forgeries by British and American bomber aircraft would have achieved nothing. It was the agents who regularly passed genuine ration cards out of Germany, so ensuring that the counterfeits were never easily detected as such, and that they always bore the correct dates of issue. It was the agents also who stole, or arranged the stealing, of unstamped sheets of ration-card coupons.

Shortly after it was formed in November 1940, Section X began planning not only the ration-card and ration-coupon operations but also what it called 'insaisissable sabotage'. By that it meant a great variety of small-scale destructive actions which did not look as though they had been done deliberately. All such sabotage – occurring in armaments factories and other places serving the Nazi war economy – was unspectacular. None involved the use of explosives, weapons or anything else that would attract the attention of the authorities.

Section X began infiltrating sabotage organisers into Germany in April 1941. From then until the end of the war in Europe these agents recruited a huge network of manual workers and other employees who systematically, day after day after day, did damage by stealth. In the section's opinion, every trade and profession provided its own particular opportunities for sabotage and passive resistance to the Hitlerite tyranny. The X officers, therefore, gave the sabotage organisers instructions on what insaisissable action should be taken by anti-Nazis in various workplaces.

In factories, machines should be allowed to overheat through inadequate oiling. The increasingly acute shortage of oil would be a plausible excuse for that happening. As each machine was allocated its own ration of oil, some of it might be poured away if nobody was watching. Transmission belt gearings should also be made to run hot. By so misusing only one gearing, a whole row of machines might be brought to a standstill. The transmission belts themselves should be given too little lubricant and it should be applied wastefully. When used on turning lathes, chisels should be pressed too hard, making them wear out prematurely. By running precision machinery too fast, holes and screw threads might be enlarged by a fraction of a millimetre so that they matched their counterparts but did not fit airtight or gas-tight. This would accelerate so-called 'wear and tear'. As noted in a policy statement, the X officers believed that tool grinding provided 'unending opportunities' for sabotage. For example, because of the shortage of fine metals, chisels were made partly of iron and partly of steel. If overheated and insufficiently cooled, the steel became soft and required more grinding. Much time would thus be wasted.

Section X also had instructions for factory transport workers. They should waste time asking unnecessary questions, such as about routes that they already knew well. They should also run needless errands, so wasting fuel, and should fritter away yet more time by pretending to misunderstand what the management had told them. As one X officer noted in a minute, wastage of working capacity, raw materials and fuel was 'a most important form of sabotage' and one most difficult to detect as such. Drivers of lorries carrying perishable goods were similarly instructed. They should 'lose' part of their loads or expose it to the rain. At night, when nobody was around, drivers might throw stones on rural roads used only by military vehicles. Clerks and others handling transport documents should shuffle the consignment labels of goods to be sent by road or rail. Through incorrect labelling, merchandise might arrive dozens or even hundreds of miles from its intended destination. Then the authorities would have the problem of finding out where the goods should have been sent to – and those who ordered them would be tearing their hair! Mis-labelling was a particularly effective sort of insaisissable sabotage if military supplies were being transported. When writing these instructions, Section X was advised by the ITWF.

Section X had instructions for others. For example, chauffeurs should waste petrol and oil, and make needless detours, preferably on rough roads. Miners should under-produce and send to the surface large amounts of useless rock along with their output of coal or iron ore. Agricultural workers should feed seed corn to livestock, kill too many of the animals, let machines rust in the fields, and sow seeds too deep or too late.

Foreigners conscripted for work in Hitler's 'Greater Germany' did, of course, have little chance of undertaking any large-scale sabotage, like blowing up arms factories. Section X was glad that that was so. It believed that such action by slave labourers would have resulted in savage reprisals by the Gestapo and would have added to the anxieties of the European governments-in-exile. However, according to a policy statement, insaisissable damage done frequently and in many workplaces in the Third Reich and the Nazi-occupied countries would make a 'major contribution to the war effort'. By contrast, isolated acts of spectacular sabotage, unrelated to Allied military objectives, would be 'mere pin-pricks', tending to 'render more difficult the primary task of quietly demoralising the German, who is the main [psychological] target'.

In October 1943 exiled French trade union leaders belonging to the Confédération Générale du Travail presented SOE and OSS's Labour Desk with ideas on organising French workers in Germany. This resulted in the formation of a joint committee to plan Mission Varlin, an operation in which French trade union activists would be infiltrated into the Reich to give sabotage instruction not only to their compatriot slave labourers but also to French prisoners of war doing manual work. Over the next two months an SOE operative in Switzerland smuggled into France more than 5,000 copies of two pamphlets – *Manuel du Saboteur* and *Manuel du Deporté en Allemagne* – for secret distribution in this operation. By February 1944, two Mission Varlin agents had reached Germany, but the principal one was killed. There were some small successes later. However, by August, more agents had been killed and money had been lost.

In March 1944, another French organisation, the Mouvement des Prisonniers de Guerre et Deportés (MPGD), sought help from RF, SOE's Free French section. Most of the assistance was given by RF. However, Section X supplied silk maps for use by agents, and cigarette-paper packages in which MPGD leaflets could be concealed. Reports received in SOE's London headquarters over the next few months showed that the MPGD was active.

In 1944 well over 7 million foreign civilians and prisoners of war were undergoing forced labour in Germany and Austria. The approximate corresponding totals earlier in the war were: 301,000 in 1939, 1,151,000 (1940), 3,069,000 (1941), 4,134,000 (1942) and 6,400,000 (1943). Between 1939 and 1944 the percentage of foreigners in the 'Greater German' workforce rose from 0.8 to 24. How many of these slave labourers engaged in insaisissable sabotage is, of course, unknown. Most of this 'quiet' gradual wrecking was done by French, Belgian and Dutch workers and almost all of it was undetected, despite the presence of Gestapo agents in factories and other workplaces. Russians and some of the other eastern Europeans were generally unresponsive to insaisissable sabotage propaganda or, more likely, it never reached them.

Why did SOE staff officers use the French word 'insaisissable'? Evidently they thought that no English word exactly expressed the sort of sabotage they had in mind. 'Insaisissable' means 'elusive' (for example, of a thief or a wild animal), 'imperceptible' or, in a legal context, 'privileged from seizure'.

Insaisissable action was by far the most important kind of sabotage without explosions, but there were also a few other sorts. One of these involved the use of forged documents to get foreign workers out of Germany, both for their own sakes and to reduce the labour forces of arms factories and the like.

Towards the end of 1942, SOE agents stole copies of two important German documents: the Urlaubschein (leave warrant) used by some foreign workers to travel between Germany and their home countries; and the Rueckkehrschein, a document issued by the President of the Berlin Labour Exchange either to permit a company to sack any employee, with or without good cause, or to allow a foreign worker to return to his homeland on compassionate grounds. Both documents were forged by PWE and in March 1943 various quantities of the counterfeits were given to SOE country sections for infiltration into Germany to help foreigners to try to return home. The genuine versions of these two documents would, of course, have been issued only to a minority of the foreigners employed in Germany and certainly not to those who were slave labourers. This forgery operation could therefore have never achieved much.

A rather more successful project was the distribution by SOE (and OSS) agents of itching powder for spreading on the underclothes and bedding of members of the German armed forces. The anonymous planners of this operation, who were perhaps inspired by the recollection of the pranks they played when schoolboys, hoped that the victims of their devilment would be soldiers about to go on front-line duty or submariners due soon to join their U-boats. The first consignment of itching powder was infiltrated into Switzerland in November 1941 and it reportedly had the desired painful effect when dusted on to the clothing of an unspecified number of German sailors in June 1942. In Norway, especially resourceful members of the Resistance persuaded laundry workers and others providing personal services for the occupying armed forces to spread the powder on clothing and bedding, and even inside contraceptives. Hospitals in the Trondheim area often had to treat soldiers incapacitated by serious pain to the more sensitive parts of the body. In some occupied countries, turning contraceptives into weapons was routine. Inserting the powder was a tedious task requiring the use of rubber gloves. But those so employed enjoyed their work. They maliciously relished the possible consequences of their endeavours and they sold the treated contraceptives to brothels at a good profit.

Major M.W. Royce of OSS tested the itching powder on himself – but not on where it would hurt the most. In December 1944 he reported that the powder, made of tiny barbed seeds of the mucuna plant, had caused 'burning pain' when he spread it liberally on his arms and other sturdier parts of the body. Washing did not give him much relief, and some of the powder accidentally got into one eye as a result of rubbing it. It 'seemed the eye was going blind,' he said. Royce also described what happened when the powder was supplied to eight locations in central Crete, where most of the German troops were billeted in village houses and three barracks. 'Our local Greeks, through contact men, spread the powder – thin and carefully.' This was a necessary precaution to prevent Nazi revenge action. Later, it was learned from townspeople that the Germans thought that their suffering was being caused by an unidentified pest. Some soldiers obtained ointment from their clinics and the German doctors 'did not seem to catch on'. In one operation the itching powder was used to torment selected individuals – a Greek mayor notorious for his collaboration with the occupation authorities, and a German sergeant 'known to have led atrocity parties'. The mayor, about sixty years old, had a wife aged about thirty-five who was suspected of being the sergeant's mistress. The itching powder was spread in the beds of all three of these people. As Major Royce explained, this would 'make sure it wouldn't miss'.[3]

# Chapter Twelve
## *Larger-scale wreckings*

Despite the special difficulties involved, Section X masterminded a few larger-scale sabotage operations – as many as it was able to. It was prevented from doing more by a scarcity of agents suitable for infiltration into Germany, and by the Gestapo's brutal efficiency in protecting armaments factories and other potential targets serving Hitler's war machine.

In November 1941, it began planning Operation Champagne, the infiltration into Germany of an agent to organise sabotage and subversive political activities in the Hamburg area. A candidate for the job was recommended to the X officers by the Combined Services Detailed Interrogation Centre. He had been captured when a crew member of the *Lauenburg*, a German armed trawler converted into a meteorological observation ship, which had been sunk five months earlier. This 25-year-old man had, as a youth, belonged to an anti-Nazi group called the Kittelsbach Piraten (Pirates).[1] As an adult his political views did not change and he was imprisoned several times, but was released in October 1940. He later joined the ship as a civilian apprentice to a locksmith at its base at Trondheim, Norway.

On 26 December 1941 the man – a Catholic whom Section X judged to be an idealist but 'somewhat unbalanced' – began training for his secret mission. Segregated from the nationals of Allied countries, he was instructed in demolition, the dissemination of propaganda, and the use of a letter code and invisible ink. He was also given a new identity and cover story. According to these, he had been captured by the British, to whom he had represented himself (truthfully) as being strongly anti-Nazi, and had been put in a special company of the Pioneer Corps. Later, so the cover story said, he had been poorly paid and discriminated against when working in a Dundee shipyard and had escaped to Norway from Aberdeen in a stolen fishing boat.

In reality, he was clandestinely dropped on the Norwegian coast on 20 April 1942 by a cutter that had been carried from Aberdeen by a trawler for all except the last 70 miles. The Nazi authorities believed the agent's cover story and flew him to Berlin three days later.

Section X eventually received reports that he had contacted members of the Norwegian Resistance and had organised unspecified acts of sabotage. However, the agent was never found after the war. If he had been, SOE would have had to honour its promise to help him obtain British nationality and suitable employment anywhere in the British Commonwealth.

Wrecking on a significant scale was done by an anti-Nazi German group called Lex, whose members were infiltrated from Switzerland by contacts with Section X. In July 1942, Lex did substantial damage to goods trains, aircraft factories and Gestapo barracks in the Vienna area. On 21 August near Steyr, it blew up a train loaded with artillery munitions. In September, Lex derailed and burned out a train carrying sixteen seaplanes and twelve Focke-Wulf aircraft to Kiel, and started fires in a Hamburg factory. It did much other railway sabotage in 1942 and 1943, including immobilising heavy locomotives by sawing through the screws on their axles. Early in 1943, Lex set on fire a drawing office at a Hamburg plant and destroyed twelve unassembled aircraft and several aero-engines in Bremerhaven by igniting stored fuel oil.

Section X received various scrappy pieces of information about other sabotage in Hitler's 'Greater Germany' in 1942. In May, contacts in Switzerland reported five train derailments in Ruhr towns. A month later, an attempt was made to destroy an aircraft factory near Vienna. In August, however, there was a major setback. The section's representative in Sweden had to leave the country when his cover was blown as a result of one of his sabotage contacts being arrested. But in September, informants in Switzerland reported that there had been 'sporadic' sabotage in Germany, including explosions, incendiary incidents and tampering with the axle boxes of trains.

From 1942 railway saboteurs often used a greasy substance, largely consisting of finely ground Carborundum, to wreck locomotives and other rolling stock. Indistinguishable at first glance from heavy motor oil, this substance – one of the many inventions by scientists working for SOE – was applied by agents who appeared to be lubricating any mechanical part that needed to be oiled. Far from making the components operate more smoothly, it soon caused them to seize up. This would almost certainly result in derailment if a train were travelling fast. SOE headquarters supplied quantities of this 'lubricant' in any containers or dispensers that would not arouse the suspicion of security staff. The first consignment of grease guns for subsequent delivery to Section X's railway saboteurs was smuggled into Switzerland in January 1942. Essential help in that difficult operation was given by contacts recommended to the section by the International Transport Workers' Federation.

In July 1943, Section X organised Operation Herd – the despatch of an agent to wreck the main railway lines on both sides of the River Rhine at selected points between Koblenz and Rüdesheim (at St Goar and Oberwesel on the left bank and at St Goarshausen and Kaub on the right bank). Carrying explosive charges, he was to be dropped by parachute over Germany, and after the operation he was to escape by his own means. SOE gave him special training in derailment and other railway sabotage. According to his cover story, he was a German NCO travelling on duty with a special permit to carry explosives. He was provided with money and the 'permit', together with other forged documents.

The operation was carried out successfully on the night of 15/16 July. On 27 July Section X received a telegram from Madrid saying that the agent had arrived in San Sebastian. He later travelled on to Portugal but was arrested there. However, after a few days, SOE's representative in Lisbon persuaded the police to release him, and he was flown back to Britain on 15 August.

In a debriefing, the agent described his experiences. On landing at 1 a.m. on 16 July he buried his personal belongings, but packed his parachute in his suitcase, which he later dropped in the Rhine. After walking for a few hours, he made two train journeys, arriving at Andernach between 4 and 5 a.m. The agent went from there to Leutesdorf by ferry. He then visited Frankfurt where he viewed the river, noting that tunnels in the vicinity were not guarded. To obtain ration cards, he went on by train to Munich, where he chatted to troops and civilians as if he were an ordinary soldier. After more circuitous travelling he arrived at Oberwesel railway station, went down to the river and stole a fishing boat from the quay at night, although it was not very dark. He then rowed across the river downstream to the first tunnel on the right bank. This took him five minutes. Next he tied up the boat and walked into the tunnel over about 150 railway sleepers, this taking him another five minutes. After clearing stones on either side of the track, he spent ten minutes laying explosive charges. Leaving the tunnel he went on in the boat to Oberlahnstein, arriving at dawn between 5 and 6 a.m. Landing near gardens above the town, he let the boat float away. He then walked to Nederlahnstein and, after more roundabout rail journeys via Harburg, he reached a suburb of Bremen in the evening.

The agent used his remaining explosives to destroy engines in the locomotive depot between Bingerbrueck and Bingen. He damped the charges and placed them in coal in tenders attached to the engines. After washing his hands in water leaking from a siding pump, he walked away.

His escape was as planned. He crossed from France into Spain after breaking through a barbed-wire fence near the border. There were no guards on the French side. Once over the frontier he hid in a maize field and changed into civilian clothes. He then walked on and was not spotted when he passed a man who was sheltering in a customs hut to keep out of the rain. At a police barracks further along the road, the agent stopped, showed his forged identity papers, gave the Nazi salute and was allowed to continue on his journey.

In September 1944, a special camp was opened to select German and Austrian prisoners of war who seemed suitable for clandestine work in their homelands. Assessing the work of Section X and the German Directorate, a minute-writer commented after the war: 'The camp functioned satisfactorily and a small but regular supply of recruits was obtained for our work.' The section's representative in the Middle East was then 'successfully infiltrating a flow of agents and couriers' into Austria. With them went sabotage instructions. X's representative in Sweden 'opened several very active lines' for the mass infiltration of black propaganda into Norway and northern Germany. This representative also helped to recruit and train agents, and to infiltrate organisers and couriers into Germany and saboteurs and couriers into Norway.

Officers of Section X were reluctant to send German Jews into the Third Reich. They believed, with good reason, that any captured Jewish agents would suffer the most bestial treatment in the Gestapo book. However, at least one German Jew did persuade SOE staff officers to employ him on a clandestine mission. How he did so is unrecorded. This brave man, Robert Philip Baker-Byrne, was originally named Rudolf Philipp Becker. He was born in Berlin in July 1910 and educated there. His experiences as a young man were mixed and troubled. After serving in the German cavalry in 1928 and 1929, he studied art history in Paris and was a company director from 1933 until February 1936, when he emigrated to Britain because of the persecution of the Jews. For about a year, until encountering financial difficulties, he ran a high-class dress designer's business in the West End of London. After that he gave French and German lessons, did a little acting (he played a Gestapo agent in *Night Train to Munich*) and was a waiter and bouncer in a seedy nightclub. His descent to destitution continued, and in 1938 and 1939 he was sleeping rough on the Thames Embankment.

Shortly after the start of the war he enlisted as a volunteer in the 251st Company of the Aliens' Pioneer Corps, was later promoted to corporal, and joined SOE in the spring of 1943 – at about the time that he changed his name to Baker-Byrne. During his initial training at Welwyn, Hertfordshire, in June, he – a bulky, overweight man – did not do well at anything requiring physical exertion. His performance in fieldcraft was also poor. But he was intelligent, precise in matters of detail, and was an excellent shot, although seemingly frightened of grenade explosions. Presumably his shortcomings were later corrected, for in March and April 1944, he attended a 'finishing course' at SOE's Special Training School (STS) 36 at Boarmans, Beaulieu, in Hampshire. Section X had briefed the school that he was to do 'lone-wolf type work in the field'. In July he went on an operations course at STS 45, at Hatherop Castle, Fairford, Gloucestershire. He was rated as not suitable for explosives work, good at weapons training, poor at 'toughening' ('very awkward indeed over obstacles and generally funks them and goes round'), quite good at industrial sabotage and fairly good at personal security. In November he completed parachute training at STS 51, at Dunham House, Dunham Massey, Cheshire, and Ringway, Manchester. Weighing 206 lb, he was regarded as rather heavy for parachuting, but he did well and was finally described as 'a reasonable risk under good conditions'.

While Baker-Byrne underwent all this training, his status within SOE was changing. In October 1943, he was transferred from the Pioneer Corps to the Royal Fusiliers and then formally seconded to SOE. In September 1944, he was promoted to second-lieutenant with an agent's commission.

On 26 November 1944, Baker-Byrne was sent on Operation Vivacious, whose objective was to sabotage a factory in a Berlin suburb that was making sighting controls for V2 rockets. Dropped by parachute near Eisenach, he travelled to Berlin but failed to carry out the mission. He escaped to Switzerland, from where he returned to Britain on 28 December.

On 13 April 1945, Baker-Byrne went on another training course. Although displaying the same strengths and weaknesses as before, on 25 April he was again parachuted into Germany, this time near Lübeck. His mission, named Operation Branston, was to organise sabotage and resistance either through contacts given him before departure or through some found on his own initiative. His main sabotage targets were submarine installations. He again failed to achieve anything and, after some adventures in battlefield areas, returned to Britain on 8 May – VE Day.

Baker-Byrne left SOE on 30 July to join the interpreters' pool of the Allied Control Commission in Germany. His training in the various techniques of clandestine warfare was like that given to other SOE agents. He experienced the sort of failures that many of them did. There was nothing unusual for an agent to have been unable, through no fault of his own, to successfully complete a sabotage operation. Nobody doubted Baker-Byrne's bravery and resourcefulness.

Some idea of how SOE-trained saboteurs operated (or how HQ hoped they would operate) can be gained from the briefings they were given. It is therefore worth examining one such briefing – that for Operation Chalgrove,[2] which envisaged the assassination of U-boat commanders as well as sabotage in the Hamburg area. The agent chosen for this mission, a 28-year-old German soldier taken prisoner in August 1944, was told to 'form bands of thugs' among 'his own contacts and sympathisers' and to incite dock workers and U-boat building yard workers to strike and sabotage.

A German Directorate minute dated 27 January 1945, described Operation Chalgrove as 'the most important it [the Directorate] has ever had'. The minute added:

It is known that U-boat successes depend entirely upon the quality of the commander. The murder of a few of these commanders would have a far-reaching effect on the efficiency of the U-boat arm and upon morale of the crews. If, as we hope, some of these murders are attributed to Germans, the propaganda effect will be enhanced and could be fully exploited by black propaganda, which is largely directed against the morale of U-boat crews. This operation is particularly urgent as the new U-boats will soon be ready to operate in strength.

The agent was given a false name. According to his cover story, he was a Hamburg dock worker returning there from Bremen. It was essential that his clothes and personal possessions should be 'well aged and not of a very good quality'. He was to wear a marine-style polo-neck pullover, a cap and an overcoat or raincoat, and should carry a suitcase 'not too big and well used'. The cover story described how the agent had been discharged from the Germany army for health reasons and had obtained employment in the Hamburg docks, but was sent initially to do similar work in Bermen. On 17 February 1945, he was told to report back to Hamburg, but, as he had a few days' leave, he had decided to return on foot or by hitch-hiking on lorries. SOE gave him forged documents – one issued in Bremen, ordering him back to Hamburg; together with a certificate exempting him from military service, a membership card of the German Labour Front and other labour papers, and civilian ration coupons. Hidden in his suitcase or about his person were two pistols, 100 rounds of ammunition, a compass, a penknife, a torch, a flask of brandy, a set of field army dressings, and lethal 'L' tablets (to swallow if under arrest and wishing to commit suicide rather than be tortured by the Gestapo). He was also given a large sum of Reichmarks, some to be concealed in his clothing.

The agent's supposed poor health was an important part of his cover story. If asked about his 'illness' he was to say that he had been exempted from military service in 1940 and had always been subject to pains in the head and fits of dizziness which sometimes made his arms twitch. He also sometimes suffered loss of memory. As dock workers should be at least fairly fit, he was to explain that his 'illness' was more mental than physical. The health side of his cover story partly tallied with what had really happened to him. Shortly after he had been taken prisoner he had had pneumonia and spent some time in hospital in Epsom. He was also clearly not robust. About 5 ft 7 in tall, he was nervous and excitable by nature.

It may seem strange that SOE chose such a man for an extraodinarily demanding assignment. To train for it he learned to parachute and was instructed in special killing methods and rudimentary sabotage. In his briefing, he was told to observe the movements of U-boat officers, note the cafés and places of entertainment that they visited, and 'try to kill as many of them as possible'. He was also advised that a good time to do serious damage to docked U-boats was during the chaos which followed air-raids. Such sabotage should include dropping special pills into batteries, interfering with pipes and electric leads, and placing dirt in lubricating oil. In U-boat building yards, cranes could be immobilised with charges placed inside the winch drums, on the gears or on the motor.

The agent was dropped into Germany on the night of 2/3 April – hopelessly late in the war to achieve any of the desired results. He did, however, get in touch with some fellow German Social Democrats and with some Dutchmen, and they began planning particular acts of sabotage. He made an informed contribution to such scheming, having been a skilled mechanic before he was conscripted into the German army in November 1937, and having subsequently served in a mines and explosives battalion. As instructed, he reported to the Allied authorities on VE Day. Demobilised in June 1945, he was given a lounge suit by SOE.

SOE's incomplete archives reveal little about the other Germans sent into their homeland on sabotage operations. However, according to *Gubbins and SOE*, by Peter Wilkinson and Joan Bright Astley, about twenty-eight former members of the German armed forces went on such missions during the final months of the war in Europe.[3]

# Chapter Thirteen
## *Black propaganda*

Section X and the German Directorate believed strongly in the effectiveness of anti-Nazi black propaganda. In its written form this comprised pamphlets, leaflets, posters and other material masquerading as having been produced by the civilian or military authorities of the Third Reich, or by German groups hostile to Hitlerism. However, in reality this literature originated in Britain in the clandestine printing works of the Political Warfare Executive or in other secret locations, such as some in Switzerland from May 1943.

As described in an SOE document written shortly after the war, the staff officers responsible for operations in Germany and Austria conducted a black propaganda campaign 'ruthlessly and unremittingly' from 1940 until the defeat of the Nazi dictatorship. In planning individual projects, these officers worked closely with PWE, including in helping it with the design and wording of the various kinds of literature involved. The SOE document expressed bluntly the purpose of black propaganda: to 'appeal to the lowest instincts, passions, prejudices and selfish egotisms of the German in the name of the highest ideals, in such a way that he may act [unwittingly] against the interests of the German war effort and in favour of ours and believe he is a great idealist in doing so'. To achieve this end 'a variety of plausible and subversive means' were used. The black propaganda had specific aims: to cause strife between the military and the Nazi Party, and between officers and men; to undermine military morale and discipline; to encourage soldiers and members of U-boat crews to make 'continual requests' for leave, to malinger ever more often, to desert and eventually to mutiny. Such appeals, when made to already disheartened members of the German armed forces, were particularly effective if the men concerned were waiting to be posted to front-line units or to U-boats that were inflicting heavy losses on Allied shipping. On the German home front, the propaganda aimed to 'incense the working population against the Nazi Party bosses' and to cause 'panic, confusion, fear of disease, premature evacuation from industrial areas, and a general loss of confidence in the administration'. This was ungentlemanly warfare at its most ungentlemanly.

The infiltration of black propaganda into Germany began in 1941. In July of that year non-Nazi Germans were urged to start passively resisting the regime, such as through working slowly and inefficiently in armaments factories and giving the Nazi authorities as little cooperation as possible without arousing suspicion.

In June 1942, SOE headquarters in Baker Street, London, received reports of Section X agents distributing literature describing the damage done in bombing raids on northern and western Germany – detailed information that Goebbels suppressed. Two months later, X's contacts in Switzerland reported the development of 'certain Catholic lines into Austria' through which black propaganda was being introduced. By September, according to these contacts, it had become a systematic practice in Germany to spread alarm and despondency after air raids.

In April 1943, it was reported in Stockholm that an unspecified number of German and Austrian troops had fled from Norway to Sweden – almost certainly influenced by black propaganda. However, in the same month, the infiltration of such literature from Sweden into some German ports had to be suspended because a Section X agent had been arrested and suborned by the Gestapo. In May, the large-scale printing of black propaganda in Switzerland began. But in the following month, X's activities in Sweden were further hampered by the arrest of several agents, including a local group leader. An X officer in Baker Street commented: 'The laborious task of rebuilding the shattered remains of this group was commenced.' In July, carefully concealed messages in code were smuggled into Austria by Section X's Middle East organiser. However, in August, another setback was reported, but it was one caused by the Allies rather than the Nazis! In the Hamburg area, the homes of a group of active collaborators with X had been destroyed in air raids and these people had been dispersed to other parts of Germany. There was yet more trouble in November. Section X's chief representative in Switzerland, a woman, was seriously compromised as a result of the arrest and interrogation of several of her contacts. But in December, with help from another SOE section, she managed to slip out of the country. Her journey back to Britain, by an unrevealed roundabout route, was often hazardous. Also in December, Section X began arranging parachute drops into Austria from the Middle East.

But operations into that country continued to be difficult. In February 1944, left-wing contacts reported that the work of subverting the Nazi administration in Austria was for the time being 'almost impossible'. In May, the situation became even worse with the tightening of controls on the border between Hitler's Greater Germany and Switzerland. In September, there was yet more bad news. Some agents based in Switzerland and contacts in the Sudetenland had been arrested, a radio operator dropped for infiltration into the Tyrol was reported missing, and a Section X party in northern Slovenia was forced to withdraw because of a German offensive. However, about the same time, more X agents were being flown from Britain and parachuted into Germany; SHAEF kept strict control on everything related to those drops.

Regardless of its operational successes and failures, Section X had by 1944 earned a reputation within the British intelligence community as a skilled provider of agents' cover stories and false documents. By the spring of that year it was, by request, giving advice on preparing these to other SOE country sections and to MI9 (the prisoner-of-war escape organisation) and SIS.

SOE relied heavily on its clandestine missions in Switzerland and Sweden. Switzerland was invaluable both to the Allies and Nazi Germany as a source of intelligence about each other's military, political and economic activities. On the anti-Hitler side, SOE, SIS, OSS, the Soviet GRU military intelligence organisation and the Lucy Ring (run by a German communist, Rudolf Rössler) all had wartime presences of various sorts in this small, strategically placed country. The Swiss too were deeply involved in espionage. Their network, the Wiking Line, had many efficient agents in Germany and their counter-intelligence service caught more than 380 spies, mostly pro-Nazi Swiss citizens but including about 100 Germans.

Deeply distrustful of Hitler, Switzerland mobilised her 435,000-strong poorly equipped army on 2 September 1939, the day after his troops crossed into Poland. In May 1940, with Swiss airspace being violated by both German and French aircraft, it was feared that a Nazi invasion was imminent. A month later, several German planes were shot down. Enraged by that, Göring sent in saboteurs to wreck Swiss military airfields, but the intruders were captured long before they could do so. Later, during bombing raids on Germany and Italy, Allied aircraft often intruded into Swiss airspace. As a result of a night-time lighting blackout imposed from November 1940 to September 1944, Swiss cities were occasionally bombed by accident.[1]

Surrounded by territory controlled by the Nazis or the Italian Fascists, Switzerland was a haven for refugees, members of

Resistance movements and escaped prisoners of war. At the end of hostilities in Europe in May 1945, about 115,000 of these fugitives from tyranny were being held in Swiss camps and many more had passed through the country during the war years. Switzerland's position was ultra-sensitive. She fulfilled treaty obligations allowing non-military goods and agricultural produce to be transported across her territory between Germany and Italy. She also, under pressure from Hitler, closed her borders to many thousands of Jews expelled from Vichy France as 'undesirable' in 1942. However, the overwhelming majority of Swiss had no illusions about the Nazis. Stalin called the Swiss 'swine' because of their commercial dealings with the Axis Powers. But Churchill thought differently. 'Of all the neutrals,' he once wrote to Foreign Secretary Anthony Eden, 'Switzerland has the greatest right to distinction. She has been the sole international force linking the hideously sundered nations and ourselves. What does it matter whether she has been able to give us the commercial advantages we desire or has given too many to the Germans, to keep herself alive? She has been a democratic state, standing for freedom in self-defence among her mountains, and in thought, in spite of race, largely on our side.'[2]

SOE and the Swiss internal security authorities cooperated closely towards the end of the European war, as documents in the Public Record Office at Kew show.[3] For example, an SOE minute dated 16 November 1944, mentioned various clandestine help given by the Swiss. In particular, crossing the frontier was made easy for SOE agents, one of whom was 'very much befriended' by the security authorities.

Like Switzerland, Sweden was important both to the Allies and the Third Reich as an espionage centre. These neutral countries feared, with good reason, that Hitler might invade them early in the war. It was only towards the end of the European conflict that they felt completely safe. The importance of Sweden in SOE's engagement in irregular warfare was explained on 20 October 1944, in a Section X document:[4]

> The SOE mission in Sweden was established initially with the object of preparing, without the knowledge of the Swedish authorities, a subversive organisation to operate only if Sweden was invaded by Germany or otherwise came under German control. Recent developments in the war have rendered these eventualities unlikely and it has been possible to make use of the SOE mission in Sweden:

(a) To assist the development of Danish and Norwegian Resistance.

(b) To obtain the unofficial support of the Swedish authorities for activities in Sweden designed to help Resistance in Norway and Denmark.

(c) To operate from Sweden into Germany.

The increased disposition of the Swedish authorities in favour of the Allies – illustrated by their action in training and arming the Norwegian and Danish police . . . – makes the development of the activities outlined above possible. . . .

Clearly, by October 1944, the Swedish government firmly favoured the Allies, clandestinely giving them valuable help in the distribution of propaganda. This was a big change from the early war years.

Black propaganda was broadcast as well as written. For example, the Political Warfare Executive ran Soldatensender Calais, a supposedly German army radio station claiming to transmit from that French port until its liberation on 30 September 1944. In a similar exercise, Kurzwellensender Atlantik broadcast to U-boat crews. These and other bogus stations were called Research Units (RUs) by PWE. They broadcast war news that Goebbels would have suppressed, mixing it with other information about which he would have had no objection. The RUs also reported rumours, known as 'sibs', about the *dolce vita* and sexual exploits of certain high-ranking officers and prominent civilian Nazis. Another topic touched upon from time to time was the plight of soldiers' and sailors' families in Germany, with dark hints that the faraway wives and girlfriends faced all manner of tribulations and temptations. They clearly needed to have their menfolk back at home as soon as possible! In compiling RU programmes, PWE worked closely with Allied intelligence organisations. For instance, it obtained detailed up-to-date information on German defeats and military problems, and on hardships on the home front.

Initially, PWE broadcast from twenty-nine short-wave transmitters on hills in southern England, but, after the United States entered the war, it also used an American 600-kilowatt medium-wave transmitter, codenamed Aspidistra, which was powerful enough to reach much of the German civilian population. Concealed in a huge hole in the Ashdown Forest in Sussex, this transmitter was described by Richard Gambier-Parry, head of SIS's radio communications, as 'a raiding dreadnought of the Ether'. As well as broadcasting its own material, it often made Goebbels' propaganda unintelligible by breaking into

German and Vichy French programmes on wavelengths controlled by the Nazis.

The Allies also disseminated propaganda overtly on a large scale throughout the war. At the outbreak of hostilities, Chamberlain's government forbade any bombing that was likely to cause civilian casualties. As a result, in large areas of Germany, the RAF was allowed to drop only leaflets expressing the Foreign Office's and the Ministry of Information's closely reasoned arguments for opposing Hitlerism. It seems this gentlemanly 'white propaganda' had little impact on the then heavily Nazified German public, although the leaflet-dropping did give aircrews much-needed training in night flying! When Churchill took over as Prime Minster in May 1940 that bombing policy was scrapped.

Most white propaganda was broadcast. The BBC led the field with transmissions to Germany and the occupied countries. Refugees, including leading figures such as Queen Wilhelmina of the Netherlands and King Haakon VII of Norway, were given airtime to boost the morale of their compatriots. This they did successfully throughout the European war. White broadcasts were also used to convey coded messages to the Resistance movements.

The BBC broadcasts to occupied Europe sometimes had unexpected consequences. For example, one to Belgium in January 1941, unintentionally started the 'V for Victory' campaign. This was the result of a Belgian commentator making an unscripted remark about 'V' and 'victoire'. In no time, Resistance fighters were daubing the letter V on countless thousands of buildings in Holland, Belgium and France. However, in May 1942, the British government judged that the campaign would encourage dangerous premature hopes of victory and the BBC stopped all mention of the campaign for the time being.

In peacetime, more than half a century after the event, it is easy to criticise black propaganda from ethical and other non-military standpoints. No doubt some RU output was of questionable value, either because it included unverifiable tittle-tattle (rather like some of what goes into today's newspaper gossip columns) or because it did not always have the desired demoralising effect on the Wehrmacht that its authors intended. However, black propaganda had one great merit – it carefully differentiated between Nazis and other Germans: Hitler and his followers were the villains; the German people were deceived victims of the villainy.

Not all white propaganda made that necessary distinction. For example, in BBC overseas broadcasts towards the end of 1940, Sir

Robert (later Baron) Vansittart slated Germans indiscriminately. Hitlerism, in his expressed opinion at that most critical period of the war, was merely the latest manifestation of the German people's historically flawed national character. These broadcasts, together with an accompanying pamphlet entitled *Black Record: Germans Past and Present*, are a sorry sequel to Lord Vansittart's distinguished diplomatic career. As Permanent Under Secretary at the Foreign Office from 1930 until the end of 1937, he strove tirelessly, in the face of much ill-informed opposition, to warn the appeasers that Hitler was a real threat to peace.

In general, the European Service of the BBC and the other broadcasters of white propaganda accurately reported the information available to them, and did not make extreme judgements. Listeners respected them for doing that. Their regard for the BBC, which by 1943 was broadcasting daily to seventeen European countries, was particularly high. Analysing the BBC's wartime output, Professor Henri Michel, a leading French war historian, writes:

The BBC's principle was the exact opposite of that of Goebbels – 'not to tell lies'. It sought its effect through being 'completely candid'. In general it tried to appeal to reason, to the critical faculties of its listeners, not to their emotions; it made great use of sarcasm, songs and humour and seldom resorted to insults or tampering with the truth except in the case of certain Aunt Sallies such as Hitler, Himmler or Göring. It made many mistakes of course – for instance, it announced the liberation of Paris 24 hours too early, which could have been costly for over-enthusiastic Parisians – but taken overall its success was colossal, as witnessed by the thousands of letters from listeners arriving via Portugal, and statements from people who had managed to escape from the occupied countries.[5]

Throughout 1944 the role being played by all kinds of anti-Nazi propaganda and sabotage was being re-examined by the Western Allies. During the previous four years enough evidence had been accumulated to convince even sceptical members of the Allied political and military leaderships that these 'weapons', together with other forms of irregular warfare, were powerful if used skilfully. It was therefore decided during the course of the year, at the highest levels in Washington and London, as well as by SHAEF, that irregular warfare against Hitler must be stepped up. Following that decision General Gubbins set up a committee on 2 August to plan the intensification of SOE activities inside Germany. He laid down that 'Germany must now be the first priority target for SOE, and all our energies and resources must be concentrated on the penetration of the Reich itself. . .' The SOE Chief (CD) added that he himself would now personally supervise Section X, instead of it being part of Brigadier Mockler-Ferryman's directorate, called the London Group.

Section X's restated or expanded objectives were:

1. The 'mass subversion' of Nazi German administration officials in occupied countries.

2. Subject to SHAEF directives, 'any activity that would cause large movements of people in Germany' or would 'create administrative chaos' through that or other means.

3. Attacks on Nazi security services, especially the SD.

4. The organisation of each country's nationals doing forced labour inside Germany.

5. The recruitment from Resistance movements of agents who, 'for money or revenge', would be willing later to go into Germany and carry out tasks specifically allotted to them.

6. The demoralisation of German troops, ideally leading to mass desertions.

7. Attacks on any Nazi German assets and holdings in occupied countries.

8. The development of new channels to disseminate black propaganda.

The SOE committee on Germany emphasised that all these objectives, together with all activities by Resistance movements, must be coordinated with conventional military operations. SHAEF's Special Force Headquarters (SFHQ), some of whose staff were co-opted from SOE and OSS, had this coordinating role.

In a statement dated 11 August 1944, less than a month after Colonel Stauffenberg's attempt on Hitler's life, Section X made this cautious assessment: 'There are, at present, no indications of active rebellious movements inside Germany. The only serious internal conflict which can be envisaged in Germany prior to the end of organised [Nazi] resistance is a clash between the Wehrmacht and the Party, including the SS. The possibility of bread riots and workers' demonstrations cannot, however, be entirely excluded.' SOE, the statement added, could assist French, Dutch, Belgian and Luxembourg Resistance representatives who were responsible for their displaced compatriots who were doing forced labour in Germany and the occupied countries. Specifically SOE could help the Resistance organise these workers into disciplined cells, and it could give aid with radio and other communications and with the dissemination of black propaganda and the organisation of sabotage.

In a broadcast on 13 September 1944, General Eisenhower appealed to foreign workers in Germany to leave their factories and to go into hiding. However, only twelve days later, a radio message from SHAEF largely nullified what he had said by warning against any premature action that would result in savage reprisals. It was stated in this second broadcast that those workers who were already organised for resistance in Germany should use 'wisely' the aid which had been given them.

SHAEF's policy related to anti-Nazi Germans was defined on 16 September 1944: SHAEF's

> . . . aim has been to exploit all forms of discontent in Germany rather than fostering any one opposition element in the country, thereby leading it to suppose that it had the backing of the Allies. . . . At the present time the internal situation does not permit more active exploits of opposition elements, owing to the power of the Gestapo and the apathy of the civilian population. Future activity is therefore to be devoted mainly towards the continued exploitation of such opposition elements as already exist, and to the development of further contacts with foreign workers. . . . There is in Germany no resistance movement which can be compared with the organisations in occupied Europe. The subversive elements in Germany are those which while opposed to the Hitler regime and ready to bring about his downfall, are not pro-Allied.[6]

Up to the summer of 1944 Section X spent much time convincing other SOE country sections, missions abroad and individual agents of the operational importance of black propaganda. Early in the war there was scarcely any sign of its effectiveness. However, there was a subsequent build-up of such evidence, and towards the end of hostilities a spate of captured German documents proved conclusively that SOE was working consistently along the right lines.

By 1944 Section X handled five sorts of black propaganda, which it categorised as Types A to F. Type A literature was represented as having been written by German groups or movements striving clandestinely to overthrow the Hitler dictatorship. In reality, all these organisations were figments of the lively imaginations of Political Warfare Executive staff, advised by X officers. The literature, often bearing the 'insignia' of these non-existent bodies, comprised pamphlets, leaflets, posters and stickers that urged people to engage in a wide variety of passive resistance to the Nazi regime. Some of the literature was intended for soldiers, U-boat crews and other members of the armed forces. It contained accurate descriptions of the urban devastation inflicted in RAF and USAAF bombing raids, with as much detailed information as the Allies had, such as the names of the streets most severely stricken. The literature encouraged servicemen to apply for compassionate leave, quoting this information as the basis for doing so. Type A pamphlets and leaflets, many bearing clever slogans that were easy to remember, were distributed by Section X agents in various ways – for example, at night time in deserted streets, and when the wind was strong, large bundles of the literature were released and blew away all over the place. When nobody was looking, pamphlets and leaflets were also left singly or in piles in cafés, buses, trains, public lavatories and indeed almost anywhere. Individual copies of the literature were posted to selected persons thought likely to give the propaganda's 'message' a wide circulation without alerting the authorities.

Black propaganda in the Type B category consisted of forged German military documents and circulars. 'Signed' by senior Wehrmacht officers, they were made to look as though they had been sent out by the OKW or other headquarters for the guidance of junior and middle-rank officers. Copies of the literature were distributed singly or in packets of different sizes in the hope, often. realised, that they would be picked up casually by NCOs, private soldiers or other junior armed forces' personnel. Agents left neat bundles of the forgeries in the waiting-rooms of railway stations or in other public places where a negligent officer might have briefly left what he regarded as bumf, intending to pick it up later. Single copies of the Type B propaganda were dropped in all sorts of public places. An agent might crumple up a circular or tear it slightly. Alternatively, he might put a cigarette burn on one corner of it, but making sure that its slogan or other message could still be read. In such mutilated condition, the single items of propaganda were made to look as though they had been thrown away by an officer who had read and memorised what the literature said. Type B propaganda comprised a great range of material encouraging indiscipline, a lowering of morale and the undermining of junior ranks' trust in their officers.

Various publications seemingly produced by the Third Reich's civilian or military authorities were categorised as Type C propaganda.

Such literature was posted to selected individuals, inserted among newspapers on news-stands, left in doctors' waiting-rooms, or indeed distributed in the way Type B was.

Although the encouragement of malingering by members of the armed forces was one of the purposes of several sorts of black propaganda, it was the sole aim of Type D material. This appeared in many innocent-looking guises, such as booklets on uncontroversial subjects. For example, one booklet was a short guide to the French language, with basic vocabulary, phrases and sentences used in everyday conversation. The 'black' message was deep within the text; in a section on medical matters in the middle of the booklet there was a brief description of how to fabricate the symptoms of various minor ailments. Other Type D products included a Wehrmacht soldier's diary and a book of lottery tickets. Agents made special efforts to get Type D items to troops awaiting transfer to front-line units and to U-boat crew members about to begin a hunt for Allied shipping. The distribution was much like that of the other categories of black propaganda. However, booklets were also put in the pockets of overcoats hanging in cloakrooms and into soldiers' kitbags if these were left around unattended.

Type E propaganda comprised anonymous stickers stuck upon lamp-posts, the outsides of buildings or any other surface where they were likely to be seen by troops. Small versions of the stickers were put on envelopes before posting. Whatever their size, the stickers carried slogans encouraging defeatist feelings already existing among many German troops towards the end of the European war.

Type F propaganda, a variant of Type E, appeared on what SOE and PWE described as 'special stickers'. The purpose of these, often achieved, was to intensify the already existing discord between the military and the SS. The few words on these stickers suggested in not the most polite language that the SS was ruining the international reputation of Germany and its army. That reasonable assertion was also expressed in stark pictorial fashion by the prominent inclusion on the stickers of a crude lavatorial swear-word, 'Scheisse'. It was provocatively printed as 'ScheiSSe', the double 'S' being an exact copy of the SS symbol. PWE and SOE hoped, with good reason, that the general public would regard this propaganda as coming from a dissident but patriotic group of unidentifiable military personnel who believed that the SS's increasingly negative influence was leading Germany on the road to a shameful defeat. With the military men under suspicion, SOE expected that the Gestapo would not be looking for culprits among the local civilian population.

Some black propaganda did not fit into the categories A to F. This miscellaneous material mainly comprised circulars and other literature, which PWE produced in an attempt (largely successful) to embarrass influential pro-Nazi citizens of neutral countries. This propaganda similarly tried to discomfit certain expatriate Germans who loudly championed Hitlerism.

Section X also devised various hoaxes. The minor ones included the posting to selected pro-Nazis of forged invitations to prestigious events for which all seats had already been booked. When the 'guests' turned up on the appointed day, they were accused of trying to gate-crash. There were angry scenes and much confusion. The most important and most successful of the hoaxes was one in which the non-existent 'Foreign Organisation of the National Socialist German Workers' Party' was made to seem to have posted a circular towards the end of July 1944 to about 500 selected Germans living in Sweden. The circular, in reality posted by the SOE mission in Stockholm, said that every German felt himself duty bound to renew his oath of loyalty in the Führer, following the recent attempt to assassinate him. To do this 'by deeds', the circular added, the Germans in Sweden must 'make a thank-offering to the Heinrich Himmler Fund'. Donations to it, either money or goods, were to be sent to a certain address in Stockholm. The circular caused confusion among expatriate Germans and acute embarrassment to those of them who were Nazis. Swedish journalists wrote indignant commentaries and asked searching questions about 'the Heinrich Himmler Fund'.

The various sorts of black propaganda were smuggled into Germany or were dropped in containers by Allied aircraft, usually on bombing raids. The smuggling was organised by representatives of Section X and the German Directorate in Stockholm, Istanbul, Berne and Italian towns, as well as by what the Directorate described mysteriously as 'our mission in the Iberian Peninsula'. According to a Directorate document written after the war in Europe, there were 'many ingenious methods of distribution by our representatives in neutral countries'. For example, the representatives in Turkey did 'excellent work and spent much time and labour' in concealing 'selected items' in what was described coyly as 'certain rubber goods', as well as in lottery-ticket envelopes, cigarette boxes, tins of food and packing cases. Most of these goods went to Germany by sea. The air-dropped containers of black propaganda were picked up by SOE agents belonging to resistance movements in Belgium, France, Holland, Poland, Norway and Denmark. It took a long time to build up groups of these agents and to train them to infiltrate the forgeries into Germany.

Section X and the German Directorate are estimated to have organised the clandestine distribution of nearly 10 million leaflets, booklets, posters, stickers and forged documents. This total does not include an unknown vast amount of black literature that was printed secretly in Nazi-occupied Europe by what the German Directorate described as 'featherweight stereos – light plastic plates enabling printing to be done direct in the field'. SOE agents used hundreds of these small and basic pieces of equipment, which were easy to carry and conceal.

Much of the black propaganda directed at members of the German armed forces gave practical advice on how to malinger or desert. Towards the end of the war in Europe, the Political Warfare Executive, with help from SOE, produced what were called 'malingering kits' – sets of pamphlets, booklets and other literature describing methods of simulating illnesses that would give men a reasonable-sounding excuse to report sick. The kits named drugs which, if taken in the doses stated, would bring on ailments or at least the appearance of illness, but would do no lasting harm.

There is plenty of documentary evidence that this black propaganda successfully encouraged widespread malingering. For example, in February 1944, an army officers' journal, *Mitteilungen für das Offizierkorps* (issue number 29), ran an article headlined 'A Frequent Trick of Enemy Propaganda'. After quoting some of the ways of persuading soldiers to pretend to be ill, it added: 'More dangerous is another method employed by both the Bolsheviks and the Anglo-Americans. Disguised as sports hints, in outward form similar to a supplement to the HDV (Army Service Rules), hints and prescriptions for the simulation of certain ailments are scattered among various apparently straightforward passages.' For instance, the forgery described 'all sorts of methods of bringing on fever' and the symptoms that 'must be pleaded for during an alleged attack of appendicitis'. The article commented: 'Naturally, the enemy knows that decent soldiers do not respond to such smart and mean invitations; he [the enemy] is concerned only with the rascals who are to be found everywhere. None the less, it is a good thing for section officers to keep a careful look out for this sort of poison, each in his own province.'

On 8 April 1944, in a circular letter classified 'Secret', the Director of Medical Services of German Army Group C paid a back-handed compliment to the writing skills of the PWE forgers:

Enemy propaganda has produced a booklet in which advice and hints on behaviour are given in a very cunning way to would-be malingerers. The booklet . . . is entitled: "How to keep myself healthy. Instructions for young and old. Instructional Press. Berlin". It contains a general introduction and the following main chapters: 1. Light injuries, (i) foot trouble, (ii) skin disease, (iii) serious digestive trouble. 2. serious illness, (i) severe backache, (ii) partial paralysis, (iii) tuberculosis, (iv) loss of memory.

How to simulate all these afflictions was described in detail in this booklet and in similar black literature. For example, this was the PWE forgers' advice on how to bring on the appearance of having an inflamed foot: 'Soak a ball of cotton of the size of a pea in turpentine and keep it overnight between your third and fourth toe. . . . Repeat this experiment with other toes. . . . Before reporting to the doctor you must wash your feet very thoroughly with soap, so that the smell of the turpentine cannot be noticed.' This was the forgers' suggested way of simulating heart disease: 'Smoke 20 to 30 cigarettes a day . . . and go on to prescribe a stiff course of digitalis tablets.' Getting these, or indeed any drugs, might be a problem. But the forgers knew how to solve it: 'If you see the chemist is hesitating, take out your pistol and put it on the table without saying a word. You will find that in most instances this proves very effective.'

The success of the 'malingering kits' is best illustrated by quoting parts of a circular letter (below) written on behalf of the Director of Medical Services of the German Armed Forces' High Command. This and similar documents were sent to medical officers at all levels of the German army command structure:

**OKW, Director of Medical**  **Berlin. April 12, 1944**
**Services. Nr. 461/44/Secret**
*Subject: Subversion in the Fighting*
*Services through Malingering*

Recently, on repeated occasions, innocently camouflaged booklets have been distributed among members of the armed forces, and drugs to be used for malingering purposes have been given to members of the armed forces. Reports from the military and criminal police and also from the Gestapo make it clear that the use made of these instructions by members of the forces has already attained larger proportions than was at first supposed. . . .

Assistant Directors of Medical Services, regimental medical officers and medical officers at recruiting centres are to be warned that when holding sick parades or primary medical inspections they must pay increased attention to the question of malingering. . . .

Investigations are to be carried out with extreme care, so that those under suspicion [of malingering] are not prematurely warned. . . . Some cases have already been tried and the death penalty has been given. . . .

for the Director of Medical Services
Wurfler,
Chief of Staff

Judging from the reference in the *Mitteilungen* article to 'the Bolsheviks and the Anglo-Americans' and an (unquoted) ambiguous mention of 'communist agents' in the OKW letter, the Nazi authorities were probably not certain whether the forgeries encouraging malingering were of Soviet or Western Allied origin.

On a few occasions German artillery fired to front-line Allied troops a complete translation of the PWE's practical advice on simulating illnesses. However, as recorded in an SOE German Directorate minute, 'Unfortunately for the Germans, although their method was thorough, it was not subtle or "black" in any way. . . .' Allied soldiers read the Nazi version of the forgeries, immediately recognised it as crude propaganda, and had a good laugh.

Some of the malingering kits were targeted at German naval personnel, particularly submariners. According to a document captured in 1944, the Flotilla Chief of the Harbour Defence Flotilla at Cherbourg was appalled when he discovered near Lyons what he described as 'a new type of enemy propaganda, extremely cleverly disguised'. Deep within the text of a bogus *Sports Manual for the Navy* were detailed instructions on what to do and say when reporting imaginary ailments to a medical officer. Also in 1944, a prisoner-of-war lieutenant-commander, who had served in U-boats, told his interrogators that the main items of Allied subversive material that had attracted his attention were the anti-SS 'ScheiSSe' stickers and a leaflet suggesting ingenious methods of obtaining six weeks' leave.

A carefully planned campaign to incite members of U-boat crews to malinger or desert was conducted in earnest from 1943. All the different sorts of black propaganda reported casualty figures as accurately as the Allies knew them and emphasised that there was only a small chance of German submariners surviving the war. That was fair comment, with no exaggeration, as the Third Reich lost 781 U-boats during the war – 66 per cent of the 1,170 commissioned and nearly 80 per cent of the estimated 1,000 that put to sea. What the

Allied forgeries did not say was that this huge submarine fleet, like its First World War predecessor, was a major threat to Britain's survival during much of the time. As a result of U-boat activity, about 2,000 Allied merchant ships, totalling about 14.5 million tons, were sunk. The German submarines were also deadly foes of Allied warships. It did not take long for that to be made plain. On the night of 13–14 October 1939, *U47* slipped through the defences of the base of the British Home Fleet at Scapa Flow in Scotland and sank the battleship *Royal Oak*, with a loss of 833 lives.

The black propaganda directed at German submariners was infiltrated into the U-boat yards of north and north-west German ports and into submarine bases in Norway. This was dangerous work, done mostly by agents and couriers based in Stockholm. However, some of the booklets about malingering reached these ports concealed in cargoes of egg powder and other imports. A German Directorate minute, written after the end of hostilities in Europe, noted rather complacently that the forgeries about desertion included 'a particularly subversive little item': a description of why a number of gallant German sailors were shot for sabotaging U-boat components. These men had been waiting to go on an obviously ill-planned operation that could result only in their own death and that of their comrades.

German submariners were also targeted through Operation Tuckbox. In this devious exercise, SOE sent food parcels through neutral countries to the relatives in Germany of captured U-boat personnel. These recipients were led to believe that the 'gifts' had been bought by their menfolk who, despite being prisoners of war, were well treated and better fed than many German civilians. In SOE's Baker Street headquarters it was hoped that Tuckbox would stimulate 'a spirit of surrender' among active German submariners and make captivity seem attractive from the point of view of the men themselves and their families. Most of the 'gifts' were made to look as though they had been sent to Germany by anonymous well-wishers in neutral countries who had received money and orders for the food parcels from named prisoners of war. It is, of course, impossible to confirm a claim by the German Directorate that Tuckbox was successful. But the operation did result in a number of PoWs' wives writing in glowing terms about their surprise and gratitude on receiving the 'gifts' from their husbands.

PWE and SOE were undoubtedly inventive and tireless in tempting U-boat personnel to desert. Also, the agents who distributed the related black propaganda took great risks in doing so, as did all other SOE agents everywhere in the Third Reich and the occupied countries. However, desertion from submarines was much more difficult than from army units, and comparatively few disillusioned U-boat crew members reached neutral countries.

Some German submariners decided to mutiny rather than desert, possibly because mutiny was a less serious offence than desertion. Stockholm newspapers reported in 1943 that 'a considerable number' of U-boat personnel, including some officers, were imprisoned in Akershus jail in Oslo, then being used as a military prison. These men were members of six crews that had refused to put to sea.

One of the most subtle and effective examples of black propaganda was a bogus 'proclamation' made to look as if it had been signed by Colonel-General von Falkenhorst,[7] Commander-in-Chief of the German armed forces in Norway. Entitled 'Deutscher Soldat', it appealed to the better nature of the German soldier, deploring 'the shameful increase in the number of cases in which men and even officers have evaded their military obligations by crossing into neutral territory and receiving asylum there'. The 'proclamation', which was given a wide clandestine circulation in Norway and was the subject of Swedish newspaper articles, also made Falkenhorst appear to reveal that, towards the end of the war, all deserters were being welcomed into 'neutral territory' (Sweden) as long as they conformed to certain reasonable standards. The occupation authorities in Norway, headed by the notorious Reich Commissioner Josef Terboven, were clearly embarrassed by the 'proclamation'. They felt manoeuvred into commenting publicly on it. But in declaring it a forgery, they gave it yet more publicity. In Sweden, however, it was generally thought to be a genuine pronouncement by Falkenhorst. In the opinion of SOE staff officers in Baker Street, it put the idea of desertion 'on the map'. Similar 'proclamations', with alterations in text to suit local situations, were circulated later in other occupied countries. They were 'signed' by the appropriate German commander-in-chief. Agents sometimes took great risks in posting these forgeries on public buildings. One seen briefly outside the town hall at Tournus, in France's Saône-et-Loire department, contained much of the information that a deserter needed to know:

Unfortunately, the Spanish authorities, basing their action on international law, are giving asylum in Spain to deserters from German military service, when these cross the Spanish frontier in civilian clothes and without personal documents, and declare themselves to be Alsatians and Lorrainers. I trust that this inexplicable attitude of the Spanish authorities will not seduce honourable German soldiers into the shameful breaking of their military oath. At this critical moment of the highest state of readiness, we must be able to depend upon every single person.

This 'proclamation' was 'signed' by Field Marshal von Rundstedt, C-in-C, West.

Section X also organised what it called a 'Führerbilt' operation. This involved the distribution of a flattering picture of Hitler, the caption underneath mentioning a military office locally where other copies of the portrait could be obtained. On the reverse side of the picture, however, the text suggested that each German soldier should make sure that his family or next-of-kin got a copy of the Führerbilt, as he himself would probably lie and rot on the Eastern Front, or at least become a cripple for life. The text then stated the number of German divisions being recalled for active service against the Russians.

Yet another black propaganda operation was the printing in Stockholm and infiltration into Norway of a German-language newspaper bearing the insignia (a red circle) of the Deutsche Freiheitspartei, a non-existent resistance group. As well as reporting news about the war and general interest topics, the paper, which had a large secret readership among German troops, appealed to 'comrades in the Wehrmacht' to desert. It also condemned the 'machinations of the Nazi war lords' and told the story of 'the heroes who sabotaged the *Scharnhorst*' and were executed by firing squad in Altenfjord.

The imaginary red-circle resistance group also 'issued' a leaflet listing German town streets known to have been destroyed in RAF bombing raids. From time to time new editions of the leaflet were produced, giving accurate up-to-date information to keep pace with the intensive bombing of Germany in the last years of the war. As German troops were strictly forbidden to listen to Allied broadcasts, they were thirsty for real news about their home towns, this being all too often denied them by Dr Goebbels. PWE and SOE therefore reasonably assumed that if a German soldier found one of the leaflets, he would not destroy it or hand it in to the military authorities until he had glanced through the list of bombed streets. If his own home were on the list, he would be tempted to apply for compassionate leave – as suggested in the leaflet. Copies of it were found on many of the soldiers who deserted to neutral countries.

Towards the end of 1944, the Political Warfare Executive and the German Directorate launched what they described as a 'Special Desertion Project'. For this an envelope full of various forged documents was produced for the benefit of the disillusioned German soldier, giving him detailed advice on how to desert and, if that were impossible, how to malinger or obtain compassionate leave without alerting the suspicion of the military authorities or the Gestapo. The main aim of this project was to encourage front-line troops to desert back to their homes in Germany, rather than make their way to an Allied unit and surrender. That sort of desertion was regarded by the Directorate as having 'a greater subversive value' than any conventional quitting of one's post. The envelope contained forgeries of all the official documents needed to give the impression that permission had been given for the soldier's journey home and for his stay there. These papers bore the required official stamps and signatures. The soldier would, however, have to make certain entries himself, such as his name, his destination and the date – but the black propaganda even gave him instructions on how to do that without making any careless mistakes. As expressed in a memorandum, the German Directorate felt confident that: 'These papers, if completed properly by the user, were foolproof, not only for getting the soldier back home but also for regularising his position in Germany.' The operation involved much work for the SOE documents section before final printing by PWE. Captured Wehrmacht records show that it was a great success.

PWE and the German Directorate organised this sophisticated 'Special Desertion Project' well. If they had not done so and if the forgeries had been less than perfect, the consquences would have been catastrophic, for the Nazi authorities regarded desertion as an offence against both the Führer personally and the Volksgemeinschaft, the Nazi concept of the 'national community'. In April 1940, Hitler declared his strong approval of the execution of deserters. An estimated 35,000 members of the Wehrmacht were charged with desertion during the war. About 22,750 of them were sentenced to death, and at least 15,000 of the sentences were carried out.[8]

Press reports in Sweden, Switzerland and other neutral countries, together with Allied intercepts of international mail, indicated that many Wehrmacht soldiers and a smaller number of U-boat crew members read the various sorts of black propaganda described above. The number of desertions by disillusioned members of Hitler's armed forces increased significantly from the beginning of 1944.

# Chapter Fourteen
## *Targeting the workers*

Some of the black propaganda circulated clandestinely by SOE agents was targeted primarily at the civilian population of Hitler's Greater Germany, particularly at workers in armaments factories and others employed in spheres of the economy directly affecting the war. The main purpose of that diverse literature – forged leaflets, stickers and the like – was to encourage passive resistance to the Nazi regime and even active opposition if events eventually allowed that.

Even during the last eighteen months of the European war the task of discrediting the dictatorship through propaganda was difficult, for the nimble-minded Dr Goebbels had a long record of spectacular success in systematically deceiving the majority of the German people. His total control since 1933 of the Third Reich's media and cultural activities, together with the brutal suppression of all opposition to the regime, gave him immense power over hearts and minds. He was therefore a formidable opponent of the Allies' overt and secret efforts at influencing German public opinion.

Much of the black propaganda sought to discredit the highly privileged members of the Nazi Party élite. These self-serving 'swine', the forgeries said, were the only beneficiaries of the dictatorship. They ignored the hardships and privations that ordinary Germans experienced as a direct or indirect result of the regime's criminal incompetence in handling matters relating both to the war and to the running of the civilian administration.

In the black literature – produced as usual with advice from SOE – the PWE forgers asked thought-provoking questions, floated ideas and provided the sorts of information that Goebbels censored. As well as giving the literature as wide a 'readership' as possible, SOE agents conducted 'whispering campaigns' – countless informal conversations in which verified anti-Nazis were told discreetly about the themes covered in the printed propaganda. Great care had to be taken, of course, that Gestapo agents and other unreliable people were not within earshot.

Relating to the Nazi Party élite, these (and many other) themes were given a wide airing, in printed form and orally:

> Are all Germans willing to work like slaves so that the 'Parteibonzen' [Nazi Party big-wigs] can drink themselves stupid, drive around in cars, pick and choose their girl friends, and live like kings?

The Party high-ups have a privileged position. They have 'diplomatic' rations (Diplomaten-Verpflegung) – three or four times the rations of a heavy manual worker. Party functionaries of military age are largely exempt from front-line service or labour service. The wives and daughters of the Party élite get cushy jobs in offices to avoid factory work. Party officials are exempt from providing billets in their homes for evacuees, all other Germans being forced by decree to take in these people. The decree exempting the high-ups from billeting is dated 17 February 1943. The high-ups have special reserved zones into which they may evacuate their families. The zones are called Focal Points of Housing Shortage (Brennpunkte des Wohnungsbedarfe) and are closed to all evacuees. They include holiday resorts: Berchtesgaden, Bischofswiesen, Gern and six others.

You [the reader of the propaganda or the listener to a whispering campaign] are not surprised to see high-ups racketeering, black marketeering and gluttonising in occupied territories while ordinary people starve, but you are surprised to see the same thing happening in Germany.

Section X agents circulated a special PWE leaflet entitled *The Victims of Berchtesgaden*. It told the story of a bombed-out German family who received short shrift from Nazi officialdom when they requested asylum in the peaceful environs of Berchtesgaden. The forgery was illustrated with what it described as 'authentic' photographs of the family. Much more serious than the telling of this sad tale was the leaflet's allegation that every bombed-out person was 'mercilessly shot' if he or she dared to turn up in the Berchtesgaden district without permission to go there. According to the leaflet, this fate befell a soldier's wife.

Some of the information in *The Victims of Berchtesgaden* was probably untrue, for, on 27 October 1943, the *Leipziger Neueste Nachrichten* (circulation 146,000), published a denial of everything in the leaflet. This it could not have done without official permission. Presumably the Nazi authorities thought that the denial, which for them would have the disadvantage of giving the leaflet more publicity, would be less of an evil than making no comment. Incidentally, eight days later, the London *Daily Mail* reported the 'Victims' story, making it known internationally.

Among PWE's most visually attractive forgeries was a brochure intended to look as though it had been published by the Mayor of Freiburg. In it he was represented as having invited people in badly bombed cities to evacuate to his most pleasant town. In 1944 the brochure was circulated in the Hanover area and some other parts of Germany, as well as among German troops in Poland. It seems that most copies of the brochure were seized by the Nazi authorities; however, a few people accepted the 'invitation'.

Other black propaganda was directed against the Nazi Party élite; it was often salacious and based largely on rumour, exaggeration or outright invention. Leaflets and broadcasts told startling tales about individual Nazi high-ups who were already thoroughly discredited because of their long records of violent crime and scarcely needed any further condemnation over their actual or supposed sexual excesses.

According to one such tale, Christian Weber, a former Munich nightclub bouncer and one of Hitler's rough-neck companions in the 1920s, organised entertainments in which naked girls on horseback gave what a Section X document described as 'spirited renderings' of Wagner's *Ride of the Valkyries*. A section report compiled in July 1942, stated: 'A particular attraction at this time was a large roulette wheel on which a naked girl had been strapped. Christian Weber, drunk as usual, was acting as croupier and set the wheel in motion. The audience of mainly SS men sat ready round the table. The gentleman opposite the girl when the wheel stops then obliges.' By then, however, the young lady was unconscious. Other black propaganda claimed that a German bomber was used as a flying brothel on the Eastern Front in 1941, and that a sixty-year-old admiral took 'a bunch of really sex-starved U-boat men' to a cabaret in which one of the entertainers, the admiral's reputed mistress, wore only a transparent raincoat. Similar propaganda described homosexual excesses.

One of the SOE whispering campaigns emphasised the great military and economic strength of the United States, with its industries out of range of German bombers. Section X agents talked privately to their trusted non-Nazi contacts about the vast number of American war-oriented goods that were being delivered to Britain. 'This is,' the agents said, '1917 all over again.' Related topics discreetly aired in this whispering campaign included the 'astonishing growth' of the RAF with American help, and the new, big bombs devastating whole streets in Kiel, Wilhelmshafen, Hamburg, Bremen, Mannheim and other cities. The Section X agents also mentioned the Nazis' concealment of enormous losses of U-boats and Luftwaffe aircraft, and of German troops drowned at sea when on the way to Norway, Crete and other countries. All this information was wholly or largely true. With it the agents included some questionable comments, such as: 'Because of food shortages, the authorities are doing away with people who are no longer of service to the State.'

In another whispering campaign, the agents suggested that, when local Nazi administrations lost control of events during the 'chaos' after air raids, those industrial workers who passively opposed the regime could safely go absent without leave. It would take a long time to find and identify bomb casualties, and generally to locate people. The agents would try to turn public anger against the local Nazi bosses by making various provocative comments on the causes of the chaos. They would express surprise over police inefficiency. 'There were,' they would say, 'so few police and those few were so old.' And they might add: 'Well, I suppose most of the police are away in the occupied territories or at the front. It is difficult for them to put a good team into the field.' The Section X agents would also express dismay over the increasingly heavy bombing by the Americans and British, and would contrast their huge combined aircraft production with the decline of Germany's plane output because so many German aircraft factories were being bombed. Perhaps as a throw-away line, the agents would comment on inadequate protection against air raids and would describe the appalling amount of bomb damage elsewhere in Germany.

In quite a different sort of whispering campaign, the agents circulated the false story that 'a famous international trade union official' (nationality unspecified) had secretly arrived in Germany and, despite Gestapo efforts to find him, was forming small cells of foreign workers. His and their aim was to hasten the inevitable collapse of the Nazi regime. He was at present collecting black lists of the worst Nazi criminals and white lists of Germans who had shown themselves humane in their treatment of foreign workers and willing to collaborate with them in overthrowing the dictatorship. When that great objective had been achieved, the anonymous trade union official's 'organisation' would hand itself over to the 'Allied Supreme Command'.

Section X, and later the German Directorate, had various other means of influencing German public opinion. For example, shortly after the Nazis had banned the *Frankfurter Zeitung* (circulation 68,000) in 1943, PWE produced a clandestine version of the newspaper, which SOE agents distributed widely in France as well as Germany. This forgery, whose layout was identical to that of its suppressed predecessor, was the subject of lively press commentaries in Britain and neutral countries.

PWE and SOE also cooperated in the production and dissemination respectively of stickers with propaganda messages for German civilians and military personnel alike. Some of these forgeries were often seen in occupied Europe as well as in Germany. One was entitled 'Es kommt der Tag' ('The Day will Come'). It showed a swastika hanging from gallows. Greatly admired by members of resistance movements, it appeared in the oddest of places. For two whole days a copy of the sticker remained attached to a German general's staff car in Greece. Early in 1945, this sticker design and two others, one of them listing Hitler's broken promises, were displayed on many buildings in Oslo.

Another of the PWE creations praised by resistance members was a sticker with the slogan 'Wir wollen einen Führer von Gottes Gnaden und keinen Mörder von Berchtesgaden' ('We want a Führer of God's choosing, not a murderer from Berchtesgaden'). It was seen from time to time in widely separated towns of Germany and the occupied countries. In August 1943, a German prisoner of war told interrogators that, despite savage counter-action by the Gestapo, much anti-Nazi propaganda was being circulated in the Third Reich, particularly among industrial workers and their families. However, he also mentioned an instance of Gestapo vengeance: some Munich students were executed after being caught pasting the 'Wir wollen . . .' sticker on walls. A German deserter, who arrived in Sweden in April 1944, said during a later interrogation that many soldiers stationed in Norway were talking openly about the war being already lost. They loved repeating the 'Wir wollen . . .' slogan whenever they thought it safe to do so.

Yet another PWE forgery targeted at both civilians and the Wehrmacht was a sticker bearing the words 'Der Führer ist in Gefahr!' ('The Führer is in danger!'). It was uncannily prophetic, as it was issued in September 1943, only ten months before the actual attempt on Hitler's life by Colonel Stauffenberg. The sticker was 'signed' by senior SS officers in Norway, Belgium and France. It contained a warning that Hitler was in danger from certain Prussian elements in the German army who were planning a Putsch to overthrow the Führer. They would then establish a military dictatorship and make peace with the Western Allies. The Nazi authorities classified the sticker as 'highly subversive' and said it was so subtly produced that the uninitiated would not realise that it was a forgery. A similar sticker, 'signed' by Erich Koch, the Gauleiter of Königsberg, was issued at about the same time.

Unlike other black propaganda aiming to intensify the Wehrmacht's already strong distrust of the SS, this 'Gefahr' project identified a source of possible opposition to Hitler – the 'certain Prussian elements' in the army. This was a grave and easily avoidable mistake; it gave the Gestapo widely circulated documentary evidence on which it could publicly justify any action against Prussian officers at any time of its own choosing. The timing of the project could hardly have been worse, although PWE and Section X could not, of course, have foreseen the July Bomb Plot.

The simplest of the black projects was a plain sticker. It had on it just one word, 'Schluss!' – meaning 'to Hell with it all!' This sticker was pasted up among others, such as ones giving German war casualty figures as up to date as the Allies knew them. In this combination the 'Schluss' sticker was outstandingly successful in helping to show ordinary German people, particularly industrial workers, that the Hitler dictatorship had wickedly deceived them since 1933 and was unworthy of any continuing support.

The 'Schluss!' slogan was seen in countless places in Germany, and also – for the enlightenment of German troops – in the occupied countries. As was intended by PWE and SOE, the easily remembered swearword was often repeated in the privacy of the home. 'Schluss!' appeared not only on stickers but was also rubber-stamped on any surface where it would be legible. SOE agents and their contacts particularly enjoyed defacing Nazi propaganda posters with this provocative word. It also brought colour to otherwise drab surroundings. For example, orange 'Schluss!' stickers enlivened the dreariness of wartime Oslo. In the last days of the Third Reich, the slogan was also a common sight on the walls of bomb-damaged buildings in Berlin.

In addition to the stickers, leaflets, pamphlets and the like, PWE and SOE strove to influence German public opinion through the medium of forged postage stamps. In one operation, a six-pfennig stamp showing Himmler's dour, bespectacled face was created by PWE in the style of a genuine three-pfennig Hitler stamp. In another project, the stamp portrayed Field Marshal Erwin von Witzleben, a long-time secret opponent of the Nazis who was given a mockery of a trial and executed with bestial cruelty shortly after the July Bomb Plot.

The purpose of the Himmler operation was to encourage rumours that he was plotting to replace Hitler as Führer. Although eventually successful, this complicated and time-consuming operation was beset with difficulties when launched early in 1942. Several thousand Himmler stamps were printed in PWE's clandestine workshops but many never reached their intended destinations in Switzerland, Portugal, Sweden and other neutral countries. A number of envelopes bearing the stamps had to be destroyed or were probably lost because of hitches in the posting arrangements. There were also communication problems between Baker Street, SOE stations and agents.

The operation was based on the hope (eventually realised) that the appearance of a few of the Himmler stamps in neutral countries would start people thinking that the forgeries were genuine stamps printed in Germany. Meanwhile, SOE spread the story that a sheet or two of the stamps had been issued prematurely and had been used by mistake. According to a variation of that tale, Himmler himself had ordered the production of this mysterious new issue of stamps; however, Hitler cancelled that order, but not before a few of the stamps had been posted.

The belated success of the operation dated from the arrival in Switzerland of a German letter postmarked Stuttgart, 23 September 1943. On the envelope was a Himmler forgery with genuine Hitler stamps on either side of it. International press comment on the significance of the new stamp then began. Soon there was widespread debate on whether the SS leader was planning a *coup d'état*. This was exactly what SOE wanted.

In 1945, the RSHA leader, Ernst Kaltenbrunner, by then a Nuremberg Trials defendant, asked his captors about the faked Himmler stamp. He said he had seen a picture of one in November or December 1943, in a Swiss philatelic magazine. Being himself a stamp collector (a relaxing hobby between drinking binges and organising mass murder), he tried to obtain a specimen of the stamp. Kaltenbrunner added that he had talked to Himmler about the forgery, but 'he had treated the matter as a joke'. Mirth, unless malicious, is not what one usually associates with the SS-Reichsführer!

Colonel Thornley, when deputy head of the German Directorate, had hoped to have Himmler interrogated on the subject of the stamp (and probably many other matters). However, his suicide prevented that, so Thornley requested in a letter to Brigadier Robin Brook that Ribbentrop be interrogated 'at the first opportunity'.[1] Unsurprisingly, there is no record of any such interrogation. The intensive questioning

Hitler and Göring in earnest conversation in April 1941. The Führerzug is in the background. (Public Record Office HS 6/624)

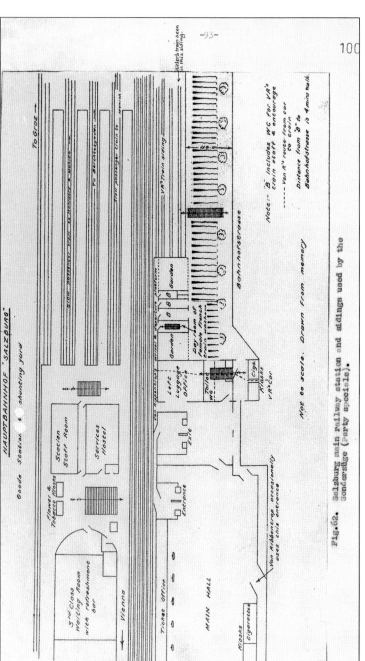

Described as 'not to scale' and 'drawn from memory', this is Section X's sketch of the layout of Salzburg's main railway

Within the figure:

HAUPTBAHNHOF "SALZBURG"

Goods Station & shunting yard

To Graz →

Slow passenger train to memmory & vienna

To Berchtesgaden

Slow passenger train to vienna

VR train siding

Flower & Tobacco Kiosks

Station Staff Room

Services Hostel

← Vienna

3rd Class Waiting Room with refreshment bar

Ticket Office

Von Ribbentrop occasionally uses this entrance

Exit

Entrance

MAIN HALL

Kiosks

Cigarettes

For Ribbentrop arrival & departure platform

Left Luggage Office

Garden

Day Room of Female Reich

B B B Garden

Toilet

Toilet

Ciga

Kiosks

VR Car

Bahnhofstrasse

Hitler's train seen in this siding

-93-

Note:- "B" includes WC for VR's train staff & entourage

------ Von R's route from car to train

Distance from "B" to Bahnhofstrasse is 4 min walk.

Not to scale. Drawn from memory.

Fig. 62. Salzburg main railway station and sidings used by the Sonderzüge (Party specials).

100

A captured German general is quoted in the Foxley papers as describing Dr Goebbels as 'a phenomenally clever and intelligent man who can play any part'. This picture, taken in the Propaganda Ministry in Berlin in 1939, shows him acting one such role: the avuncular giver of presents to ethnic German children who had reportedly left Poland after its seizure and partition by Nazi Germany and the Soviet Union at the start of the Second World War. Goebbel's propaganda message was that these children and their parents had been saved from Polish 'persecution' by invading German troops. (Imperial War Museum HU 40080)

## 'COURT' PHOTOGRAPHER

Heinrich Hoffmann (1885–1957) was the Führer's personal photographer. Between 1919 and 1945 he took 2.5 million photographs of Hitler and other leading Nazis. (He probably took the one above.) But he was far more than a photographer. He made a big contribution to the dictator's personality cult, coaching him to be a spellbinding and photogenic orator. He also helped make Hitler rich. It was on Hoffmann's suggestion that the Führer earned a royalty from the sale of every postage stamp bearing his portrait. Hitler first met Eva Braun when she was working in Hoffmann's photographer's shop in Munich. In 1938 the Führer appointed him a professor. In 1947 a West German court found the millionaire Hoffmann guilty of being a Nazi profiteer. It sentenced him to ten years' imprisonment and stripped him of his professorship. The sentence was later reduced to three years but then raised to five in 1950.

Hitler investing General Rommel in March 1942 with the high militar
award of 'Oak Leaves with Diamonds to the Knight's Cross of the Iro
Cross'. In June that year he was promoted to field marshal – Nazi Germany'

youngest – after his capture of Tobruk. A late convert to the need to depose the Führer, Rommel was forced to commit suicide on 14 October 1944. (Imperial War Museum HU 40165)

A side view of the Berghof. With good reason, Eva Braun called th[e] luxurious villa 'the Grand Hotel'. (Imperial War Museum HU 63535)

The Berghof's Great Study had a huge picture window that gave Hitler [a] splendid view of the Bavarian Alps. (Imperial War Museum HU 63538)

Göring's house on the Berghof estate. (Imperial War Museum HU 63543)

The uniforms of Gruppenführer (major-general) Tiefenbacher (left) and an Unterscharführer (sergeant) of the SS Führerbegleitkommando. (Public Record Office HS 6/624)

The tunnel entrance to the Eagle's Nest, photographed shortly after war. Carved out of solid rock by slave labourers, the tunnel led to a lift that took Hitler and his guests to this mountain-top house.
(Imperial War Museum HU 63555)

The Eagle's Nest, which survived the war unscathed. A major tourist attraction providing the finest views of the Bavarian Alps, it is today called by its original name, the Kehlsteinhaus. (Imperial War Museum HU 63553)

Martin Bormann, a Little Foxley. (Imperial War Museum NYP 77063)

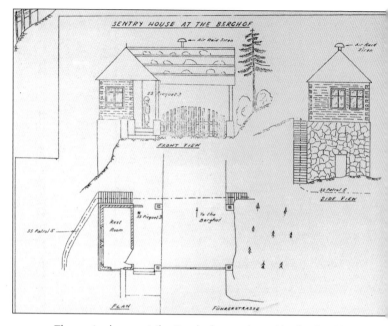

The sentry house at the Berghof as envisaged by Section X.
(Public Record Office HS 6/624).

Reinhard Heydrich, whose
assassination by SOE-trained
Czechoslovaks in Prague in 1942
was exploited by the Gestapo to
organise a series of mass murders
(Imperial War Museum STT 773)

Rudolf Hess, eating a modest meal in his cell while he was on trial at Nuremberg after the war. Probably the most bizarre idea ever conceived by an SOE officer was that Hess might have been persuaded to take part in a Little Foxley operation, perhaps when hypnotised. Unsurprisingly, the idea was never taken seriously. (Imperial War Museum HU 26596)

Berchtesgaden and the Bavarian Alps. (Public Record Office HS6/624)

Otto Skorzeny, another Little Foxley. (Imperial War Museum HU 46178)

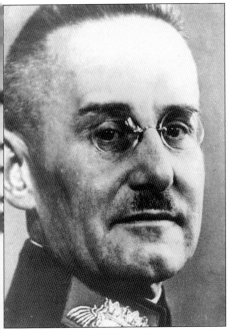

General Franz Halder, the subject of a PWE forgery operation. (Imperial War Museum MH 10933)

A triumphant Hitler in his heyday. But later, when the tide of war turned against him, he never risked assassination by riding through crowded streets in a motorcade. (Public Record Office HS 6/624)

# How to produce a temporary paralysis:

**I.**

1) Before going to bed wrap a round stone, eraser or short piece of rubber tubing in gauze tissue and fasten firmly to exert pressure on spot x (x is the spot where your "funnybone" is located) with tight bandage and allow to remain over night. Take bandage off in the morning.

2) Repeat for several days in succession until there is a numb feeling in your forearm and hand. The numbness and lack of strength which remains for only a few minutes after the first treatments, will last for an increasing length of time in the course of further treatment.

3) When a sufficient degree of paralysis has resulted report to doctor. Describe exactly what you feel; tell him that the condition which started suddenly is becoming worse and worse in the course of time.

4) Continue bandaging your arm from time to time to keep up paralysis, but under no circumstances let the doctor find any traces of the bandage. If there are bandage marks on your arm better not report until they are gone which is usually the case after 24 hours at the latest.

Fig. 1
Right arm.
⊗ marks nerve at location of "funnybone".

Fig. 2
Left arm. rear view.

Fig. 3
Right leg, rear view. Nerve coloured red.

'How to produce temporary paralysis'. This was one of several examples of Nazi propaganda showing Allied troops how to simulate illnesses – just what PWE was doing in booklets secretly distributed among German soldiers by agents of Section X.

What would Joe think of me?' Can the far-away wife or girlfriend be trusted? This picture appeared in another Nazi pamphlet encouraging Allied soldiers to desert. Meanwhile, PWE was targeting German troops with the same desertion message.

ES KOMMT DER TAG!

A PWE-forged sticker with the slogan 'Es kommt der Tag' ('The day will come'). Widely circulated towards the end of the war in Europe, it was greatly admired by members of resistance movements and was a terrifying warning to the Nazis. (Public Record Office) of the former Foreign Minister (he, like Kaltenbrunner, was hanged as a war criminal in 1946) was on subjects more serious than mere postage stamps.

Swiss, Swedish, Turkish, Indian, American and British newspapers, together with several philatelic magazines, reported on the Himmler stamp.[2] The few specimens that reached the international stamp market were sold at sky-high prices. The stamp was also the topic of baseless rumours. One of these was that the Nazi authorities issued not only the six-pfennig Himmler stamp but also other new stamps, in other denominations, featuring Goebbels and Robert Ley, leader of the German Labour Front (DAF).

PWE made the Witzleben forgery to look like a Nazi German commemorative stamp. There were many such special issues of stamps in the Third Reich. Those who bought them, along with ordinary stamps, associated themselves with the charity or official event then being commemorated. In April 1945, the Swiss press published a picture of the Witzleben counterfeit next to DAF commemorative stamps on which its design was based.

Field Marshal von Witzleben had participated in three schemes to depose Hitler and would have been Commander-in-Chief of the Wehrmacht if the July Bomb Plot had succeeded. He was rightly regarded as a man of integrity, even by those who disagreed with his old-fashioned values. His character was summed up by Dr Hans Bernd Gisevius, Vice-Consul in Zurich from 1940 to 1944: 'Witzleben was a man of refreshing simplicity. Political ruses . . . were alien to him. Perhaps not too widely read, certainly no connoisseur of the fine arts, he was rooted in the noble traditions of the old Prussian officer corps, dedicated to country life, a passionate huntsman.'[3]

Born in Breslau, in Silesia (now Wroclaw, in Poland), in December 1881, Witzleben was an army officer from the age of nineteen. He served on the Western Front in the First World War. Possessing no intrinsic interest in politics, he would almost certainly have remained nothing more than a career officer if the Nazis had not come to power. Ironically, it was under Hitler (during the massive rearmament programme) that his promotion became rapid. Between February 1934 and July 1940, he advanced in rank from major-general to field marshal. But in March 1942, when he was on sick leave, Hitler made him retire. Witzleben was always deeply distrustful of the Nazis, but what hardened his opposition to them was their framing of Colonel-General Werner von Fritsch, the army Commander-in-Chief, on a fabricated charge of homosexuality in January 1938. (Although soon acquitted by a military court, Fritsch was not reinstated. He was, however, later given the honorary rank of colonel. He was killed by a stray bullet in Poland in September 1939.)

In one of his stormiest tantrums, Hitler demanded merciless treatment of those who had conspired to kill him. Obeying that order with relish, Judge Roland Freisler, President of the Nazis' special People's Court, went to extreme lengths to humiliate Witzleben and other Bomb Plot defendants – three generals and four other officers – who were arraigned with him. During their trial in Berlin on 7 and 8 August 1944, they were already broken men, having been given a brutal preparation for it by the Gestapo. The men had been kitted out in a jumble of old clothes. They were deprived of braces to keep their trousers up, had not been allowed to shave, and were in a generally unkempt condition. All this had been deliberately arranged, for Goebbels had ordered the making of a film of the trial and the subsequent executions in which the defendants' ordeals would be shown in distressing detail.

Field Marshal von Witzleben, a revered figure in the Wehrmacht, suffered an especially savage humiliation. His false teeth having been confiscated, he looked like a sick old tramp, struggling to hold up his trousers. Judge Freisler, a former communist, regarded Andrei Vishinsky, chief prosecutor in the pre-war Soviet show trials, as his role model. In the style of Vishinsky, he shouted at Witzleben: 'You dirty old man, why do you keep fiddling with your trousers?' Freisler ranted at the Field Marshal and his seven co-defendants in this fashion throughout the trial, being cheered for his efforts by the handpicked people sitting in the body of the court. After this sordid pretence of justice, in which even the defence lawyers joined in condemning the defendants, Witzleben and the others were declared 'guilty', as they always knew they would be. Bomb Plot conspirators 'must be hanged like cattle', Hitler had demanded. That is exactly what happened in prison immediately after the show trial. Stripped to the waist, the eight defendants were strung up from meat hooks screwed into the ceiling. With nooses made of piano wire round their necks, the men dangled in excruciating pain. Their slow deaths were recorded on the film ordered by Goebbels. Processed immediately, it was shown to Hitler in a private screening later that day.

According to Allen Dulles, head of OSS operations in Europe from November 1942, the film was originally thirty miles long. Goebbels arranged for a version cut to eight miles in length to be shown to selected military audiences. He presumably thought the film would be a warning to those tempted to oppose the Führer. However, when it was screened at the Lichterfelde cadet school, the men refused to watch and walked out. Soon after this the Nazis stopped showing the film. However, the show-trial section eventually fell into Allied hands and was screened at the Nuremberg Trials. The section showing the terrible executions is believed to have been destroyed by the Nazis.[4]

That the Political Warfare Executive forged a German charity stamp featuring Field Marshal von Witzleben, a man highly respected in the Wehrmacht and by civilians, was perhaps a skilful move to counter Dr Goebbels' propaganda. The stamp, if seen by many Germans, would have highlighted the fragility of the Hitler dictatorship in the last months of the Third Reich.

PWE and SOE conducted another operation involving a prominent German military leader – Colonel-General Franz Halder (1884–1972), Chief of the Army General Staff from September 1938 to September 1942. In this black propaganda project, a leaflet advocated that Bavaria should break away from the Third Reich and become a separate state. Readers of the leaflet – circulated in Bavaria in May 1942 – were invited to express their opinion on the continuation of the war and on the 'giving of Bavarian blood and food to Prussian interests. . . .' On the leaflet there was a slip which the readers were asked to tear off, mark with a cross, and send to General Halder, himself a Bavarian. Some of the slips did reach the general, probably to his acute embarrassment. Shortly after the end of hostilities in Europe, German Directorate officers speculated that the leaflet might have contributed to Hitler's decision to dismiss Halder. However, there is no evidence that it did so, and it is much more likely that the dictator was making him a scapegoat for recent setbacks on the Eastern Front.

There seems to have been some woolly thinking in planning this operation. Halder was a capable general, which Hitler recognised by awarding him the Knight's Cross after the conquest of Poland. But he was also, in private, bitterly critical of the Nazis and of the Führer personally. Halder might well, therefore, have been much more useful to the Allies if he had remained in office, in the centre of military decision-making.

At various times Halder supported schemes to depose Hitler, but he never took effective action to further such plans. A devout Christian (a Protestant in Catholic Bavaria), he was constantly torn between his devotion to the army and his desire to rid Germany of the Nazis. As a result, he was often under great stress. Occasionally this made him weep, so wrecking his normally stern exterior, for he was the very model of a 1940s German general, with pince-nez spectacles, cropped hair and clipped moustache. On 21 July 1944, the day after the Bomb Plot, Halder, his wife and daughter were arrested by the Gestapo. Between 7 February and 30 April 1945, he was held in concentration camps, and would probably have been executed if the war had gone on longer. From 1948 to 1961 he headed the Historical Liaison Group of the American army's Historical Division.

# Chapter Fifteen

## *Ungentlemanly warfare*

The Ministry of Economic Warfare was correctly nicknamed the 'Ministry of Ungentlemanly Warfare'. It supervised operations by Section X and the German Directorate that were undeniably ungentlemanly – not that any sort of warfare is gentlemanly in any real meaning of the word. But the Second World War, the most terrible conflict ever, was a total war and almost everything that did not violate the Geneva Conventions and other international agreements was regarded by the Allied leaders as an acceptable method of defeating Hitler. It is also undeniable that the different sorts of sabotage organised by SOE's London headquarters did an unquantifiably large amount of damage to the Nazi war economy without much killing or wounding of civilians. It is therefore arguable that if more resources had been allocated to SOE-type selective wrecking, there would have been less need in 1944 and 1945 to rely so heavily on the area bombing of German cities – a strategy that resulted in large-scale civilian casualties. In Hamburg, for instance, about 55,000 people were killed, and in Dresden the total, which included many displaced persons, is roughly estimated to have been 50,000. About 49,000 were killed in Berlin. According to German statistics released in 1962, an estimated 539,000 civilians in the Third Reich died as a result of bombing and other air action.

Although the Allied leaders regarded SOE's sabotage as an effective weapon, they did not fund it on the scale that Baker Street wanted and it had its critics at the centre of the decision-making process. One of these was Marshal of the Royal Air Force Sir Charles Portal, Chief of Britain's Air Staff from October 1940 to December 1945. Referring to the relative merits of sabotage and the huge bombing raids on Germany in 1944 and 1945, he said: 'My bombing offensive is not a gamble. Its dividend is certain. It is a gilt-edged investment. I cannot divert aircraft from a certainty to a gamble [the parachuting of saboteurs] which may be a gold mine and may be completely worthless.'[1]

The argument supporting at least some area bombing was, of course, strong. V1 and V2 weapons were still falling on south-eastern England,[2] Stalin saw the bombing as a major help to Soviet forces advancing towards Berlin, and the war-weary people of all the combatant nations were anxious that the conflict did not last a minute longer than it needed to. However, area bombing as well as sabotage was sometimes a gamble. This was vividly illustrated in an SOE operation conducted after the RAF had done only slight damage in a series of raids in 1943 on the Peugeot car factory at Sochaux, France – a large plant which was being forced to manufacture tank turrets and vehicles for the German army. With the secret cooperation of the Peugeot management and after discussions between the Ministry of Economic Warfare, the Chiefs of Staff and RAF Bomber Command, SOE agents were infiltrated into the factory and placed explosives in the transformer hall and on a few machines that were hard to replace. All the most important machinery was destroyed in subsequent explosions shortly after midnight when the workforce was absent. Some weeks later, replacement presses for the manufacture of the tank turrets arrived from Germany on canal barges. Its French crew fled, its German guards were overpowered, and the barge and its contents were blown up, blocking the canal and making recovery of the remaining machinery difficult. Weeks later still, two more presses arrived from Germany, this time on lorries, with armed SS guards patrolling the route. However, the saboteurs, with grenades and home-made bombs, destroyed the machinery as it was entering the factory yard, unprotected by the SS men. All this destruction was done without totally wrecking the car plant and without causing civilian casualties. In a 'successful' night-time raid, when most aircraft would have found precision bombing impossible because of anti-aircraft fire and technological limitations, the factory and nearby residential property would almost certainly have been largely or wholly flattened, causing heavy loss of life.

Early in 1941 Sir Charles Portal had expressed his general disapproval of SOE saboteurs and assassins. He had written in a minute: 'I think that the dropping of men dressed in civilian clothes for the purpose of killing members of the opposing forces is not an operation with which the Royal Air Force should be associated.' He added that there was a 'vast difference in ethics' between that sort of action and the 'time-honoured operations of the dropping of a spy from the air'.[3] It was criticism like Portal's from him and a few other key members of the Allied leadership that SOE had to contend with throughout the war.

The various sorts of sabotage without explosions also seldom resulted in the loss of civilian life. The insaisissable wrecking of factory machinery was always done stealthily, the saboteurs taking as many precautions as possible to ensure that they were not being watched by Gestapo informers. On all but a relatively few occasions, the Nazi authorities had great difficulty in taking effective action against the different kinds of 'quiet' sabotage.

It is, of course, impossible to estimate accurately the effectiveness of Allied propaganda, black or white. However, Dr Goebbels paid the Political Warfare Executive a compliment of sorts by replaying some of the subversive themes expressed in the black literature secretly circulated by SOE agents. Or perhaps it was the other way round – PWE was stealing a few of the Reich Propaganda Minister's bright ideas?

Some Nazi propaganda leaflets quoted from letters actually or supposedly written by British prisoners of war. One such excerpt from Rifleman —— to a relation (probably his father) in Belfast said: 'I've had very good attention all the time I've been in hospital, everyone has been very good to me, the doctors certainly know their job . . . but we have made friends with lots of German chaps, we have some fine times trying to teach each other our different languages.' The same propaganda message – that being a PoW was much better than the rigours and dangers of front-line army life – was also expressed in an illustrated leaflet entitled *Somewhere in Germany.* An attractive montage of photographs showed Scottish soldiers playing bagpipes, other troops praising the toilet and laundry facilities in an unnamed Stalag, spectators at a sports meeting ('the German guards are very friendly,' the caption said), and PoWs preparing to decorate their rooms 'according to their own taste'. Yet another picture was of a British medical officer delighted by the Germans having given him a clinic equipped with all the drugs and equipment that he needed.

Other Nazi propaganda material used the PWE theme that the wives and girlfriends of soldiers far from home were succumbing to temptations. One leaflet, directed at American soldiers, showed a glamorous young lady about to make a telephone call. She was thinking, so the caption said: 'What about calling up Sam Levy . . . Joe is so far away over there on the front and I'd love to go out and have a good time again. There's so little chance of Joe coming home. Well, I guess I'll just give Sam a call, he'll take me out.' Other examples of this sort of Nazi propaganda pictured the wives and girlfriends being seduced by lecherous men in bars or bedrooms, and wounded soldiers returning home and being shunned by their womenfolk; one Propaganda Ministry slogan said: 'Gentleman prefer blondes, but blondes don't like cripples.' A variant of this material inciting desertion was targeted at Allied soldiers who had small children. For example, the cover of one Nazi booklet showed a sad little girl saying: 'Come back home alive, Daddy!'

Much of the Propaganda Ministry output was, of course, violently anti-Semitic. It also represented Roosevelt, Churchill and other Allied leaders as monsters. Yet other literature sought to create ill feeling between the British and the Americans, between the Canadians and the British, and between other British Commonwealth members and the British. A few illustrated leaflets explained in detail how to simulate illnesses – an idea almost certainly taken from PWE black propaganda. In view of the Nazi racial policies, the most provocative of Goebbels' literature targeted at Allied troops was a leaflet addressed to 'Colored Soldiers in the U.S. Forces!' It said: 'The white population in the U.S.A. do not allow you to pray in their churches, although you are American citizens. In Germany anything like this would be impossible. Colored people living in Germany can always go to any church they like. . . COME OVER TO US if you are fed up with this war and want to get home safe and sound. . . You will be well treated as a prisoner-of-war in a German camp. . . DON'T HESITATE. If you wait too long, it may be too late.'

Apart from the anti-Semitic effusions and a few other crudities, the Nazi propaganda literature was skilfully produced, attractively illustrated and had themes that might have appealed to some demoralised Allied soldiers. However, Dr Goebbels' sustained efforts to subvert the Allies, military and civilian, were almost totally unsuccessful. For example, the wartime broadcasts from Germany by William Joyce, a leading member of the British Union of Fascists, were listened to in Britain for their entertainment value; his nasal voice and insinuating manner earned him the nickname 'Lord Haw-Haw'.

In contrast to all the output sponsored by Goebbels, Allied propaganda often hit its targets. The Nazi authorities, at least once, admitted as much. Addressing a meeting of Gauleiters in Munich on 7 November 1943, Colonel-General Alfred Jodl, Chief of the Operations Staff of the German High Command, deplored the 'devil of subversion' in Germany, causing the country to be 'strained to the utmost'. Delivered eighteen months before the end of the European war, this was a handsome back-handed tribute to the effectiveness of Allied psychological warfare. Jodl clearly had no illusions about the vulnerability of the dictatorship that he served so diligently.

It would therefore seem that if the Allies had effectively armed anti-Nazis in Germany towards the end of the conflict, there might have been a widespread and successful rebellion against the Hitler regime. 'The Fomenting of Revolution in Germany' was the subject of an undated minute written anonymously by a Section X officer, probably in 1944. Concerning 'arming the opposition', it said:

At the right moment it will be effective to drop loaded arms and ammunition among working parties of prisoners employed outside concentration camps. It must be repeated, however, that it is not expected that use will be made of these weapons unless and until Germany has suffered some heavy reverse.

We can expect no aid from the [German] army until the later stages of the revolution; <u>we must rely upon the workmen of Germany</u> [The minute-writer, or somebody else, underlined these words in pencil.] At present the workman feels discontented, but helpless under the terror, and his attitude of mind is emphasised by his doubt whether the Allies are capable of defeating Germany.

The writer added that the revolution against the Hitler dictatorship would occur only after a German military reverse.

The most effective method of impressing the population that such a reverse has in fact been suffered is unquestionably by a succession of bombing raids on open towns and cities whose population contains a high percentage of artisans.

The writer concluded:

Revolution is produced by a state of mind resulting from an intolerable oppression of the body. It is the considered opinion of this Section that revolution can be fostered in Germany and will indubitably break out when, but only when, the fear of physical retribution from outside eclipses the fear of terrorism by the present regime. . . .

The large-scale arming of anti-Nazi Germans, foreign slave labourers and prisoners of war was considered a possibility by some Allied leaders, including Churchill, but only 'at the right time'. Towards the end of 1941, Professor Frederick Lindemann (Lord Cherwell), Churchill's chief scientific adviser,[4] envisaged the dropping over Germany of vast numbers of inexpensive and easily operated devices that could be used to cause explosions or fires. Initially called the Moon project, Lindemann's idea was gradually developed as Operation Braddock.[5] By 1942 various devices, such as pencil incendiaries and phosphorus pellets wrapped in moist cotton, had been produced. One proposal was that they should be dropped in packages also containing a railway-line cutting charge and a cheap automatic pistol of a sort then being manufactured in bulk in the United States; it was thought that a saboteur might have to use such a weapon to defend himself, but, if it were found in his possession by the Gestapo, his fate would have been sealed. However, the final decision was that the main effort should be put into the invention and mass production of an incendiary device which would be small and easy to carry, hide and ignite.

In a letter to Churchill in October 1943, Lord Selborne, a keen advocate of Braddock, reported that 2.5 million of these devices were 'ready for use' and production was continuing at a rate of 300,000 a month. He added that a Lancaster bomber could carry about 10,000 of them to any target within 600 miles. Fifty Lancasters could drop 500,000 over western Germany. They would float down on pieces of card, and attached to them would be printed instructions on their use in eleven languages – English, German, French, Dutch, Italian, Greek, Russian, Polish, Czech, Serb and Serbo-Croat. Selborne explained that the instructions would be 'foolproof' and that the devices could be put in places such as a lorry, woodshed, haystack and the packing rooms of a factory, post office or railway station. By 1943 about 6.7 million prisoners of war and 'forced workers' were in Germany. Many were employed on farms or in factories. If only one per cent of the 2.5 million incendiaries were picked up by hands willing to use them, 25,000 fires would break out in Germany. Selborne suggested that 50 Lancasters should undertake an 'initial shower' of the devices 'at a very early date'. This needed to be followed by 'weekly showers' by 25 Lancasters, coordinated with black propaganda broadcasts by PWE in support of the operation. He thought that the Nazi authorities' efforts in collecting as many of the incendiaries as possible would involve a nationwide search in woods and fields and on roof tops, and would be a great tax on manpower resources. Selborne added: 'Now that the Nazis' morale and the Nazis' fortress are beginning to crack, there is reason to hope that a considerable number of forced workers, and possibly even anti-Nazi Germans, might feel that this gave them the opportunity of directly contributing to the termination of their misery. If Gauleiters' houses were burned down, food supplies and factories were destroyed on a large scale, etc., the results on German morale might be profound.'

A person wishing to activate one of the incendiaries would, as described in the printed instructions, remove a covering piece of protective tape and press a part of the device clearly marked with a red spot. This would crush a tube within the mechanism. The finder of the incendiary would also choose when to ignite it. The instructions informed him about a range of time settings between fifteen minutes and thirty-four hours. Allied radio broadcasts urged the finders to hide the devices and to use them later when it was safe to do so.

Acting on Professor Lindemann's advice, Churchill had authorised the research into the feasibility of Braddock. Nevertheless, the British Chiefs of Staff repeatedly saw reasons for delaying the start of the operation. Their viewpoint was, for example, expressed thus in a letter to Churchill on 29 April 1943: 'The degree of resistance of forced foreign labour and anti-Axis elements in Germany has not yet risen to a point at which, in our view, success is sufficiently probable to justify the necessary diversion of aircraft from the bomber offensive. Moreover, if aircraft could be diverted from bombing the Axis, they would be far more usefully employed in the Battle of the Atlantic.'

In May 1944, General Eisenhower expressed belief that Braddock might become 'a valuable weapon' in the exploitation of the impending Normandy invasion if it were used at the psychological moment. He emphasised, however, that the operation should begin only when Nazi control over foreign workers was diminishing and when severe retaliation was less likely than at present. Two months later, on 24 July, Lord Selborne was still pressing Braddock's cause. In a letter to Churchill, he recalled a previously expressed view that the operation should not start until rioting had begun in German towns. It now seemed, he said, that rioting had occurred in 'various parts' and that Germany was in 'a turmoil', though the Nazis had 'the upper hand'. In these circumstances he suggested 'a preliminary shower' of 500,000 incendiaries on the Ruhr.

However, it was not until 25 September that Operation Braddock began, and the American bombers involved were permitted to drop only 250,000 of the devices. Small numbers were dropped later. For example, a mere 3,500 of the incendiaries fell on the night of 20–21 February 1945. Churchill did not like that. He wrote to Portal seventeen days later: 'We have three-and-three-quarter million Braddock incendiaries ready, and the foreign workers in Germany must be very restive by now. Surely the time has come to use this weapon.'

It could be argued that Braddock was potentially the most important irregular warfare operation on German territory. If undertaken as its planners had intended, it might have significantly shortened the European war. In the event, the comparatively few incendiaries that were dropped were little more than an irritant to the Nazis. No armaments factories or Gauleiters' houses burst into flames. The operation was the victim of conflicting schools of thought within the Allied leadership.

Do you, the reader, think that Section X and the German Directorate achieved much? Operations Foxley and Foxley II turned out to be pipe-dreams. Braddock was a reality, but only just so. However, SOE's staff officers dealing with clandestine activities in Germany and Austria should not be judged on their handling of these projects – work that took up only a tiny fraction of their time. Their main contribution to the Allied war effort was masterminding many successful sabotage operations and cooperating with the Political Warfare Executive in ensuring that black propaganda was widely disseminated. Section X and the German Directorate engaged in almost all the different sorts of this ungentlemanly warfare.

# Appendix A
# *Germans opposing Hitler*

Fortunately for Hitler and tragically for the Allied war effort, as well as for humanity in general, the organisations, movements and individuals comprising the active German opposition to Nazi tyranny had no joint policy. Indeed, they had little or nothing in common except their hatred of the regime. However, the brave men and women engaged in this clandestine resistance came from all walks of life. Notable among them were influential figures as diverse as generals, Abwehr intelligence officers, senior government officials, members of the banned political parties and trade unions, clergy and lawyers. Surprisingly few of these people were security conscious. For example, it was not uncommon for conspirators to keep diaries and talk about sensitive matters on the telephone. As a result, the Gestapo eventually identified most of the Germans who seriously threatened to topple the Nazi dictatorship. The Gestapo's revenge was barbaric.

The most important anti-Hitler group in Germany was the Kreisau Circle, co-founded in 1933 by Count Helmuth von Moltke and named after his Silesian estate (now Krzyzowa in Poland). Its twenty-five or so core members were lawyers, clergy, academics and other professional people of all non-Nazi political persuasions except communism. For most of the time the Kreisau Circle was only a secret discussion group, planning a democratic post-Hitler Germany based on Christian principles. The many other opposition groups included Neu Beginnen (composed of Social Democrats), the White Rose, the right-wing Freiburg Circle, the communist Gruppe Herbert Baum and the Solf Circle (named after one of its leaders, Hanna Solf, widow of a former Ambassador to Japan).

Prominent members of the German Resistance (Der Widerstand) included:

*General Ludwig Beck* (born 1880). Nominal military leader of the Bomb Plot of July 1944. He was one of the principal planners of pre-war German rearmament, initially as head of the Truppenamt, Hitler's unannounced military staff organisation set up in October 1933 in violation of the Versailles Treaty, and then as Chief of the General

Staff from July 1935 to August 1938, when he resigned in protest against Hitler's imminent action against Czechoslovakia. Beck was arrested and forced to commit suicide after the discovery of the Bomb Plot.

*Dietrich Bonhöffer* (b. 1906). A prominent Lutheran pastor and theologian. On a visit to Stockholm in May 1942, he and Bishop George Bell of Chichester discussed proposals by influential German anti-Nazi conspirators for a negotiated peace with the Allies if Hitler were overthrown. Bonhöffer was imprisoned from April 1943, most of the time in concentration camps, until his execution in April 1945.

*Klaus Bonhöffer* (b. 1901), a brother of Dietrich. A lawyer working for the Lufthansa airline, he was in clandestine contact with Social Democrats, trade unions and the Confessional Church. He was shot dead by the SS on the night of 22/23 April 1945.

*Admiral Wilhelm Canaris* (b. 1887). Head of the Abwehr, the OKW's intelligence and counter-intelligence organisation from January 1935 to June 1944. He used Abwehr contacts to pass information to the Allies and to save many Jews from extermination. However, though hating the Nazis and regarding Hitler as mad, he shrank from personal involvement in the Bomb Plot. Nevertheless, he was arrested after it and was hanged in Flossenbürg concentration camp in April 1945.

*Alfred Delp* (b. 1907). A Jesuit priest, theologian and editor. Executed in February 1945 for being active in the Kreisau Circle.

*Hans von Dohnanyi* (b. 1902). A lawyer, he successively held senior posts in the Ministry of Justice and the Abwehr. These enabled him to compile a record of Nazi crimes from 1933 and to play a major role in anti-Hitler plotting, particularly as an intermediary between Beck, Wilhelm Leuschner and other leading conspirators and in attempts through the Vatican to obtain a negotiated peace with the Allies. Arrested in April 1943, Dohnanyi is believed to have been executed in Sachsenhausen concentration camp in April 1945.

*(Johann) Georg Elser* (b. 1903). A skilled artisan, he nearly succeeded in killing Hitler with a time-bomb in the Bürgerbäukeller, Munich, in November 1939. Arrested shortly afterwards, he was murdered by the Gestapo on 9 April 1945.

*General Erich Fellgiebel* (b. 1886). Commander of Signal Troops, 1939–44. Executed on 4 September 1944 for his part in the Bomb Plot.

*Dr Hans Bernd Gisevius* (1904–74). Vice-Consul in Zurich, 1940–4, and an Abwehr agent. Early in 1943 he contacted Allen Dulles, head of the OSS's European office in Berne, Switzerland.

*Dr Karl Friedrich Gördeler* (b. 1884). The nominal civilian leader of the plot to kill Hitler in July 1944. Most of the plotters wanted him to be Chancellor in a post-Nazi government. Mayor of Leipzig, 1930–7, Price Commissioner, 1931–2 and 1934–5. He was tortured and hanged in Plötzensee prison, February 1945.

*Hans-Bernd von Haeften* (b. 1905). Lawyer, diplomat and Kreisau Circle member. Executed on 15 August 1944.

*Lieutenant Werner von Haeften* (b. 1909). Brother of Hans-Bernd. Colonel Stauffenberg's aide-de-camp when the Rastenburg bomb exploded on 20 July 1944. A few hours later he was executed, together with Stauffenberg, General Friedrich Olbricht and Colonel Albrecht Mertz von Quirnheim.

*Baron Ulrich von Hassell* (b. 1881). Ambassador in Rome, 1932–8, and son-in-law of Admiral Alfred von Tirpitz, founder of the Imperial German Navy. Hassell was the July 1944 plotters' proposed Foreign Minister in a post-Hitler government. Involved in anti-Nazi schemes over many years, he was hanged in September 1944.

*Dr Theodor Haubach* (b. 1896). A Social Democratic politician and journalist belonging to the Kreisau Circle. Hanged in January 1945.

*Dr Albrecht Haushofer* (b. 1903). Professor, Institute of Political Geography and Geopolitics, Berlin. He had some influence on Rudolf Hess, who allowed him to travel; he used this privilege for anti-Nazi purposes. Wrote poetry when held in Moabit prison. Murdered by the SS on 22 April 1945.

*Count Wolf Heinrich von Helldorf* (b. 1896). President of the Berlin police, 1935–44. Co-conspirator with Gisevius and SS officer Artur

Nebe, head of the Criminal Investigation Police. Hanged in August 1944. (Nebe executed in March 1945.)

*General Erich Hoepner* (b. 1886). Dismissed by Hitler in January 1942 for refusing to obey absurd and inhuman orders. Later in the Resistance. Hanged in August 1944.

*Professor Jens Jessen* (b. 1895). Political scientist, Berlin University. A right-wing member of the Kreisau Circle, he had been a qualified admirer of the Nazis in their early years. Executed in November 1944.

*Captain Friedrich Karl Klausing* (b. 1920). Colonel Stauffenerg's adjutant. Executed on 8 August 1944.

*Ewald von Kleist-Schmenzin* (b. 1890). A wealthy farmer and monarchist who in 1933 openly expressed anti-Nazi views, believing that his high social status would protect him from persecution. At Beck's request, he visited London for political talks in 1938. Executed in April 1945. (His son, Lieutenant Ewald Heinrich von Kleist, a collaborator with Colonel Stauffenberg, volunteered to assassinate Hitler.)

*Dr Julius Leber* (b. 1891). Member of the Reichstag, 1924–33. A highly respected Social Democrat, journalist and former concentration camp prisoner, he was Stauffenberg's nominee to be Chancellor in a post-Hitler government. Executed in January 1945.

*Wilhelm Leuschner* (b. 1890). Trade union leader and associate of Leber. Hanged in September 1944.

*Colonel Albrecht Mertz von Quirnheim* (b. 1905). General Olbricht's Chief of Staff. Executed on 20 July 1944, along with Olbricht, Stauffenberg and Lieutenant Werner von Haeften, shortly after the discovery of the Bomb Plot.

*Count Helmuth James von Moltke* (b. 1907). Co-founder of the Kreisau Circle. Worked from 1939 to 1944 as a military and international lawyer for the Armed Forces' High Command; his military ancestors included Field Marshal von Moltke of the 1870–1 Franco-Prussian War. Executed in January 1945.

*Dr Josef Müller* (1898–1979). A Catholic lawyer and Abwehr officer from 1939 to 1943, he was a Resistance emissary to the Vatican.

*Martin Niemöller* (1892–1984). Lutheran pastor and concentration camp prisoner from 1937 to 1945.

*General Friedrich Olbricht* (b. 1888). Head of the Reserve Army's supply section and deputy to General Friedrich Fromm, Commander of the Reserve Army. Olbricht was deeply engaged in anti-Hitler conspiracies from February 1943. However, on 20 July 1944, when he learned at the War Ministry that Stauffenberg's bomb had failed to kill Hitler, he lost his nerve. Fromm, whom he had arrested, was released and took control of the situation. Shortly afterwards Olbricht, Stauffenberg, Colonel Mertz von Quirnheim and Lieutenant Werner von Haeften were executed on Fromm's orders. (Fromm, who for a while had seemed sympathetic to the conspirators, was hanged in March 1945.)

*Major-General Hans Oster* (b. 1888). An Abwehr officer from 1933 and Canaris' deputy from 1938 to 1943. In May 1940, he informed the Dutch military attaché in Berlin of the impending invasions of Norway, Denmark, Belgium and Holland. He also used his influential official position to save the lives of many Jews and to prick the consciences of generals and others in an effort to prevent a range of Nazi atrocities. Implicated in the Bomb Plot, he was executed in Flossenbürg concentration camp on 9 April 1945.

*Dr Friedrich Perels* (b. 1910). A lawyer active in the Confessional Church. Arrested in October 1944, he was taken from his cell on the night of 22/23 April 1945, and shot dead by the SS.

*Professor Johannes Popitz* (b. 1884). Finance Minister of Prussia, 1933–44. A right-wing Resistance member and former Nazi, he perhaps had a moderating influence on Himmler, whom he met on 26 August 1943. Executed in February 1945.

*Professor Adolf Reichwein* (b. 1898). Educationist, historian and economist, a Social Democrat member of the Kreisau Circle. Executed in October 1944 for his part in the Bomb Plot.

*Field Marshal Erwin Rommel* (b. 1891). A brilliant strategist and an inspiring leader, he was respected by German and Allied troops alike, not least because of his chivalrous treatment of prisoners of war. He was aware of the Bomb Plot, but was a late convert to the need to depose Hitler, preferring that he should be imprisoned rather than assassinated. Rommel was forced to commit suicide on 14 October 1944.

*Dr Hjalmar Schacht* (1877–1970). The mastermind of Germany's pre-war economic recovery. President of the Reichsbank, 1923–30 and 1933–9, Economics Minister, 1934–7, and Minister without Portfolio until January 1943. Although pro-Nazi in 1930, he was active in the Resistance from 1938 and was arrested after the failure of the Bomb Plot. He spent the rest of the European war in concentration camps. Acquitted at the Nuremberg Trials.

*Hans and Sophie Scholl* (b. 1918 and 1921 respectively). Brother and sister, they belonged to the White Rose, a group of pamphleteering anti-Nazi students, scientists and artists who regarded Hitler as 'the anti-Christ'. Hans, Sophie and other members of the group were executed in February 1943.

*Count Fritz-Dietlof von der Schulenburg* (b. 1902). A left-wing member of the Kreisau Circle and a former Nazi, he held several influential appointments, including Vice-President of the Berlin police from 1937 to 1940. Executed in August 1944.

*Captain Count Ulrich-Wilhelm Schwerin von Schwanenfeld* (b. 1902). He was Field Marshal Witzleben's assistant adjutant in Paris in 1941 and later held influential military posts in Berlin. Believing as early as 1935 in the need to kill Hitler, he maintained contact with the Kreisau Circle and anti-Nazi members of the Abwehr. Executed in September 1944.

*Count Berthold Schenk von Stauffenberg* (b. 1905). A Doctor of Law who had worked in the early 1930s at the International Court of Justice in The Hague, he was a senior legal adviser to the Naval High Command from the start of the war until 20 July 1944. Executed on 10 August 1944.

*Colonel Count Claus Schenk von Stauffenberg* (b. 1907), brother of Berthold. He narrowly failed to kill Hitler with a bomb which he planted in a briefing hut at the Rastenburg FHQ on 20 July 1944. A few hours later, that night, he and three of his fellow conspirators, General Olbricht, Colonel Mertz von Quirnheim and Lieutenant Haeften, were executed in the courtyard of the War Ministry. Stauffenberg, a Catholic, was one of many religiously motivated members of the Resistance. The bomb, which he concealed in a briefcase, was made of a kilogram of plastic explosive obtained from SOE, although it had no hand in planning the explosion. He made the assassination attempt despite having lost his right eye, right arm and part of his left hand through war wounds in north Africa in April 1943.

*Major-General Helmuth Stieff* (b. 1901). Head of the Army High Command's organisation department, 1942–4. Executed on 8 August 1944.

*General Karl-Heinrich von Stülpnagel* (b. 1886). Military commander in France, 1942–4. A long-time friend of Beck. Executed in August 1944.

*Brigadier Henning von Tresckow* (b. 1901). Pro-Hitler before he came to power. A staff officer in Army Group Centre, 1941–3. Chief of Staff, Second Army, from November 1943. A close collaborator with Colonel Stauffenberg. He committed suicide after the failure of the Bomb Plot.

*Adam von Trott zu Solz* (b. 1909). Studied at Oxford University, 1932–3. Lawyer and widely travelled diplomat, both before and during the war. Advised the Kreisau Circle on foreign policy and made fruitless attempts to persuade the Allies to take the German Resistance seriously. Joined the Nazi Party in 1940 to provide cover for his clandestine activities. Executed in August 1944.

*Josef Wirmer* (b. 1901). A left-wing Centre Party member and lawyer, acting before 1933 on behalf of Catholic students. He also gave legal advice to Jews. His house was a meeting place for Resistance activists of various backgrounds. Executed in September 1944.

*Field Marshal Erwin von Witzleben* (b. 1881). Commander-in-Chief West for about a year until March 1942, when he retired because of ill-health. Having taken part in coup plots in 1938–9 and 1943–4, he agreed to command the army in a post-Hitler Germany. Executed in August 1944.

*Count Peter Yorck von Wartenburg* (b. 1904). A lawyer and government official, he served in the OKW Defence Economy Office from 1942. A co-founder of the Keisau Circle and close associate of his cousin, Colonel Stauffenberg. Executed in August 1944.

# Appendix B

## *No shortage of would-be assassins*

A German historian, Peter Hoffmann,[1] has said that at least forty-six attempts to kill Hitler were made between 1921 and 1945. In 1933 alone, the year he came to power, there were ten such attempts which the police investigated as being seriously intended. There were also various plots to depose the Nazi dictatorship bloodlessly or with a minimum of bloodshed.

It is fixed in many people's minds that the well-publicised Bomb Plot of 20 July 1944, was the only assassination attempt in which Hitler's life was seriously threatened. That is not so. In November 1939, the dictator had narrowly missed being killed by a bomb made and detonated by Georg Elser, a small shy man who, although being a communist sympathiser, acted alone.[2]

A highly skilled joiner who had worked in clock and armature factories, he concealed the bomb in a hole in a pillar inside Munich's Bürgerbäukeller beer-hall. He spent thirty-five nights secretly digging the hole, into which he placed the bomb on 1 November, priming it on the following night. On 5 November he set the fuse to explode the bomb on 8 November at 9.20 p.m. when Hitler was due to make his annual speech to fellow participants in the 1923 'Beer-Hall Putsch'.[3] However, in the event the dictator addressed the meeting (delivering an anti-British tirade) from 8.10 p.m. to 9.07 p.m. He then left. The bomb exploded as planned, killing eight people and wounding sixty-three. But by then Elser had already been arrested near the Swiss frontier. He spent the next five years in captivity, mainly in concentration camps, and was murdered by the Gestapo on 9 April 1945.

Conspicuously courageous men like the aristocrat Colonel Stauffenberg and the artisan Elser personified the disunity of the German Resistance (Der Widerstand). It was the perceived ineffectiveness of the German Resistance that caused the Allied leaders, political and military, to regard it as being incapable of killing Hitler or indeed of playing any significant part in the war effort. Whether the Allies were correct in making that assessment is a matter of debate. Countless thousands of words have been said and written on that question, which remains controversial even now, so long after the event. That the Allies did not take Der Widerstand seriously is resented by some present-day Germans, understandably so. However, the matter has been examined dispassionately by Germans as much as by others.

For instance, speaking at a conference organised by the Goethe House in New York in April 1988, Willy Brandt, the former West German Chancellor, commented on the 'limited effectiveness' of the 'other Germany' during the twelve years of the Nazi dictatorship. 'When I was a young man,' he said:

> we referred to ourselves as the 'opposition'. Of course, we knew about the diversity of those opposing the Nazis, and we were aware of their inadequacy . . . there was very little resistance deserving of the name that was not soon discovered, with the means available to the totalitarian regime at the time, or even destroyed before it got started. One of the major differences between resistance in Germany and similar movements that emerged in several of the countries occupied after 1939 was that the latter acted mainly in defence of their own national interests. In the case of Germany, those who were against the Nazis constantly ran the risk of being misinterpreted as if they were anti-nationalists; and this is, in fact, how some foreign observers of contempoary events described them, even after 1945. . . .
>
> All those individuals and groups who risked their lives by refusing to submit to tyranny may not have been able to stop enforced political conformity in Germany, nor were they able to prevent the Second World War or the Holocaust. But they certainly bore testimony against the notion of collective guilt by an entire nation, and they did so not only at the beginning but also towards the end of Nazi tyranny.

Another contributor to the Goethe House conference, Peter Hoffmann, the historian, stated: 'Between 1933 and 1945 about three million Germans were held for political reasons in concentration camps and prisons. Tens of thousands were executed, after being sentenced to death by a court; more were simply murdered in camps and prisons. These numbers reveal the potential for popular resistance in Germany society – and what happened to it.' In Hoffman's opinion, 'the most active (and continuously active) centre of resistance' was the Abwehr [the OKW's intelligence and counter-intelligence organisation], but it was 'frustrated by lack of military support'. Eventually the anti-Nazis within the Abwehr plotted to kill Hitler and then move Reserve Army units to take over the government. 'In the meantime,' he added, 'the [Abwehr] centre was active in saving Jews and other potential victims and in maintaining and establishing contact with enemy powers. But saving Jews became its undoing: the centre was broken up by arrests in April 1943.'[4]

Hoffmann justifiably criticised the failure of anti-Nazi army officers to give their Abwehr opposite-numbers the support they needed. However, elements within the Wehrmacht, not just ones within the Reserve Army, did plot to topple the Hitler regime. They were appalled by what Hoffmann has called 'the wanton sacrifice' of the Sixth Army in Stalingrad in January–February 1943. This was the result of the dictator's order to the army commander, Field Marshal Paulus, to continue fighting regardless of the consquences – these turning out to be an estimated 70,000 German soldiers killed and a vast number of others wounded or taken prisoner (the captives included Paulus and twenty-four other generals).

Hitler's characteristic decision-making on this occasion was obviously criminal and militarily mad. From after the Battle of Stalingrad until the end of the Third Reich, many officers were willing to remove the Führer from the scene if the unlikely chance of doing so ever arose. Some thought they saw such an opportunity.

Several officers of Army Detachment Lanz in the Kharkov area of the Ukraine decided in February 1943, that when Hitler made an expected imminent visit to Army Group B headquarters at Poltava, they would arrest and kill him. However, the dictator changed his travel plans without warning, as he often did, and instead visited Army Group South's headquarters at Saporozhe on 17 February. On 13 March Hitler conferred with Field Marshal von Kluge at Army Group Centre's headquarters near Smolensk, where there were about six members of Kluge's staff, led by his operations officer, Colonel Henning von Tresckow, who were prepared to go to any lengths to be rid of their detested and discredited Führer. These conspirators planned to have him riddled with submachine-gun bullets while he was having lunch with Kluge. However, these would-be assassins would have had to begin firing immediately they had opened the dining-room door, giving them no opportunity to take accurate aim. Although the field marshal shared the conspirators' opinion of Hitler, he refused to allow this particular method of killing him. There was an excellent reason for this: Kluge himself would be sitting next to the Führer! However, it was thought that all was not lost. During the lunch Tresckow asked a staff officer who travelled on Hitler's personal aircraft to deliver a small parcel to another officer at Army

High Command headquarters. Tresckow said that 'bottles of spirits' were in the parcel, but in fact it contained two mines with a 30-minute fuse. Lieutenant Fabian von Schlabrendorff, another of the plotters, started the fuse before handing over the parcel shortly before the plane took off. However, the mines did not explode. If they had done so, they would have blown a huge hole in the fuselage, almost certainly causing the aircraft to crash. Fortunately, the parcel was not opened. Schlabrendorff flew to Berlin on the next flight and, saying that a great mistake had been made, retrieved the parcel. He found that the fuse had functioned, but it had not ignited the explosive, probably because the temperature on Hitler's aircraft had been too low to do so.

Some conspirators were prepared to die themselves when killing the dictator. One such plotter willing to make the supreme sacrifice was Colonel Baron Rudolph-Christoph von Gersdorff, a counter-intelligence officer at Army Group Centre headquarters. On 21 March 1943, he was required to visit Berlin to take part in the annual Heroes' Memorial ceremonies at which Hitler opened an exhibition of captured arms and ammunition. Gersdorff, who was to lead a small group accompanying the dictator as he examined the exhibits, decided to carry in his overcoat pockets the two mines that had failed to explode in the aircraft. Schlabrendorff had now given them 10-minute fuses, which Gersdorff set shortly before Hitler entered the exhibition rooms. In the event, however, the Führer rushed through the rooms in no more than two minutes, not looking at a single exhibit. Gersdorff also sped away – to a lavatory where he defused the mines!

Towards the end of 1943 another officer, Captain Baron Axel von dem Bussche, volunteered to assassinate Hitler in an explosion in which he too expected to die. It was planned that he would be granted leave from his tank regiment and put in charge of a demonstration of new infantry equipment in Berlin that Hitler was to watch. But before that could happen the equipment was destroyed in an air raid. Shortly after returning to his unit in January 1944, Bussche lost a leg in combat and was in hospital for a long time. Learning of this, Lieutenant Ewald Heinrich von Kleist suggested that he kill the Führer and himself at the next equipment demonstration. However, when the event was staged in July, he was refused permission to attend. Yet another would-be assassin was Captain Eberhard von Breitenbuch, who hoped to shoot Hitler with a pistol. He accompanied Field Marshal Busch to a conference with the dictator in March 1944, but was unexpectedly forbidden to enter the conference room.

Some would-be assassins of Hitler were non-Germans. For example, a 22-year-old Swiss theological student, Maurice Bavaud, tried to shoot him in Munich on 9 November 1938, the anniversary of the 1923 Beer-hall Putsch. This was a year before Elser's assassination attempt.

Pretending to be an admirer of the Führer, Bavaud had made several previous visits to various parts of Germany, including Berchtesgaden. But he had never got anywhere near his quarry, who was always elusive and almost always heavily guarded. He therefore decided that his only chance of succeeding in what had become an obsessive mission was to kill Hitler at the Putsch anniversary celebrations when he marched through the streets of Munich at the head of a parade of fellow Putsch veterans. Claiming to be the correspondent of a Swiss newspaper, Bavaud, with a revolver in his overcoat pocket, was given a front-row seat overlooking part of the parade route. But when Hitler came in view, the Stormtroopers who lined the street gave the Nazi salute, their extended right arms obscuring Bavaud's intended line of fire. Leaving his revolver in his pocket, he was not caught then, and he hoped to have another shot at the Führer later. Eventually, however, having run out of money, this extraordinarily determined young man had to try to go home. Unfortunately, while he was still in Germany, he was arrested after being found to be carrying an invalid railway ticket. Under intense interrogation, he revealed his intention to kill Hitler. Sentenced to death by a People's Court, he was beheaded in May 1941.

Those non-Germans who seriously planned to assassinate Hitler before the war did not include any UK citizens. However, the British Military Attaché in Berlin from 1937 to 1939, Colonel (later Lieutenant-General) F. Noel Mason-Macfarlane[5], declared his desire to kill that "arch-thug" who, he believed, was hell-bent on military aggression at any costs.

Mason-Macfarlane, whose repeated condemnation of Chamberlain's appeasement policy earned him many enemies in high places, expressed his feelings in April 1939 in a private conversation with Ewan Butler, *The Times* correspondent in Berlin. Both men were looking out of the windows of Mason-Macfarlane's lounge in his residence overlooking the Charlottenburger Chaussee. They saw workmen hanging up swastika banners near the platform from which Hitler was due to watch a grand military parade celebrating the anniversary of his birthday on 20 April. An "easy rifle shot," the colonel said, adding; "I could pick the bastard off from here as easy as winking, and what's more I'm thinking of doing it." He was, of course, speaking in the full knowledge that there was no chance of him being given permission to do the deed. Later, the British Government position was made plain when Lord Halifax, the Foreign Secretary, declared that assassination was not "a substitute for diplomacy."

# Appendix C
## *The July Bomb Plot*

Colonel Count Claus von Stauffenberg, Chief of Staff of the Reserve Army, made three attempts to assassintate Hitler in July 1944. On 6 July he visited the Berghof carrying a large quantity of plastic explosive. It seems he had hoped that Major-General Helmuth Stieff, head of the Army High Command's organisation department, would use the explosive to kill the Führer on the following day. However, Stieff withdrew an earlier offer to be the assassin, and Stauffenberg resolved to do the deed himself and also to lead the July Bomb Plot conspirators. There was evidently no opportunity to kill Hitler during this Berghof visit.

Stauffenberg returned to the Obersalzberg on 11 July to report to the Führer on the formation of a new combat unit to serve on the Eastern Front. This time he did not try to kill Hitler because some of the leading conspirators had insisted that Göring and Himmler, neither of whom were present on this occasion, must also die in the planned explosion. These conspirators believed that with Hitler, Göring and Himmler dead, the Nazi regime would collapse. Four days later, Stauffenberg attended a conference called by the Führer at the Rastenburg FHQ (the Wolf's Lair). When Göring and Himmler did not turn up for this meeting, Stauffenberg decided that he would ignite his plastic explosive regardless. However, he had no opportunity to set off the fuse.

On the morning of 20 July Colonel Stauffenberg again visited the Wolf's Lair. He had been summoned there to report on the 'blocking divisions' that the Reserve Army was forming to strengthen the Eastern Front. The colonel and his adjutant, Lieutenant Werner von Haeften, arrived at the Wolf's Lair airfield at about 10 a.m. and then had breakfast at the FHQ commandant's headquarters. From 11 a.m. Stauffenberg attended several conferences with officers on Hitler's personal staff in preparation for a noon briefing at which he was to deliver his report. The last of these preparatory meetings was chaired by Field Marshal Keitel in his office hut. Hitler's bunker, in which he slept, and his office hut were in another compound some distance away. As Keitel's briefing ended just as the Führer's one was due to begin, the field marshal was worried that he might be late in arriving at Hitler's hut.

When the officers were on the point of leaving to attend the noon briefing, Stauffenberg said to Keitel's adjutant that he wished to have a brief wash and change his shirt. He was shown where to go but reappeared shortly afterwards, looking for Haeften. It was reasonable to expect that a one-armed man like Stauffenberg needed the help of his aide when changing a shirt. Meanwhile, Haeften, his nerves on edge because he was carrying a package containing plastic explosive, put the package down briefly, unattended. A sergeant noticed what he had done and asked questions. Haeften explained that his colonel 'needed this for the Führer's situation briefing'. No more questions were asked. Stauffenberg and Haeften then went into a washroom and, unobserved, the one-armed colonel, helped by his adjutant, began setting the fuses on two packages of explosive. Each package contained about a kilo of the plastic – thought by the conspirators to be enough to kill everybody in Hitler's briefing room.

Meanwhile, Keitel, with other officers, stood outside his hut waiting for Stauffenberg. The sergeant, who had noticed the package, was sent back into the hut to inform the colonel that he should hurry, as he was needed at the Führer's briefing session. The sergeant found Stauffenberg and Haeften whispering to each other and handling an object that he did not recognise. When the sergeant spoke, Stauffenberg snapped back that he was 'on his way' and Keitel's adjutant called from outside the hut 'Stauffenberg, do hurry up!' The sergeant closely watched the conspirators leave.

As a result of the two men being interrupted when setting the fuses, Stauffenberg managed to put only one bomb, containing only half of the explosive, in his briefcase. If the whole amount had exploded in Hitler's briefing hut, everybody in it would have been killed. On his way, late, to the briefing, Stauffenberg was glowered at by Keitel's adjutant. This impatient officer tried to seize the colonel's briefcase in order to carry it for him, but Stauffenberg pulled it quickly out of his reach.

When Stauffenberg entered Hitler's briefing hut he asked Keitel's adjutant to put the briefcase near the Führer, as he wished to hear everything Hitler said. He explained that his hearing had been impaired by his war wounds.

The briefing had begun when Stauffenberg entered. Hitler was sitting on a stool half way along the edge of a heavy, oblong map table. Everybody else was standing round the table. Lieutenant-General Adolf Heusinger was reporting on the situation on the Eastern

Front. Including the late arrivals, there were now twenty-four people in the room.

After only a few minutes, Stauffenberg mumbled something about a telephone call and pointed to Keitel's adjutant. The two men left the room together, and Stauffenberg asked to be connected to General Erich Fellgiebel, commander of Signal Troops. A sergeant made the connection and the adjutant returned to the briefing. Stauffenberg lifted the telephone receiver, put it down immediately and left the hut. He walked to a bunker where Fellgiebel and Haeften were waiting for him, together with a car and its driver. A couple of minutes later, at about 12.50 p.m., there was a massive explosion in the briefing hut. Stauffenberg and Haeften told the driver to take them to the airfield. The colonel bluffed his way through the first checkpoint. Gruffly declaring something about 'Führer's orders', he was waved on. The second checkpoint was also passed through easily, but at the third one there were obstacles on the road and the NCO in charge refused to allow anybody to pass. However, Stauffenberg did continue on his journey, but only after he had spoken on the checkpoint telephone to an officer on the FHQ commandant's staff with whom he had had breakfast. At the airfield he boarded a Heinkel He 111 aircraft provided by another of the conspirators, General Eduard Wagner, the Quartermaster General.

When making their escape in their car Stauffenberg and Haeften had passed within about 30 metres of Hitler's briefing hut, and it looked to them as though the building had been totally wrecked. However, the impact of the explosion had been less severe than the conspirators expected because the hut was flimsily built and all five of its windows were open on the hot summer's day. Four people died as a result of the explosion. Everybody inside the hut was burned or bruised and many eardrums were pierced.

General Fellgiebel had a similar view of the damage and, to his dismay, he also saw Hitler, with his hair singed and his clothes in shreds, walking towards his bunker. From the communications bunker Fellgiebel telephoned General Fritz Thiele, chief signals officer of the Army High Command and a fellow conspirator: 'Something fearful has occurred. The Führer is alive.'

On hearing this news, Generals Thiele and Friedrich Olbricht, deputy commander of the Reserve Army, took no immediate action. They went to lunch, returning at about 3 p.m., when Stauffenberg was arriving in Berlin. Haeften telephoned the plotters' headquarters to say that Hitler was dead. Olbricht then appealed to General Friedrich Fromm, Commander-in-Chief of the Reserve Army, to issue the

Valkyrie orders to seize control of the government. Fromm refused to do so, and Oldbricht and Colonel Albrecht Mertz von Quirnheim issued the orders themselves, at about 4 p.m. Fromm then telephoned Keitel and was told that Hitler had survived the assassination attempt. This prompted Fromm to suggest that Stauffenberg shoot himself. When he refused to do so, Fromm tried to have him arrested, but the plotters arrested Fromm. Stauffenberg then took over leadership of the coup attempt, but it was not until four hours after the Wolf's Lair explosion that the conspirators sent out orders and proclamations claiming that the army had taken over executive powers. The timing of all this was disastrous, the arrival of the orders coinciding with broadcast announcements that the attempt on Hitler's life had failed. There was only a small, short-lived positive response to the plotters' appeals. A few radio stations were occupied and, in Paris, Gestapo officers were arrested.

By midnight the revolt had been crushed. Fromm was freed and ordered the execution of Stauffenberg, Haeften, Olbricht and Mertz von Quirnheim. Most of the other military plotters were arrested during the night. Fromm too was arrested, being suspected of supporting the conspirators, and he was executed in March 1945.

If more thought had been given to every aspect of the planning, the Bomb Plot would have been successful – and would have changed the course of the war, for better or for worse. As it was, not enough plastic explosive was used, and the different groups of conspirators – at the Rastenburg headquarters, in Berlin and elsewhere – did not work as a team. What an extraordinary decision by Generals Thiele and Olbricht to go to lunch when they did!

# Appendix D
## *The Wolf's Lair*

Although Colonel Stauffenberg had narrowly failed to kill Hitler at the Rastenburg Führerhauptquartier, and although the dictator often stayed there for long periods, Section X never thought of it as a possible scene of an assassination, and in consequence there is no description of Rastenburg in the Foxley papers. Unless he had a cast-iron official reason for visiting this most isolated and bleak of the FHQs, an agent would have had no chance of getting anywhere near the Führer. It seems that this fact was realised by SOE staff officers in Baker Street, even by those of them who were uncritically enthusiastic about Operation Foxley.

Hitler himself gave the Rastenburg FHQ its codename, the Wolf's Lair (Wolfschanze). As he once told one of his secretaries, 'Wolf' was his own alias during what he called his 'years of struggle', when he was an insignificant political agitator shortly after the First World War. The idea of building a heavily fortified forward headquarters in East Prussia, in which to plan the invasion of the Soviet Union, was conceived in September 1940. Hitler put the task of finding a site for this ultra-secret project in the hands of a group of staff officers and engineers led by Fritz Todt, the Minister of Weapons and Munitions and the head of the labour organisation bearing his name. Two months later, Todt found what Hitler considered was the right location: the so-called Gorlitz pine forest, east of Rastenburg town. Thousands of Organisation Todt workers took seven months to construct the FHQ, a vast complex of mainly concrete buildings, and its accompanying infrastructure, including many roads.

While the building work was going on, the Nazi authorities tried to conceal the future function of the project, claiming at different times that it was merely to be a camp, Anlage Nord, or a chemical factory, the Chemische Werke Askania. The work was completed on 23 June 1941, the day after the start of the invasion of Russia.

Because the 'forest' was less than 2,000 metres long and contained fields and other open spaces, camouflage netting was spread over large areas to hide those of the concrete buildings that would otherwise be visible from the air. Railway station buildings in Gorlitz, a small town south of the forest, were enlarged, and a rail line was extended, with sidings leading to the FHQ. It was there that Hitler stepped off his Special Train, the Führerzug.

The headquarters covered about 2½ square kilometres. It was surrounded by a high barbed-wire fence and protected by sentries, patrolling troops, machine-gun towers, concrete gun emplacements, anti-aircraft guns, tanks and a minefield containing more than 50,000 mines. In September 1944, with the Soviet army not far away, Hitler personally ordered a mass of additional weapons for the FHQ. These included 500 anti-tank rocket-launchers, 200 submachine-guns, 250 pistols and large quantities of brass truncheons, combat knives and ammunition.

The FHQ was divided into four security zones, each with a checkpoint manned by armed guards. Zone Number Four was a reception area. The headquarters proper functioned in the inner zones, numbered one to three. Somebody with an appointment in the FHQ had to be checked through Zone Four and at least one other zone. Some visitors had their identity papers scrutinised at the entrances of all four zones. Hitler worked, ate and slept in Zone One, where security was tighter than anywhere else. The only visitors to it were leading Nazis and their entourages, together with an invited few others. Everybody entering this zone had to have a special pass.

Security Zone Number One contained many and various concrete bunkers and wooden huts, including the one in which Stauffenberg's bomb exploded. All these utilitarian buildings were hidden from the view of overflying aircraft by camouflage netting spread between the tops of surrounding trees and over roads inside the zone. Other means of disguise included artificial moss on roofs, rustic paintings on walls, and trees and foliage between buildings. The Führerzug was also hidden from aerial view when it stopped at Gorliz or on the Wolf's Lair rail sidings.

Although called bunkers, these ugly structures were at ground level and had only two or three small rooms in which everybody lived and worked. Even the Führerbunker, the principal building in Zone One, was spartan – a far cry from the home comforts of the Berghof. Hitler also had one of the many huts. Other Zone One buildings included guests' quarters, offices, barracks and other military and RSD accommodation, a few houses, two tea-houses, a cinema and even a sauna. Those with accommodation near the dictator included Göring, Bormann, Keitel and Colonel-General Alfred Jodl, the OKW's Chief of Operations Staff.

The Zone Two buildings included houses for the Army Leadership

Staff (WFSt), the FHQ commandant and naval and Luftwaffe liaison officers, garages and drivers' accommodation, barracks, a teleprinter exchange, messes and administrative buildings. Most army officers slept in huts around an inn, patronised by the general public until it was incorporated in the FHQ complex. Zone Three had accommodation and offices for liaison staff and others, including Albert Speer, who was Armaments Minister and head of Organisation Todt after Todt's death in an aircraft crash in February 1942.

The whole overcrowded complex of bunkers, houses, huts and other buildings – a total of about sixty – was often thoroughly uncomfortable for the vast majority of people living there. In hot weather the swampy ground of the FHQ swarmed with mosquitoes and flies, and the humidity was almost unbearable.

Hitler's staff were glad to leave the Wolf's Lair. So was he, but only after being persuaded to go by those few to whom he listened, and by the sound of Soviet gunfire in the distance. The Führer, who had so often ordered his generals to defend every square inch of ground irrespective of the circumstances, himself retreated on 20 November 1944 – to save his skin. He never returned to the Wolf's Lair or Berghof and spent what little was left of his wretched life in the Reich Chancellery bunker in Berlin – a place as depressing as his East Prussian FHQ.

# Appendix E
# *Hitler's health*

SOE was well informed about Hitler's failing health. However, much more was learned about it after the war from German army officers and others who had observed him at close hand.

It is clear from their eye-witness reports and from documentary sources that he was an increasingly sick man from 1943. He began being under severe nervous strain towards the end of 1942 as a result of acrimonious confrontations with his generals over what they correctly regarded as his strategic blundering.

From 1943 his bouts of hypochondria and insomnia became more acute, these being worsened by Dr Morell's pills and injections. He also became increasingly reclusive, depending for occasional company only on a chosen sycophantic few, such as his 'personal adjutants' and secretarial staff, Bormann, Morell and Eva Braun. According to some postwar accounts, eventually he even gave up listening to Wagner.

Göring is quoted as saying in 1943 that Hitler had aged fifteen years since the start of the war. Goebbels commented similarly. Referring to the dictator's long visits to the Rastenburg FHQ, the Propaganda Minister wrote: 'It is tragic that the Führer has become such a recluse and leads such an unhealthy life. He never gets out into the fresh air – he does not relax. He sits in his bunker, worries and broods. If one could only transfer him to other surroundings! . . . the loneliness of general headquarters and the whole method of working there naturally have a depressing effect upon the Führer.'[1] After visiting Hitler on 20 February 1943, General Heinz Guderian reported: 'When I saw him for the first time after a space of thirteen months, I noted the change in his condition. The left hand trembled, his posture was stooped, his gaze rigid, the eyes bulged slightly and were dull, the cheeks had red spots. His irritability had increased. He lost control when angry and then was unpredictable in words and evaluations.'[2]

In 1944, even before the July Bomb Plot, Hitler had dizzy spells and his balance was unsteady – possibly the result of Parkinson's disease. His condition worsened after the Rastenburg explosion, which ruptured both ear-drums.[3] He developed infective jaundice, had acute headaches, and his temper tantrums became even more frequent. An electrocardiogram indicated that his coronary blood-flow was impaired and that he had high blood pressure. By the autumn of 1944 he was often exhausted, even after having a rest. His shoulders drooped, his gait was slow and shuffling, he needed a large magnifying glass to study maps and documents, and sometimes his hands trembled so violently that he had to clutch them between his knees.

Captain Gerhardt Boldt, aide-de-camp to General Hans Krebs, Nazi Germany's last Chief of the Army General Staff, described Hitler's physical appearance when he saw him in February 1945: 'His head was slightly wobbling. His left arm hung slackly and his hand trembled a good deal. There was an indescribable flickering glow in his eyes, creating a fearsome and wholly unnatural effect. His face and the parts around his eyes gave the impression of total exhaustion. All his movements were those of a senile man.'[4]

When a young man, Hitler was acutely neurotic. At Ypres in October 1918, as a corporal in the Kaiser's army, he was a war casualty. He claimed that he had been gassed and indeed there had been a British gas attack on his unit. However, Professor Karl Wilmans, a psychiatrist at Heidelberg University, believed that Hitler had suffered only hysterical blindness. He was undoubtedly unable to see for a short while and, according to his medical records from Pasewalk military hospital, this was caused by mustard-gas poisoning.

In November 1923, after the Munich Putsch, the future dictator was medically examined in prison and found to be in poor health generally. In particular, he had rotten teeth (later, ably repaired), neck boils and localised eczema. In 1933, at about the time he became Chancellor, Hitler had severe abdominal pains after meals. For the rest of his life he often took excessive quantities of proprietory anti-wind pills, risking poisoning from their ingredients of strychnine and atropine.

Before and during the 1939–45 war, it was widely rumoured that Hitler had a congenital malformation of his sex organs. According to the most lurid of these rumours, he possessed only one testicle. Dr Fritz Redlich, Professor Emeritus of Psychiatry at the University of California in Los Angeles, who has made an exhaustive study of the Führer's mental and physical health, writes in *Hitler: Diagnosis of a Destructive Prophet*: 'Weighing the pros and cons, it is likely that Hitler had a genital defect.' The professor points out, however, that the single-testicle assertion is based only on the results of a Soviet post-mortem examination of the charred remains of Hitler's body and circumstantial evidence reported while he was alive.[5]

The Führer reportedly had a horror of being examined undressed by any doctor other than Morell or other favoured charlatans. He also hated being X-rayed, even when dressed.

# Appendix F
## *Climate and topography*

The Foxley papers state:

> The climate of Berchtesgaden is in general colder in winter and hotter in summer and autumn than in England. The chief characteristic of the weather is that it is fairly stable. When it rains, it usually goes on for several days or weeks – similarly in the case of snow. . . . When it is fine it usually stays fine for several days. Snow falls fairly early because of the altitude, sometimes as early as September. . . . Fog is very rare, and normally occurs either in the valley, coming no higher than the Gutshof, or the heights surrounding the Kehlstein. It is very rare that the Berghof and the SS barracks are wrapped in fog. . . .
>
> Obersalzberg lies in an amphitheatre of the Bavarian Alps adjacent to the former Austrian frontier. The dominating peaks and ranges are, in the north-west the Untersberg (1,973 metres), in the south-west the Lattengebirge and Watzmann peaks, in the south the Hoher Göll (2,522 metres) and in the east the Rossfeld ridge (1,608 metres). Here the bare limestone peaks and glacier-scaped slopes of the Alps give way to a jumble of pine-clad foothills, interspersed with wide stretches of open grass- and meadow-land.
>
> The Bad Reichenhall-Berchtesgaden-Hallein area is drained in the east by the Salzach, in the west by the Saalach and in the centre by the Ache which, on leaving the Nonntal defile (the route taken by Hitler when travelling from the Obersalzberg to Schloss Klessheim) enters the Salzberg plain near St Leonhard to flow into the Salzach south of Anif. The greater part of the Obersalzberg as well as the road from the Berghof as far as Grödig (on the way to Schloss Klessheim) is very hilly and densely wooded and should therefore afford good cover, even in winter, as most of the trees are of the non-deciduous variety. Since the route taken to Schloss Klessheim makes use of the Autobahn which skirts the Maxglan suburb of Salzburg, the attempt would have to be made from the woods between the Obersalzberg and Grödig or in the vicinity of the teahouse on the Mooslaner Kopf. . . .

The entire area of the Obersalzberg is for the most part very heavily wooded and, being also extremely hilly, is a difficult area to guard. This is also true of the area immediately around Hitler's residence – the Berghof – which is known as the Führergebiet. . .

The Foxley papers add that the woods near the Rodelbahn, behind the Mooslaner Kopf, north of the Berghof and round the Kehlstein are particularly thick. Concluding their description of the topography of the Obersalzberg, the papers say: 'Except above the 1,400-metre line of the Kehlstein, which is a very tricky area to climb, the entire Führergebiet is passable on foot. In winter the lower slopes of the Kehlstein are passable on skis, and a very good skier could negotiate the slopes of the Rodelbahn. Ski-ing on the Führerstrasse in the vicinity of the Berghof is forbidden.'

# Appendix G
## *Skorzeny's career*

**The Foxley papers record that Major H.B. Court (L/BX) minuted on 16 March 1945:**

. . . Skorzeny did not apparently take part in the coup against the capital following Italy's capitulation, concentrating rather on the rescue of Mussolini; the scene of his first attempt (by torpedo boat) took place at the island of St Maddalena, off Sardinia, but was too late as Mussolini had been removed to the Gran Sasso by seaplane half an hour before Skorzeny's arrival.

Although officially the Germans take credit for discovering the presence of Mussolini at Gran Sasso, they appear to have stumbled on the Duce's new prison from a chance remark by an Italian mechanic on the Grosseto airfield to General Student to the effect that Mussolini had landed there . . . [the previous day] and left under escort by car for the Gran Sasso.

Mussolini's prison on the small, boulder-strewn plateau surrounded by cliffs and precipices in the northern Abbruzzi, known as the Gran Sasso, was a newly built but unoccupied hotel, approached only by a mountain railway and goat tracks.

There are two versions of the rescue – one official and the other unofficial and factual. According to the official account, reconnaissance showed that the station at the foot of the mountain railway was occupied by Badoglio's troops (in point of fact Carabinieri, i.e. police), and it was decided to land airborne troops on the plateau itself.

Ten gliders took part in the operation (for the planning of which General Student was largely responsible) with Skorzeny in the tenth glider accompanied by a Carabinieri colonel whom he is said to have bribed. As the gliders flew over the target Skorzeny ordered his pilot to drop out of formation and land so that he could be first on the scene. The Carabinieri colonel was the first out of Skorzeny's glider and he ordered the Carabinieri guarding the hotel not to fire. Not a shot was fired or a casualty incurred among the company which subsequently landed. So much for the unofficial and factual version of the rescue.

According to the official account, the paratroops landed almost simultaneously at 1410 hours on 12 September 1943, led by Skorzeny, who with two men rushed into the hotel through the door of a cellar housing the telephone exchange and radio station, which he immediately put out of action. As he could not get into the hotel itself, Skorzeny ran out and swung himself up on his companion's shoulders to a balcony guarded, as he then found, by two Carabinieri with a machine-gun. At the same instant Mussolini showed himself at a window above the balcony and, shouting to the Duce to keep back, Skorzeny kicked away the machine-gun from the Carabinieri.

Mussolini's gaoler then appeared at the window but quickly put up his hands on seeing the machine-pistols pointed at him from below by the rest of the party who had in the meantime landed; he surrendered to Skorzeny as the latter entered the room. Skorzeny then informed Mussolini that he had been rescued and, conducting him to a Fieseler Storch, accompanied him to the Pratica di Mare airfield in Rome where they both transferred to a He 111 for Munich.

The only points in which the official and unofficial versions agree is the difficulty of landing in so confined an area and in the fact that not a single shot was fired, due, according to the official version, to Skorzeny's valour and Italian cowardice, but actually to the presence of the Carabinieri colonel who accompanied Skorzeny's glider.

The manner in which Skorzeny 'cashed in' (to the tune of a Ritterkreuz) on the exploit on arrival at Munich in saying that he had done the job though two-thirds of the paratroops had gone to their deaths (when in fact not one casualty occurred) reflects the unscrupulous nature of the man.

The next twelve months saw Skorzeny active in most of the European countries still occupied by Germany, e.g. [an] abortive project to kidnap Pétain (November 1943); [a] raid on Tito's HQ by SS-Verbände (paratroops from the Div. Brandenburg); organisation of [an] anti-Allied resistance movement in Paris where, with his adjutant, Major Maumann, Skorzeny took over the Abwehr Abteilung II set-up from Baron Freytag-Loringhoven (February 1944); organisation of sabotage and counter-sabotage in Denmark (March 1944) and France (Toulon, June 1944); promoted Obersturmbannführer (June 1944); Skorzeny is alleged to have forestalled the attempt of the Hungarian army to break away by kidnapping the Regent, Horthy (Ocobter 1944); ordered the attack on the Nijmegen bridges [on] 26/27 and 28/29 September 1944, by the swimming saboteurs; returned end of September 1944, to Amt VI to direct operations in Greece (ELAS).

*Unternehmen Greif.* This operation, which formed part of Rundstedt's counter-offensive of 16 December 1944, is by far the most ambitious yet staged by Skorzeny. The project provided for the infiltration of the Allied lines by a special tank formation, the 150 Panzerbrigade, with American and camouflaged German tanks and 30 four-man Jeep parties from the Einheit Stielau; both units wore American uniforms and carried American equipment, all vehicles bearing American markings.

The objectives were two-fold. Firstly, after advancing through the breaches made in the Allied defences on the Namur-Liège sector by the SS armoured spearheads, to seize the bridges over the Meuse and to spread confusion on Allied communications by 'retreating' along vital roads and blocking traffic by simulated breakdowns or, with the help of Einheit Stielau units, spreading wild stories of the German breakthrough as they sped past; secondly, to open the way for Skorzeny's party, which it is alleged by an officer of Einheit Stielau captured in Liège, was to make contact with German left-behind agents and French collaborators in Paris preliminary to the kidnapping or assassination of Eisenhower and other high Allied commanders.

It [the operation] failed on three accounts, viz. lack of adequate preparation, the dropping of the paratroops in the wrong place and the failure of the 150 Panzerbrigade and armoured spearheads to break through and open the way for Skorzeny's *coup de main* party.

The preliminary plans for Internehmen Greif were hatched at Friedenthal where English-speaking officers and ORs of the Wehrmacht were called upon to report early in November 1944. Here these volunteers were divided into four groups according to their proficiency in English (with an American accent) prior to their formation into Einheit Stielau. Group I was given a special training in American army organisation, identification, army slang, vehicle markings, close-order drill and the general appearance and behaviour of the American officer and OR at the Dolmetscherschule at Friedenthal. Groups II and III were given much the same training plus instruction in demolition and signalling at Gravenwoehr (Bavaria) where 150 Panzerbrigade was forming. Many of the men were sent to American P/W camps (Limburg, Küstrin) to converse with American soldiers and study them. On returning to Gravenwoehr instruction was given on ways and means of infiltrating the American lines. Group IV was sent to Gravenwoehr as a reserve company for Einheit Stielau.

The 150 Panzerbrigade consisted of HQ with sigs. section and medical detachment, tank battalion, AA troop, artillery unit, a company of Panzergrenadiers, a paratroop regiment (Fallschirmjäger-Regiment z.b.V. Hermann Göring) and Einheit Stielau. The total strength of the brigade was about 3,000–3,200 all ranks, including 200 officers and men of Einheit Stielau. The tank battalion (800–1,000 all ranks) consisted of three tank companies, a reconnaissance company and supply column with a total of 20–21 tanks (six Shermans, six Tigers and six Panthers), all with US markings, and six German armoured semi-tracked reconnaissance cars. The parachute regiment[1] consisted of two battalions, each with HQ company, heavy company and three rifle companies with a total regimental strength of between 800 and 1,000 all ranks.

Skorzeny's codename as commander of the 150 Panzerbrigade and Einheit Stielau was Solar, his HQ being known as Stab Solar. Apart from the 60 officers and men to accompany Skorzeny on his mission to Paris, Einheit Stielau was organised into 30 four-man Jeep parties, viz., 10 radio reconnaissance patrols to report on approaches to the Meuse bridges, 10 destroyer parties (with communications, message centres and headquarters as targets) and 10 sabotage parties to destroy dams and bridges. These men were provided with false AGO cards or paybooks to pose as members of the US army.

150 Panzerbrigade moved from Gravenwoehr to Münster-Eifel [on] 5 December and Einheit Stielau on 8 December. The operation began by the emplaning of the Kampfgruppe von der Heyde at 0300 hours on 16 December at Paderborn. Its task was to sever the Eupen-Malmédy road. Provided with only two days' rations, they were to be relieved by Panzer troops by 1500 hours [on] 17 December. Due to strong winds and poor atmospheric conditions only 300 men were dropped anywhere near the Eupen-Malmédy road, while their containers were scattered far and wide. None of the radio equipment dropped was found and the unit was thus completely cut off. They waited until 19 December, when they had been for two days without food, for the arrival of the Panzers and subsequently surrendered with their commander at Monschau. In the meantime only a few isolated Jeep parties had succeeded in infiltrating the American lines, many being destroyed by artillery fire before getting through; this was largely due to the failure of the 12 SS Panzer Division to force a gap in the lines through which the parties could penetrate; the result, it would appear, was that Skorzeny's party never actually started on its mission. The few Jeep parties that did get through were soon rounded up owing to the effective counter-measures which were taken following the interrogation of prisoners.

This irregular type of warfare is foreign to the herd instinct of the average German who seems to lose his head in abnormal circumstances.[2] Tasks of this nature require men of strong character, but Skorzeny appears to have called upon anyone who could speak English in forming Einheit Stielau. Prisoners captured from this unit alleged that they had no idea of what they were in for, having joined as they thought to become interpreters. This and the hope of escaping the firing squad may explain the willingness with which they talked and betrayed the whole scheme. . .

# *Chronology*

*1933*
**30 Jan**    Hitler becomes Chancellor of Germany.
**Feb**       Non-Nazi political meetings banned. The Reichstag fire.
**March**     First concentration camps opened. Goebbels appointed Propaganda Minister.
**April**     Jewish shops officially boycotted. Jews banned from holding professional posts.
**May**       All trade unions dissolved. Nazis form German Labour Front. Goebbels organises nationwide book-burning.
**July**      Non-Nazi political parties outlawed.
**Sept**      Reich Chamber of Culture formed, headed by Goebbels.

*1934*
**Jan**       Third Reich and Poland sign ten-year Non-Aggression Pact.
**30 June**   'Night of the Long Knives'.
**25 July**   Chancellor Dollfuss of Austria murdered.
**2 Aug**     President Hindenburg dies. Hitler declares himself Führer of the German State and supreme commander of the armed forces; its members are henceforward required to swear a personal oath of loyalty to Hitler.
**Oct**       All workers required to join German Labour Front.

*1935*
**March**     The Saar rejoins Germany. Hitler renounces Treaty of Versailles disarmament clauses. Conscription introduced.
**Sept**      Nuremberg laws on Jews promulgated. Swastika banner becomes national flag.

*1936*
**March**     Germany reoccupies the Rhineland.

| | |
|---|---|
| **June** | Himmler appointed head of police. |
| **July** | German–Austrian agreement signed, recognising Austrian sovereignty. |
| **Nov** | Germany and Japan sign Anti-Comintern Pact. |
| **Dec** | Hitler Youth made a State organisation. |

*1937*

| | |
|---|---|
| **March** | Pope Pius XI issues encyclical on Germany entitled 'Mit brennender Sorge' ('With Deep Anxiety'). |
| **May** | Chamberlain becomes British Prime Minister. |

*1938*

| | |
|---|---|
| **11–12 March** | Chancellor von Schuschnigg of Austria resigns. Germany annexes Austria (The Anschluss). |
| *March* | *SIS forms Section D. Foreign Office forms EH.* |
| **29 Sept** | Munich Agreement. |
| **5 Oct** | Germany occupies Sudetenland. |
| *Oct* | *War Office's GS(R) section, later renamed MI(R), begins research into irregular warfare.* |
| **9 Nov** | Kristallnacht – organised attacks on Jews, synagogues and Jewish property throughout Germany. |
| **Dec** | German–French Non-Aggression Pact signed. |

*1939*

| | |
|---|---|
| **14 March** | Czechoslovakia dismembered. Germany occupies Bohemia and Moravia. Slovakia declares its 'independence'. |
| **23 March** | Germany occupies Memel. |
| **22 May** | Pact of Steel: German–Italian military alliance. |
| **23 Aug** | Nazi-Soviet Non-Aggression Pact signed. |
| **1 Sept** | Germany invades Poland. |
| **3 Sept** | Britain and France declare war on Germany. |
| **17 Sept** | Soviet Union invades Poland. |
| **28 Sept** | Poland partitioned. Nazi-Soviet Friendship Treaty signed. |
| *8 Nov* | *Georg Elser narrowly fails to assassinate Hitler in Munich.* |
| **30 Nov** | USSR invades Finland. |

*1940*

| | |
|---|---|
| **12 March** | Soviet–Finnish war ends. |

| | |
|---|---|
| **9 April** | Germany invades Denmark and Norway. |
| **10 May** | Germany invades Belgium, Holland and Luxembourg. Churchill becomes British Prime Minister. |
| **28 May–3 June** | Dunkirk evacuation. |
| **10 June** | Italy declares war on Britain and France. |
| **14 June** | German troops enter Paris. |
| **22–24 June** | German and Italian armistices with Vichy French. |
| **30 June** | German occupation of the Channel Islands begins. |
| **10 July–31 Oct** | Battle of Britain. |
| *22 July* | *SOE formed, merging Section D, MI(R) and EH.* |
| **Sept** | Italy invades British Somaliland and Egypt. |
| **28 Oct** | Italy invades Greece from Albania. |
| *18 Nov* | *Section X formed.* |
| **9 Dec** | First British Western Desert offensive begins. |

*1941*

| | |
|---|---|
| **6–8 April** | German, Italian and Bulgarian forces invade Yugoslavia and Greece. |
| **10 May** | Hess flies to Scotland. |
| **10 May–1 June** | Germans capture Crete. |
| **22 June** | Germany invades USSR. |
| **16 July** | Germans capture Smolensk. |
| *Sept* | *PWE formally established.* |
| **19 Sept** | Germans capture Kiev. |
| **19 Oct** | State of siege in Moscow. |
| **18 Nov** | Second British Western Desert offensive begins. |
| **6 Dec** | Soviet counter-offensive outside Moscow begins. |
| **7–8 Dec** | Japanese attack Pearl Harbor and invade Malaya and Thailand. Britain and US declare war on Japan. |
| **11 Dec** | Germany and Italy declare war on US. |

*1942*

| | |
|---|---|
| **20 Jan** | Nazi intention to exterminate all Jews is declared at Wannsee Conference. |
| **21 Jan–1 July** | German counter-offensive in North Africa. |
| **1 March** | Russians launch new offensive in Crimea. |
| **26 April** | Hitler receives title of 'Supreme Law Lord' with absolute powers of punishment and dismissal. |
| **26 May** | German counter-offensive in Western Desert. |
| *27 May* | *Heydrich wounded in Prague by SOE-trained Czechoslovaks. He dies on 4 June.* |

| | |
|---|---|
| **30–31 May** | First RAF 1,000-bomber raid on Cologne. |
| **1–2 June** | 1,036 RAF bombers raid Essen and Ruhr. |
| *10 June* | *Announcement of total destruction of Czech village Lidiče as reprisal for assassination of Heydrich.* |
| **21 June–5 Aug** | Germans capture Tobruk, Mersa Matruh, Sevastopol, Rostov and Voroshilovsk. |
| **23 Oct** | Battle of El Alamein begins. |
| **7–8 Nov** | American and British troops land on north-west African coast. |
| **27 Nov** | Germans enter Toulon. French warships in its harbour scuttled by their crews. |

| | |
|---|---|
| *1943* | |
| **14–24 Jan** | Casablanca Conference. Roosevelt tells Press that the Axis Powers will be required to accept only 'unconditional surrender' terms. |
| **23 Jan** | 8th Army enters Tripoli. |
| **2 Feb** | Completion of German 6th Army's defeat at Stalingrad; more than 146,000 Germans reported dead. |
| **25–26 Feb** | RAF start round-the-clock bombing. Allied air forces make 2,000 sorties in 48 hours. |
| *28 Feb* | *SOE's Operation Gunnerside. Norwegian saboteurs destroy heavy water plant at Norsk Hydro.* |
| **1–28 March** | Big RAF raids on Berlin and Essen. |
| **April–May** | Massacre of Warsaw ghetto; at least 56,000 Jews reported murdered. |
| **13 May** | Last Axis forces in Tunisia surrender. |
| **9 June** | Announcement: 291,000 Axis prisoners taken in North African campaign. |
| **9–10 July** | Allies invade Sicily. |
| **24–30 July** | Big RAF and USAAF bombing raids on Hamburg, with massive civilian casualties. |
| **25–26 July** | Mussolini resigns and is arrested. Marshal Badoglio appointed Italian Prime Minister. The new Italian cabinet dissolves Fascist Party and repeals Fascist legislation. |
| **17 Aug** | Sicily totally in Allied control. |
| **8 Sept** | Unconditional surrender by Italy. |
| **9 Sept** | Allied forces land at Salerno. |
| **12–15 Sept** | German paratroops free Mussolini from Gran Sasso. Mussolini reappoints himself Fascist leader. |

| | |
|---|---|
| **13 Oct** | Italy declares war on Germany. |
| **6 Nov** | Kiev liberated. |
| *7 Nov* | *Colonel-General Jodl speaks to Gauleiters in Munich of the 'devil of subversion' in Germany, the country being 'strained to the utmost.'* |
| **28 Nov–1 Dec** | Tehran Conference. |
| **2–30 Dec** | Massive RAF bombing raids on Berlin. |

*1944*

| | |
|---|---|
| **1–31 Jan** | More big RAF raids on Berlin. |
| **22 Jan** | Anzio landings. |
| **27 Jan** | Leningrad blockade lifted. |
| **18–23 March** | Huge RAF bombing raids on Frankfurt. |
| **18–29 April and** | |
| **7–24 May** | Big American bombing raids on Berlin. |
| **5–6 June** | Allied airborne troops land behind German defences in Normandy. Widespread activity by French Resistance. |
| **6 June** | D-Day. |
| **10 June** | Montgomery sets up HQ in Normandy. |
| **13–14 June** | V1 flying bombs begin landing in Britain. |
| **26 June** | Cherbourg liberated. |
| **28 June** | Philippe Henriot, Vichy Propaganda Minister, assassinated in Paris. |
| **9 July** | Caen liberated. |
| **11 July** | Mikolajczyk, Polish Prime Minister, states that Polish Underground Army in open conflict with Germans. |
| *20 July* | *The Bomb Plot. Colonel Stauffenberg narrowly fails to assassinate Hitler at East Prussian FHQ. Stauffenberg and other plotters executed in Berlin. Himmler appointed commander of Reserve Army.* |
| **24–27 July** | Lublin and Lvov liberated. |
| **25 July** | Goebbels appointed Plenipotentiary for Total War. |
| *4 Aug* | *Purge of German army announced. Court of Honour formed to investigate antecedents of field marshals and generals and to discover who participated in Bomb Plot.* |
| **9–10 Aug** | Le Mans, Nantes and Angers liberated. Eisenhower establishes HQ in France. |
| **13 Aug** | Italy-based Allied bombers drop arms and ammunition to Polish Resistance in Warsaw. |

| | |
|---|---|
| **15 Aug** | Allied forces land on south coast of France between Toulon and Nice. |
| **17–28 Aug** | Chartres, Orléans, Paris, Grenoble, Marseilles, Cannes, Avignon and Toulon liberated. |
| **24 Aug** | Martial law proclaimed in Slovakia after Resistance forces begin open warfare. |
| **27 Aug** | RAF bomb Homberg-Meerbeck oil refinery in Ruhr (first big daylight raid over Germany). |
| **31 Aug–11 Sept** | Amiens, Nice, Bordeaux, Dieppe, Brussels, Antwerp, Lille, Ostend, Bruges, Luxembourg City and Dijon liberated. |
| **7 Sept** | Announcement: Since 13 June about 8,000 V1 bombs launched, about 2,300 reached London. |
| **8 Sept** | First V2 rocket lands in Britain (Chiswick, London). |
| **11 Sept** | American troops cross German frontier. British troops cross Dutch frontier. |
| *13 Sept* | *Eisenhower appeals to foreign workers in Germany to leave factories and go into hiding.* |
| **14 Sept** | Soviet aircraft begin dropping arms and supplies to Polish Home Army in Warsaw. |
| **15 Sept** | Maastricht, Nancy and Epinal liberated. |
| **16–21 Sept** | General strike in Denmark in protest against deportation of 190 Danish prisoners to Germany. |
| **17 Sept** | First Allied Airborne Army lands in Holland. |
| **18 Sept** | US troops occupy Brest after prolonged fighting. |
| **25–7 Sept** | Withdrawal of remnants of 1st Airborne Division from Arnhem, with about 7,000 casualties. |
| **30 Sept** | Calais liberated. |
| **3 Oct** | Warsaw falls after sixty-three days' fighting. |
| **5 Oct** | British forces land on Greek mainland and islands and in Albania. |
| **14 Oct** | Athens liberated. |
| **18 Oct** | Announcement that Soviet army has entered Czechoslovakia. |
| **20 Oct** | Belgrade and Dubrovnik liberated. |
| **23 Oct** | Soviet troops enter East Prussia. |
| *30 Oct* | *Section X renamed the German Directorate.* |
| **22–24 Nov** | Müllhouse and Strasbourg captured. |
| **16 Dec** | Germans begin Ardennes offensive. |

*1945*

| | |
|---|---|
| **1 Jan** | 800 German aircraft attack Western-Front Allied airfields and Brussels, losing 188 planes. |
| **2 Jan** | Saboteurs wreck Copenhagen radio factory making parts for V2 rockets. |
| **11 Jan** | Soviet forces enter Warsaw. |
| **12 Jan** | Announcement: US war casualties total 646,398, including 138,393 killed. |
| **3 Feb** | Heavy US bombing raid on Berlin. |
| **4–11 Feb** | Yalta Conference. Belgium totally clear of German forces. |
| **8 Feb** | Announcement: British civilian war casualties from September 1939 to 30 September 1944, total 136,646, including 57,468 killed. |
| **13–15 Feb** | Heavy RAF and USAAF bombing raids on Dresden. |
| **23 Feb** | Poznan liberated. |
| **9–20 March** | Bonn, Brandenburg, Worms and Saarbrücken captured. |
| **23–24 March** | 21 Army Group crosses Lower Rhine at four places and 40,000 airborne troops land. |
| *31 March* | *Eisenhower calls on German troops to surrender.* |
| **7–11 April** | Göttingen, Hanover, Wiemar and Essen captured. |
| **12 April** | Roosevelt dies. Truman sworn in as US President. |
| **13 April** | Vienna captured. |
| **16 April** | Hitler gives his last Order of the Day to armies on the Eastern Front: 'He who orders retreat . . . must be shot on the spot.' |
| **18 April** | Ruhr pocket collapses, 325,000 prisoners taken. |
| **20 April** | Nuremberg captured. Announcement: 60,585 UK civilians killed in air raids since start of war. |
| **21 April** | Stuttgart captured. |
| **23 April** | Announcement: Soviet forces have penetrated northern and eastern defences of Berlin. In a telegram to Hitler, Göring proposes to take over the leadership. Hitler orders Göring's arrest. |
| **24 April** | Count Bernadotte of the Swedish Red Cross gives British a verbal message from Himmler offering to surrender to the Americans and British only. |
| **26 April** | Bremen surrenders. Pétain arrested. |
| **27 April** | Western Allies reject Himmler's armistice offer. |

|              | Announcement: 1,052 V2 rockets fell on Britain, killing 2,754 people. |
|--------------|--------------|
| **28 April**    | Mussolini and twelve members of his cabinet executed by partisans. |
| **28–29 April** | Hitler marries Eva Braun and appoints Dönitz as his successor. |
| **30 April**    | Hitler and Eva Braun commit suicide. Munich captured. |
| **1 May**       | Hamburg radio announces Hitler has 'fallen in Berlin, fighting for Germany'. Goebbels and his wife commit suicide after having their children murdered. |
| **2 May**       | Berlin surrenders to Soviet forces. German armies in Italy surrender. Laval arrested. |
| **4 May**       | Berchtesgaden and Salzburg captured. |
| **6 May**       | German forces in Denmark and Holland surrender. |
| **7 May**       | Third Reich surrenders unconditionally. Breslau captured after 82-day siege. |
| **8 May**       | VE Day. Germans in Prague surrender to Czechoslovak National Army. |
| **9 May**       | Final act of capitulation ratified in Berlin. German forces in the Channel Islands surrender. |
| **10 May**      | Soviet troops occupy Prague. Announcement: US casualties in European war totalled 800,000, of whom 150,00 were killed. |
| **12 May**      | German forces in Crete surrender. |
| **14 May**      | Austrian republic re-established. |
| **23 May**      | All members of Dönitz's 'acting German Government' are arrested along with members of German High Command at his Flensburg HQ. Himmler commits suicide. |
| **29 May**      | Churchill reports total casualties of British Commonwealth armed forces from outbreak of war to 28 February 1945: 1,128,315, of whom 307,210 were killed. |

# *Notes*

## Introduction

1. The fire started in a stationery store as a result of an accident.
2. Unofficially called MI6.
3. Eisenhower's tribute to the French Resistance is mentioned in E.H. Cookridge *Inside SOE*, p. 605.
4. Not to be confused with the Inter-Services Liaison Department (ISLD), one of SIS's cover-names during the Second World War.
5. A résumé of Lord Selborne's memorandum is published in J.G. Beevor, *SOE: Recollections and Reflections, 1940–1945*, pp. 244–6.
6. The future Sir Robin Brook (1908–98), CMG, OBE, and the holder of American, French and Belgian honours. He was a star pupil of John Maynard Keynes, the economist, at Cambridge University. At the 1936 Berlin Olympics he competed in the British sabre team – and refused to march past Hitler in a parade of athletes. Brook served in SOE from July 1941 to November 1945. He was recruited by Dalton, who made him one of his three assistants (the others being Hugh Gaitskell and Christopher Mayhew). Later, he supervised SOE activities in France, Belgium and Holland. After the war he had a distinguished career in merchant banking and was a leading administrator of good causes.

## 1. Operation Foxley – and much more

1. Through this greatest of Hitler's countless strategic blunders he ended his invaluable alliance with Stalin. It had dated from the signing in Moscow on 23 August 1939 of the Non-Aggression Pact between Nazi Germany and the communist USSR. In accord with the Pact's secret protocol, Germany invaded Poland on the following 1 September, so making the Second World War inevitable, and the Soviet Union joined in the aggression sixteen days later. As a result of negotiations related to the Pact, the Soviet authorities provided the Nazi war economy with huge amounts of raw materials, including oil, iron ore, scrap iron, platinum and manganese. See A. Rossi, *The Russo-German Alliance, August 1939–June 1941* (London, Chapman and Hall, 1950), p. 112.

2. The rank of Obersturmbannführer in the SS was equivalent to lieutenant-colonel in the British and American Armies.
3. PWE was formally set up in September 1941. It was answerable to the Foreign Secretary, the Minister of Information and the Minister of Economic Warfare. For cover purposes, PWE used the notepaper of the Foreign Office's Political Intelligence Department – so sometimes confusing researchers after the war!
4. The fellow refugees with whom Dr Demuth was in contact included: Ludwig Loewy of the Loewy Engineering Co., Ltd, of Kingsway, London, and his partner, K. Guttenstein – consulting engineers in the Rhineland for many years, they had a detailed knowledge of many German factories; Hans O. Mankiewitz, a former industrial adviser to the Deutsche Bank; H. Edgar Landauer, a former general manager of the Reichs-Kredit-Gesellschaft; Walter Joseph Loeb, a former President of the Thuringian State Bank and chief adviser to the Shell Group in Germany and the Middle East – after moving to Amsterdam in 1933, he resumed his business career and did relief work for refugees; Engelbert Broda, a chemist, with knowledge of armaments, metals, lubricating oils and paper-making; Dr Anthony Fried, formerly of the Skoda Works, Prague, who had information on electric power plants, the chemical and gas industries, oil and aluminium; P.A. Rosin, a former professor at Berlin Technical High School (knowledge of machine tools, petrol and oil, ceramics, copper, textiles and sugar factories); J.H. Lothar (rolling mills, mining and chemistry). PRO file HS6 699.
5. PRO file HS6 691.
6. Forerunner of the Central Intelligence Agency (CIA).
7. Stephenson (1896–1989) was awarded the MC, the DFC with two bars and the Croix de Guerre avec Palmes for his First World War service. In one of his dogfights he shot down an aircraft belonging to a flight led by Lothar von Richthofen, brother of the 'Red Baron', Manfred von Richthofen. For his Second World War service Stephenson was decorated with the US's Medal for Merit and membership of France's Légion d'Honneur.
8. F.H. Hinsley and C.A.G. Simkins, *British Intelligence in the Second World War*, vol. 1, p. 51.
9. Ibid., p. 56.
10. Christopher Andrew, *Secret Service* (Sceptre edition), pp. 646–7.

## 2. Hitler's train a target

1. M.R.D. Foot, *SOE*, pp. 264–5.
2. Schloss Klessheim, a Baroque palace built for Archbishop Johann Ernst von Thun between 1700 and 1709, the interior being completed in 1732. The Kavalierhaus in the park belonging to the Schloss was built in 1880.
3. The Rastenburg FHQ was used by Hitler and the Armed Forces' High Command (OKW) from 23 June 1941 to 20 November 1944.
4. The PIAT (Projector Infantry Anti-Tank), a British hand-held weapon firing a small anti-tank bomb.
5. Charles Cruickshank, *SOE in Scandinavia*, p. 19.

## 3. The Führer's mountain retreat

1. What little that remained of the ground-level part of the Berghof was destroyed by the Bavarian authorities in 1952 at the request of the American army. However, much of the villa's complex of subterranean rooms survived. Also undamaged was the Eagle's Nest, now again called the Kehlsteinhaus. It is an important tourist attraction, providing splendid bird's-eye views of the surrounding terrain. Even more impressive is the luxurious InterContinental Hotel and its huge spa. The hotel, on the site of Göring's villa, is next to the Dokumentation Obersalzberg - an exhibition about the Berchesgaden area during the Third Reich and Nazi rule in general. The documents on display are commendably candid about subjects which many Germans formerly seldom discussed in public, such as the Holocaust and the fact that Hitler enjoyed widespread admiration in pre-war Germany.
2. The sale of about 230,000 copies of *Mein Kampf* made Hitler rich even before he came to power. The book was originally in two volumes, the first appearing in 1925 and the second in 1926. These were combined in a 'people's edition' in 1930. By the end of 1933, when he had been in office eleven months, about 1.5 million copies had been sold. Total sales during his lifetime are conservatively estimated at 8 million. However, it was not until early in 1939 that complete English-language editions were published in Britain and the United States. Before then only abridged English-language versions were available, these diluting Hitler's menacing message.
3. His first wife, Karin, having died in 1931, Göring married actress Emmy Sonnemann in 1935. Her husband being bachelor Hitler's chosen successor as Führer, she was the most important woman

member of the Nazi inner circle but had no political role. She died in 1973.

4. Some reports say that Eva Braun had blonde hair. For example, when he was interrogated after the war Field Marshal Keitel described her as a 'dark blonde'. He also said that she was 'very slender, elegant in appearance' and had 'quite nice legs'. (Quoted from a Nuremberg Trials document, *Nazi Conspiracy and Aggression*, Supplement B. The 42 volumes of Nuremberg Trials documents are entitled *Trial of the Major War Criminals before the International Military Tribunal, Nuremburg, 14 November 1945 to 1 October 1946*. In the immediate postwar years these books were sold, but not published, by HM Stationery Office, London.)

5. Spitzy writing in his book *How We Squandered the Reich*, p. 89.

6. They included Hauptsturmführer Schwieger, Smoke Unit commander; Obersturmführer Vater, a former SA (Brownshirt) Stormtrooper, responsible for looking after visitors to the Berghof; Vater's three assistants, Weiss, Schneider and Buschmann; Herbert Döhring and his wife, respectively major-domo and housekeeper at the Berghof; and Frau Schafytzel, Hitler's personal cook.

7. The Foxley papers list various sorts of passes used in May 1944: 1. The Berghof estate entry pass. It was inspected by SS Pickets 1 to 6 and by any RSD personnel; 2. The Führerstrasse pass, relating to the part of the road closed to the general public, from Posten Teugelbrunn to Posten Antenberg. A variant of this pass had to be shown to SS Picket 8 and the Teugelbrunn, Berghof and Antenberg civilian pickets. Führerstrasse passes were issued to German and Czech workers employed in the area and to various inhabitants of the estate, such as those at the Gutshof and the Haus and Atelier Speer; 3. The Auerstrasse pass, needed to leave the Führerstrasse and enter the SS barracks area; 4. The Theaterhalle pass. It was issued to every inhabitant of the Obersalzberg and had to be shown before seeing stage performances; 5. A pass to enter Göring's house. It was needed by his visitors and by everybody who worked in the SS barracks and the Vordereck. Officers visiting him had to show evidence that they had been invited. Those needing to see him in a hurry had to obtain a temporary pass from the RSD. Entry to the Eagle's Nest was allowed only if a pass bore a special imprint.

8. The AA gun sites included one at Schonau, one near Dürreck and two in Berchtesgaden town.

## 4. The tea-house and road plots

1. The American Bazooka rocket-launcher. A small shoulder-carried anti-tank weapon with an effective range of about 137 metres. It was first used in North Africa in 1942.
2. The Foxley papers also mention an alternative route across the Larosbach to the east of Obersalzberg.
3. The special forces' unit formed in October 1941 by David Stirling. More than half a century later it is still called upon from time to time to engage in dangerous covert operations.
4. An article in *The Times* magazine of 22 February 1997 was based on Captain Leighton-Langer's research. He later wrote two books, *X Steht für unbekannt: Deutsche und Osterreicher in den Britischen Streitkraften im Zweiten Weltkrieg* and *The King's Own Loyal Enemy Aliens*. Helen Fry's *The King's Most Loyal Enemy Aliens* (Sutton Publishing 2007) is the most recent full study of this subject. Dr. Fry is an honorary research fellow in the Department of Hebrew and Jewish Studies at University College, London.

## 5. Foxley thoroughly re-examined

1. Duff Cooper (1890–1954) was Ambassador to France from September 1944 to 1947. When First Lord of the Admiralty in 1938 he resigned from the Chamberlain government over its appeasement policy. His posts in the wartime coalition government including Minister of Information and Chancellor of the Duchy of Lancaster. He was created Viscount Norwich in 1952.
2. Ismay (1887–1965) was Chief of Staff to Churchill, in his capacity as Minister of Defence, and Deputy Secretary (Military) to the War Cabinet from 1940 to 1945. He was created a baron in 1947.
3. According to Hinsley and Simkins, *British Intelligence in the Second World War*, volume 3, part 2, Hitler was asleep until noon on D-Day and until the afternoon did not consent to two armoured divisions, the 12th SS-Panzer and Panzer Lehr, being moved as ordered by Field Marshal von Rundstedt, Commander-in-Chief, West. On 17 June Hitler met Field Marshals von Rundstedt and Rommel at Soissons, demanding that every square inch of ground be defended. The dictator and these two field marshals conferred again on 29 June at Berchtesgaden.
4. The legend is also said to relate to Frederick the Second (1194–1250), Barbarossa's grandson.

### 6. Chemicals, bacteria and Hess

1. This was a characteristic effusion by Hess, delivered in June 1934: 'The National Socialism of all of us is anchored in uncritical loyalty, in the surrender to the Führer that does not ask the why in individual cases, in the silent execution of his orders.'

### 7. Four Little Foxleys

1. The SD agents held by the British included Simone Desirent and Hugo La Haye, captured by 7th Armoured Division, and Jean F. Fixel and Pierre M. Sweerts, captured by 21st Army Group.
2. Ludwig Nebe, captured by 6th Army Group, and Alfred Naujocks and Fritz Wilhelm Lorenz, captured by 1st Army Group, were SD agents held by the Americans.
3. In September 1943, according to the Foxley papers, the guard contingent at the Sachsenhausen concentration camp's barracks comprised about twenty ethnic Germans from Romania. They wore SS uniforms. At the same time about 200 political prisoners, together with Poles and Russians from the concentration camp, were doing forced labour in the barracks. All these prisoners were later reportedly murdered on Skorzeny's orders. The camp, opened in 1936, was where an estimated 100,000 people died. One of its inmates was Kurt von Schuschnigg (1897–1977), Chancellor of Austria when it was occupied by Hitler in March 1938.
4. The Propaganda Ministry, the Gauleiter headquarters and his office as Reichverteidigungs Kommissar, all in Berlin; and his Munich office as Reichspropagandaleiter der NSDAP (Nazi Party).
5. The Foxley papers mention these military establishments at Bernau: Wehr-Bezirks-Kommando; Wehr-Melde-Amt; Heeres-Standort-Verwaltung; Offiziers-Anwarter-Schule; Landesschutzen-Bataillon 311; Reserve-Lazarett; and Wehrmacht-Gefangnis-Abteilung.
6. Goebbels and his wife had a suicide pact. There are several versions of what happened. According to two of these, they were either shot by an SS man on Goebbels' orders or he himself did the shooting. Frau Goebbels readily agreed to her own death but was briefly unnerved before consenting to the murder of her children.
7. The Foxley papers give the general's name as 'Ramke'. This is perhaps a mis-spelling of 'Ramcke'. Major-General Hermann Ramcke (1889–1968) was a paratroop commander captured by the Americans in Brest in 1944.

## 8. The Himmler problem

1. Born in October 1900, Himmler had a Catholic upbringing. He was an army officer cadet at the end of the First World War. Later, he gained a diploma in agriculture and was briefly a fertiliser salesman. His stern father was a schoolmaster who had been tutor to the Bavarian Crown Prince.

2. The Allies' demand that Nazi Germany (and the other Axis Powers) would be allowed only unconditional terms of surrender was first made by Roosevelt at a press conference held after the Casablanca Conference in January 1943. Churchill immediately agreed with what Roosevelt had said, and Stalin, who did not attend that summit meeting, soon did so too.

3. Eisenhower wrote in his book *Crusade in Europe* (first published in 1948): 'For many weeks [towards the end of the war in Europe] we had been receiving reports that the Nazi intention, in extremity, was to withdraw the cream of the SS, Gestapo, and other organisations fanatically devoted to Hitler, into the mountains of southern Bavaria, western Austria and northern Italy. There they expected to block the tortuous mountain passes and to hold out indefinitely against the Allies. Such a stronghold could always be reduced, by eventual starvation if in no other way. But if the [Nazi] German was permitted to establish the redoubt he might possibly force us to engage in a long drawn out guerrilla type of warfare, or a costly siege. Thus he could keep alive his desperate hope that through disagreement among the Allies he might yet be able to secure terms more favourable than those of unconditional surrender. The evidence was clear that the Nazi intended to make the attempt and I decided to give him no opportunity to carry it out.'

4. The report did not name the type of jet aircraft. Presumably it was the Messerschmitt 262. The world's first operational jet fighter, it could fly at 540 mph at 20,000 feet. Developed from a design project conceived in December 1938, the Me 262 was not put into production until 1943, and its first fighter unit was not formed until November 1944. Of the 1,433 Me 262s built, only about 220 were used operationally and many of those unsuccessfully as bombers, the role for them favoured by Hitler. The Me 262 out-performed its Allied counterparts. It would have been a deadly weapon if it had always been used as its designers intended.

5. SS-Obergruppenführer Eric von dem Bach-Zelewski (d. 1972) was a ruthless specialist in anti-partisan warfare. Hitler said of

him: 'Von dem Bach is so clever. He can do anything, get around anything.'
6. On 12 March 1945, at the SS sanatorium at Hohenlychen, Himmler and Kersten signed an agreement on the treatment of concentration camp prisoners. It stated: 'It was decided: 1. That concentration camps will not be blown up. 2. On the approach of Allied troops, a white flag will be hoisted. 3. No more Jews will be killed, and Jews will be treated like other prisoners. 4. Sweden is allowed to send food parcels to individual Jewish prisoners.'
7. One of the intelligence reports mentioned an unsupported claim that the SS had penetrated the Freies Deutschland (Free Germany) organisation and supplied weapons to about 200 of its 'turned' agents in Cologne, Koblenz and Bonn. The National Committee of Free Germany was a mainly propaganda organisation run by German communist emigrants under the Kremlin's direction. Some of the officers of the German Sixth Army, which surrendered at Stalingrad in January–February 1943, belonged to a branch of the organisation, the Federation of German Officers; their commander-in-chief, Field Marshal Paulus, joined after the July Bomb Plot.
8. *The Sound of Music*, starring Julie Andrews and Christopher Plummer, is a colourful, tuneful but sentimental version of events.
9. On 16 March 1945, the US army captured Bitche after hard fighting in the Vosges mountains, and the Soviet army captured Griefenhagen and many other places south of Stettin.

## 9. Searching for the unfindable?

1. Major Smith (born in Portsmouth in April 1910) worked for the National Provincial Bank from 1926 to 1939. Joining the Territorial Army in 1934, he was sent to France on the outbreak of war. When commanding 23 Field Battery, Royal Artillery, in July 1941, he was severely wounded. He was in hospital until August 1942 and later had postings in Britain, lastly with SOE from November 1944 to October 1945.
2. Julian Amery gives an amusing account of the Vilmar story in his book *Approach March* (London, Hutchinson, 1973), pp. 240–1.
3. Quoted by William L. Shirer in *The Rise and Fall of the Third Reich*, p. 12.
4. *How We Squandered the Reich*, pp. 85–6.
5. Article, 'Life with Hitler and his Mistress', *Daily Telegraph*, 23 September 1997.

6.  *Killing Hitler* by Roger Moorhouse, p. 171, and *OSS: The Secret History of America's First Central Intelligence Agency* by Richard Harris Smith, p.222.

## 10. The SOE plotters

1.  Through its SOE Adviser, Duncan Stuart.
2.  During the Second World War most members of the FANY, a women's service, were drivers or did welfare work. This was good cover for some members to serve in SOE. Most of these were radio operators or cipher clerks, but more than seventy were trained as agents. One of the bravest FANYs was the Anglo-French Violette Szabo (1921–45), a former shop assistant executed in Ravensbrück concentration camp. Her actions in support of French Resistance groups earned her a posthumous George Cross.

## 11. Sabotage without explosions

1.  The districts of Eupen and Malmédy, the subject of a border dispute, were ceded to Belgium by the Treaty of Versailles in 1919. That decision was confirmed by the League of Nations in 1925. However, in May 1940 Hitler illegally declared these districts 'reunited' with Germany.
2.  Dated 14 January and 3 February 1944.
3.  Minute by Major Royce to Colonel Dolbey, Cairo, 4 December 1944, in PRO file HS6/696.

## 12. Larger-scale wreckings

1.  Groups of anti-Nazi teenagers, known as 'Pirates', sprang up spontaneously in several German cities in the late 1930s. They adopted the edelweiss, the small alpine flowering plant, as their emblem. Often they dressed informally and behaved generally in ways that the Hitler Youth censured. However, the Nazi authorities failed to suppress the Pirates, as there were so many of them. But the Gestapo made an example of some members, such as those who daubed 'Down with Hitler!' slogans on walls. They were executed or sent to concentration camps. The regime was less worried by other youth groups collectively known as the 'Swing Movement'. They were apolitical but enjoyed American and British dance tunes and what the Nazis called 'Negro music'.

2. Described in PRO file HS6/674.
3. *Gubbins and SOE*, p. 229. Sir Peter Wilkinson (1914–2000) held various important posts in SOE. He served during the war in Poland, France, Italy and the Balkans, being awarded the DSO and OBE. Demobilised in 1947 with lieutenant-colonel's rank, he joined the Diplomatic Service. His subsequent appointments included Ambassador to Vietnam, 1966–7, and Ambassador to Austria, 1970–1.

## 13. Black propaganda

1. Straying off course into Swiss airspace, American aircraft caused serious bomb damage in Schaffhausen in April 1944. In 1949, the US Government paid $62 million compensation for this and other accidental bombing in Switzerland.
2. Churchill's *The Second World War: Triumph and Tragedy*, volume six, p. 616 (London, 1954).
3. In PRO file HS6/693.
4. The draft of a Chiefs of Staff directive.
5. Quoted from Michel's *The Shadow War: Resistance in Europe 1939–1945*, pp. 91–2. According to this book, on 1 January 1943, the daily distribution of the foreign-language broadcasting time of the BBC's European Service included five-and-a-half hours to France, five hours to Germany and Austria, four-and-a-quarter hours to Italy, two-and-a-half hours to Holland and two hours and ten minutes to Poland. Other countries received shorter transmissions. Albania, for instance, had only fifteen minutes.
6. A letter by the Chief, Ops C Sub-Section – G–3 Division (Forward) – to the Chief, Ops Section, dated 16 September 1944, and an attached document by a Special Forces Headquarters' liaison officer (SHAEF/17240/25/ Ops C), PRO file HS 6/635.
7. Colonel-General Nikolaus von Falkenhorst (1885–1968) was dismissed from his post in Norway on 18 December 1944. In 1946 a British military tribunal sentenced him to death for his complicity in the execution of a group of British prisoners of war. The sentence was later reduced to twenty years' imprisonment. He was released in July 1953 because of ill health.
8. *The Oxford Companion to the Second World War*, p. 297.

**14. Targeting the workers**

1. Letter in PRO file HS6/641.
2. Publications which reported on the Himmler stamp included *Berner Briefmarken-Zeitung*, *Journal Philatelique*, *Basler Nationalzeitung* and *Journal de Genève* (Switzerland); *Dagens Nyheter* and *Svenska Dagbladet* (Sweden); *Stamp* (New York); *Journal d'Orient* (Istanbul); *Evening News*, *Evening Standard*, *Daily Mirror* and the Stanley Gibbons stamp magazine (London); and *Weekly Illustrated* (India).
3. From Gisevius's book *Bis zum bitteren Ende*, vol. 2, p. 143 (Zurich, 1946); *To the Bitter End* (Boston, 1947).
4. Information about the film in Dulles's book *Germany's Underground*, p. 83 (New York, 1947).

**15. Ungentlemanly warfare**

1. Quoted by Patrick Howarth in his book *Undercover: The Men and Women of the Special Operations Executive*, p. 225. Sir Charles (later Viscount) Portal (1893–1971) was a member of the British Chiefs of Staff and the Combined Chiefs of Staff Committees. He strongly favoured night-time area bombing but also saw the value of precision bombing in daylight. Eisenhower, when President of the United States, described Portal as the greatest British wartime leader, 'greater even than Churchill'. (*The Dictionary of National Biography, 1971–1980*, p. 685.)
2. The last V2 to reach Britain fell on Orpington, Kent, as late as 27 March 1945.
3. Howarth, *Undercover*, pp. 224–5.
4. A distinguished physicist and former director of the Clarendon Laboratory, Oxford, Lindemann (1886–1957) had a great influence on policy-making throughout the Second World War. Born in Germany of French Alsatian ancestry, he was a friend of Churchill from 1921. He was created a baron in 1941.
5. Papers on Operation Braddock are in PRO files HS6/637 and HS6/718 to 722.

**Appendix B. No shortage of would-be assassins**

1. Writing in his book *Hitler's Personal Security*, pp. 268–9.
2. It has been claimed that Elser was a mere Gestapo stooge, employed to kill certain dissident Nazis. Dr Hans Bernd Gisevius, Vice-Consul in Zurich from 1940 to 1944 and an Abwehr agent

working for the Resistance, testified at the Nuremberg Trials that Elser had genuinely attempted to assassinate Hitler.

3. The Nazis' clumsy attempt on 8–9 November 1923, to overthrow the Bavarian state government as an intended first step towards seizing power in the whole of Germany. For his part in the Putsch Hitler was sentenced to five years' imprisonment but served only nine months.

4. Brandt's and Hoffmann's contributions to the Goethe House conference are quoted from *Contending with Hitler: Varieties of German Resistance in the Third Reich*, pp. 9, 10, 122 and 123.

5 Lt.-Gen. Sir (Frank) Noel Mason-Macfarlane (1889-1953) was awarded the Military Cross with two bars and the *Croix de Guerre* during the First World War. He twice observed the German Army in action before the Second World War: during the annexation of Austria and during the dismemberment of Czechoslovakia when troops occupied Bohemia and Moravia. His knowledge of Hitler's military strength and of pre-war Nazi politics was unrivalled. He was erudite and deep thinking as well as brave; he spoke German and French fluently, with some knowledge of Russian, Hungarian and Spanish.

The Director of Military Intelligence with the British Expeditionary Force in 1939–1940, he led the British military mission to Moscow in 1941 and 1942, was Governor and C-in-C, Gibraltar, 1942–1944; and chief commissioner of the Allied Control Commission for Italy, 1944. When a boy and young man he was injured in accidents which resulted in him being severely disabled long before the end of the war. Nevertheless. he was elected Labour MP for North Paddington in 1945, attending the House of Commons in a wheelchair until pain forced him to give up in 1946.

Ewan Butler's wartime army service included a secondment to SOE in 1941. From 1943 to 1945 he was Assistant Military Attaché in Stockholm. A lieutenant-colonel, he was twice mentioned in Dispatches and was awarded the US Medal of Freedom with Bronze Palm. After the war he returned to journalism, later becoming a full-time writer of books.

## Appendix E. Hitler's health

1. Quoted in 'The Wolf's Lair', an article by I.M. Baxter in *Military Illustrated*, November 1998 (no. 126).
2. H. Guderian, *Erinnerungen eines Soldaten* (Stuttgart, 1979), p. 402.

3. The Bomb Plot explosion also caused minor burns, one of which turned septic and was treated with captured British penicillin. By mid-September Hitler had recovered from the bomb injuries.

4. G. Boldt, *In the Shelter with Hitler* (London, 1948).

5. The post-mortem examination of 'a male corpse disfigured by fire' (Hitler's body) was conducted in May 1945, by a commission comprising five Soviet military doctors; the two principal ones were Lieutenant-Colonel F.I. Shkaravski, Chief Expert, Forensic Medicine, First Byelorussian Front, Medical Service; and Lieutenant-Colonel N.A. Krayevski, Chief Anatomical Pathologist, Red Army Medical Service. The commission report stated: 'The genital member is scorched. In the scrotum, which is singed but preserved, only the right testicle was found. . . . The left testicle could not be found either in the scrotum or on the spermatic cord inside the inguinal canal, nor in the small pelvis.' From F. Redlich, *Hitler: Diagnosis of a Destructive Prophet*, pp. 229 and 374–9.

## Appendix G. Skorzeny's career

1. Though called Fallschirmjäger-Regiment z.b.V. Hermann Göring, it was in no way connected with the Hermann Göring Division. This unit (or at any rate part of it) appears to have gone into action under the name of its commander as Kampfgruppe von der Heydte. One company of this regiment is also said to have participated in Horthy's abduction.

2. As instanced by the ease with which some Jeep parties gave themselves up rather than fight it out, as they could have done in some cases with every chance of getting away with it. [Some of Major Court's footnotes have been omitted, and the punctuation in his minute (probably written in haste) has been altered.]

# Bibliography

Of the books listed below, the reader may find these six particularly informative: *The Oxford Companion to the Second World War*, *SOE* by M.R.D. Foot, *Undercover* by Patrick Howarth, *The Shadow of War* by Henri Michel, *Gubbins and SOE* by Peter Wilkinson and Joan Bright Astley and *The Secret History of SOE* by William Mackenzie.

## Primary Sources

The PRO files numbered HS6 623 to HS6 625 contain the Operation Foxley documents. One file, HS6 626, relates to Operation Foxley II (the Little Foxleys). Including those not released to the public, there are 1,013 files in the Western European batch of SOE papers. All are in the HS6 series. The countries concerned: Austria (files 1–24), Belgium (25–303), the Channel Islands (304), Eire (305–7, not released), France (308–616), Germany (617–722), Holland (723–74), Italy (775–908), Liechtenstein (909–11), Spain (912–1004; these files also concern Portugal, Gibraltar and Spanish Morocco) and Switzerland (1005–13). There are also papers concerning Germany, Austria and the Sudetenland in the SOE Headquarters Files numbered HS7 145–148 and HS7 253, with descriptions of sabotage and subversion.

## Secondary Sources

Andrew, Christopher, *Secret Service*, London, Heinemann, 1985; Sceptre, 1986.

Baigent, Michael and Leigh, Richard, *Secret Germany*, London, Jonathan Cape, 1994.

Beevor, J.G., *SOE: Recollections and Reflections, 1940–1945*, London, Bodley Head, 1981.

von Boeselager, Philipp, *Valkyrie: The Plot to kill Hitler,* London, Weldenfeld and Nicolson 2009 (tr. from the French by Steven Rendall). Originally published as *Nous voulious tuer Hitler: Le dernier survivant du complot du 20 juillet 1944*, Paris, Editions Perrin.

Boyce, Fredric, and Everett, Douglas, *SOE: The Scientific Secrets* (Foreword by M.R.D. Foot), Stroud, Sutton Publishing, 2004

Bullock, Alan, *Hitler: A Study in Tyranny*, London, New York, etc., Penguin, 1990.

Butler, Ewan, *Mason-Mac: The Life of Lieutenant-General Sir Noel Mason-Macfarlane*, London, Macmillan, 1972.

Charman, Terry, *The German Home Front, 1939–45*, London, Barrie & Jenkins, 1989.

Cookridge, E.H., *Inside SOE*, London, Arthur Barker, 1966.

Cruickshank, Charles, *SOE in Scandinavia*, Oxford University Press, 1986.

Dear, I.C.B., *Sabotage and Subversion: Stories from the Files of the SOE and OSS*, London, Arms and Armour, 1996.

—— and Foot, M.R.D. (eds) *The Oxford Companion to the Second World War*, Oxford, New York, Oxford University Press, 1995.

Eisenhower, General Dwight D., *Crusade in Europe*, London, Heinemann, 1948. New York, Da Capo Paperback, 1993.

Falconer, Jonathan, *Bomber Command Handbook, 1939–1945*, Stroud, Sutton Publishing, 1998.

Fest, Joachim, *Plotting Hitler's Death*, London, Weidenfeld and Nicolson, and New York, Metropolitan Books, 1996.

Fischer, Klaus P., *Nazi Germany: A New History*, London, Constable, 1995.

Fitzgibbon, Constantine, *To Kill Hitler: The Officers' Plot, July, 1944*, Stevenage, Herts, Spa Books, 1994.

Foot, M.R.D., *Resistance*, London, Granada, 1979.

—— *SOE, An Outline History of Special Operations Executive, 1940–46*, London, Pimlico, 1999.

—— and Langley, J.M., *MI 9: Escape and Evasion, 1939–1945*, London, Bodley Head, 1979.

Fry, Helen, *The King's Most Loyal Enemy Aliens: Germans who fought for Britain in the Second World War*, Stroud, Sutton Publishing, 2007.

Garnett, David, *The Secret History of PWE: The Political Warfare Executive*, London, Little, Brown, 2002.

Gaskin, Hilary, *Eyewitnesses at Nuremberg*, London, Arms & Armour, 1990.

Gilbert, Martin, *Second World War*, London, Phoenix, 1989.

Gill, Anton, *An Honourable Defeat*, London, Heinemann, 1994.

*The Goebbels Diaries* ed. and tr. by Louis P. Lochner, London, Hamish Hamilton, 1948.

Henderson, Nevile, *Failure of a Mission*, London, Hodder & Stoughton, 1940.

Hinsley, F.H., and Simkins, C.A.G., *British Intelligence in the Second World War* vol. 4, London, HMSO, 1990, Appendix I, 'The German Intelligence Services', pp. 295–303. Also the other volumes in this official history.

Hoffmann, Peter, *German Resistance to Hitler*, Cambridge, Mass., and London, Harvard University Press, 1994.

——— *Hitler's Personal Security*, London, Macmillan, 1979.

Howarth, Patrick, *Undercover: The Men and Women of the Special Operations Executive*, London, and Boston, Mass., Routledge & Kegan Paul, 1980.

Kershaw, Ian, *Hitler 1889–1936: Hubris*, London, Allen Lane/ Penguin, 1998.

——— *Hitler: Profiles in Power*, Longman Group UK., 1991.

———*Hitler 1936–1945. Nemesis*, London, Allen Lane/ Penguin, 2000.

———*Luck of the Devil: The Story of Operation Valkyrie* (an adapted extract from *Hitler: 1936-1945, Nemesis*). London, Penguin, 2009.

*The Memoirs of Dr Felix Kersten*, tr. by Ernst Morwitz, Garden City, New York, Doubleday, 1947.

Kirk, Tim, *The Longman Companion to Nazi Germany*, London, New York, Longman, 1995.

Lande, D.A., *Resistance: Occupied Europe and its Defiance of Hitler*, Osceola, WI, USA, MBI Publishing Company, 2000.

Large, David Clay (ed.), *Contending with Hitler: Varieties of German Resistance in the Third Reich*, Washington DC, German Historical Institute, and Cambridge University Press, 1994.

Leber, Annedore, *Conscience in Revolt*, Boulder, Colorado, U.S.A., and Oxford, Westview Press, 1994.

Leighton-Langer, Peter, *The King's Own Loyal Enemy Aliens*, London, Vallentine Mitchell, 2006.

Mackenzie, William (W.J.M.), *The Secret History of SOE: The Special Operations Executive 1940–1945*, London, St Ermin's Press, 2000.

Medawar, Jean, and Pyke, David, *Hitler's Gift: Scientists who fled Nazi Germany*, London, Piatkus, 2001.

Meehan, Patricia, *The Unnecessary War*, London, Sinclair-Stevenson, 1995.

Michel, Henri, tr. from the French by Richard Barry, *The Shadow War: Resistance in Europe, 1939–1945*, London, History Book Club, 1972. French title: *La Guerre de l'ombre* (Editions Bernard Grasset).

Moorhouse, Roger, *Killing Hitler: The Third Reich and the Plots against the Führer*, London, Jonathan Cape, 2006.

Overy, Richard, *The Penguin Historical Atlas of the Third Reich*, London, New York, etc., Penguin, 1996.

Petrova, Ada, and Watson, Peter, *The Death of Hitler: The Final Words from Russia's Secret Archives*, London, Richard Cohen, 1995.

Redlich, Fritz, M.D., *Hitler: Diagnosis of a Destructive Prophet*, New York and Oxford, Oxford University Press, 1999.

Rigden, Denis (Introduction), *SOE Syllabus: Lessons in Ungentlemanly Warfare, World War II*, Kew, National Archives, 2004. (North American edition: *How to be a Spy: The World War II SOE Training Manual*, Toronto, Dundurn Group, 2004).

von Schlabrendorff, Fabian, *Revolt against Hitler*, London, Eyre & Spottiswoode, 1948.

Seaman, Mark (Introduction), *Secret Agent's Handbook of Special Devices, World War II*, Kew, Public Record Office, 2000.

Shirer, William L., *The Rise and Fall of the Third Reich*, London, Mandarin, 1996.

Snowman, Daniel, *The Hitler Emigres: The Cultural Impact on Britain of Refugees from Nazism*, London, Pimlico, 2003.

Snyder, Louis L., *Encyclopedia of the Third Reich*, London, Robert Hale, 1995.

Spitzy, Reinhard, tr. by G.T. Waddington, *How We Squandered the Reich*, Wilby, Norwich, Michael Russell, 1997.

Stafford, David, *Secret Agent: The True Story of the Special Operations Executive*, London, BBC, 2000.

—— *Churchill and Secret Service*, London, John Murray, 1997.

Strawson, John, *Churchill and Hitler: In Victory and Defeat*, London, Constable, 1997.

Sweet-Escott, Bickham, *Baker Street Irregular*, London, Methuen, 1965.

Taylor, James, and Shaw, Warren, *The Penguin Dictionary of the Third Reich*, London, New York, etc., Penguin, 1997.

Taylor, Dr Philip M., *Munitions of the Mind* (war propaganda), Wellingborough, Northamptonshire, Patrick Stephens, 1990.

Tunney, Christopher, *A Biographical Dictionary of World War II*, London, J.M. Dent, 1972.

Tusa, Ann, and Tusa, John, *The Nuremberg Trial*, London, Macmillan, 1983.

Weitz, John, *Hitler's Diplomat* (Ribbentrop), London, Weidenfeld & Nicolson, 1992.

Whiting, Charles, *Skorzeny: The Most Dangerous Man in Europe*, London, Leo Cooper, 1998.

Wilkinson, Peter, and Bright Astley, Joan, *Gubbins and SOE*, London, Leo Cooper, 1993.

# *Index*

Visit our website and discover thousands of other History Press books.

**www.thehistorypress.co.uk**